THE MODEL WIFE,
Nineteenth-Century Style

THE MODEL WIFE,
Nineteenth-Century Style

RONA RANDALL

The Herbert Press

ACKNOWLEDGEMENTS

The author and publisher are grateful to the following for permission to reproduce illustrations in their collections: Abbot Hall Art Gallery, Kendal, Cumbria, p. 196; BBC Hulton Picture Library, p. 51; British Library, pp. 169, 179; British Library Newspaper Library, Colindale, pp. 184 *left*, 191, 210; Guildhall Art Gallery, City of London, p. 29; Illustrated London News Picture Library, pp. 161, 163 *bottom*; J. Hadfield, pp. 31, 118; Mary Evans Picture Library, pp. 17, 20, 23, 40, 55, 66, 170, 202, 203, 216, 219; Museum of London, pp. 26, 61, 159, 164, 173, 175; Private Collection, frontispiece; Punch, p. 28; SDL Limited, Distributors of Singer Sewing Machines, p. 141; The Board of Trustees of the Victoria & Albert Museum, pp. 110 *right*, 114, 163 *top*.

First published in Great Britain 1989 by
The Herbert Press Ltd, 46 Northchurch Road, London N1 4EJ

Designed by Pauline Harrison
Set in Imprint
Printed and bound in Great Britain by
Butler & Tanner Ltd, Frome and London

British Library Cataloguing in Publication Data:
Randall, Rona
    The model wife, nineteenth century style
    1. Great Britain. Society. Role of women,
    1800–1912
    I. Title
    305.4′2′0941

ISBN 0–906969–84–0

Jacket: *Changing Homes* 1862 (detail) by George Elgar Hicks.
    THE GEFFRYE MUSEUM

Frontispiece: *Boudoir of an English Lady* by Nicholas Chevalier 1873 (detail)

CONTENTS

BY THE SAME AUTHOR

Non-Fiction

JORDAN AND THE HOLY LAND
(Foreword by King Hussein of Jordan)

Fiction

THE POTTER'S NIECE
THE DRAYTON LEGACY
CURTAIN CALL
THE LADIES OF HANOVER SQUARE
THE MATING DANCE
THE EAGLE AT THE GATE
WATCHMAN'S STONE
DRAGONMEDE
etc.

FOREWORD
Delving into the Past

AS AN HISTORICAL NOVELIST, one of my most enjoyable tasks is hunting for authenticity in domestic detail. How did people live, dress, bring up their children, run their households, control their servants, feed the sick, balance their domestic budgets? What did they eat and how did they cook it? What of manners and morals? What of the social round?

Reference libraries, archives, old newspapers, memoirs, letters – all provide valuable information, but one of the most exciting chases is in second-hand bookshops, equalled only by country auction rooms specializing in junk sales. Here one can stumble on volumes from the past in which unknown housewives recorded favourite recipes and household hints; labours of love, laboriously penned. In this way a treasure-trove of domestic lore has spanned generations, particularly from the nineteenth century.

It is impossible not to hoard these gems of wisdom. I have been guilty in this respect ever since I wrote my first historical novel many years ago. In passing them on I hope to present a picture of nineteenth-century life from the woman's point of view, where necessary using a modification of their terminology in the interest of clarity without, I hope, losing their period flavour.

I am indebted to these diligent ladies, for they bequeathed a legacy which lifts up the curtain on a world we can now glimpse as fascinated spectators – and learn quite a lot in the process.

So let's take that curtain up ...

RONA RANDALL

*To my sister Joyce, and to the
memory of our mother and father,
with love*

1 ❧ THE RIGHT THING, THE RIGHT WAY

Warnings & Advice to the Bride-to-be

T HE 1830S AND 1840S SAW THE BEGINNING of a spate of manuals devoted to the place of women in the home and in society. The aim of these journals and their many successors throughout the century was to stress the desirability of becoming a model wife socially as well as domestically, and to provide the reader with guidelines and advice on etiquette and correct behaviour in all circumstances – suggesting, perhaps, that some women were liable to forget what their true role really was? After all, there were some shocking examples of women getting above themselves – Mary Ann Evans (1819–80) for example, who, unblessed by matrimony, lived openly with a married man – the literary critic George Henry Lewis – and chose to write under the masculine name of George Eliot; or the scandalous Ouïda (1839–1908), whose earnings as a writer of ridiculous romantic novels enabled her to live in luxury in Langham Place, squandering no less than £200 a week on hothouse flowers and entertaining lavishly, and who even refused to leave her male guests alone with their port after dinner but remained with them, drinking and smoking as no respectable woman should.

Respectability was of prime importance, but there were many vital things which brides-to-be had to learn before advancing to the more practical matters of housewifery. The basic rules of social etiquette would have been instilled into them at their governesses' knees, but marriage elevated them to the rank of hostesses and therefore demanded more sophisticated knowledge. When an invaluable little work entitled *Hints on Etiquette and the Usages of Society, with a Glance at Bad Habits* appeared in 1834, it became essential reading for all socially ambitious brides and determined mothers.

The author, Αγωγός ('leader' – but surely a female pseudonym?) stressed that it was '... not written for those who *do* but for those who do *not* know what is proper', and defined etiquette as 'the barrier which society draws around itself as a protection against offences the "law" cannot touch – a shield against the intrusion of the impertinent, the improper, and the vulgar. . . .' The rulings of this much-read volume were final and absolute, and therefore to be memorized by conscientious brides and ambitious hostesses.

Starting with the important matter of introductions, *Αγωγός* advised: 'Never introduce people to each other without a previous understanding that it will be agreeable to both.' The explanation for this was simple:

> There are many reasons why people ought never to be introduced to the acquaintance of each other, without the consent of each party previously obtained. A man may suit the taste, and be agreeable enough to *one*, without being equally so to the *rest* of his friends – nay, as it often happens, decidedly unpleasing; a stupid person may be delighted with the society of a man of learning or talent, to whom in return such an acquaintance may prove annoyance and a clog, as one incapable of offering an interchange of thought, or an idea worth listening to.

Poor bride-to-be, threatened with social failure if her dinner guests failed to harmonize! Not even when thrust into an unexpected situation dare she deviate from the accepted ruling: 'Should you, whilst walking with your friend, meet an acquaintance, never introduce them.' The risk of either proving not to be a kindred spirit with the other was apparently too great. So, too, was the risk of taking an uninvited friend to the home of another:

> Be cautious how you take an intimate friend *uninvited* even to the house of those with whom you may be equally intimate, as there is always a feeling of jealousy that another should share your thoughts and feelings to the same extent as themselves, although good breeding will induce them to behave *civilly* to your friend on your account.

In providing these warnings about the pitfalls of introductions, *Αγωγός* only touched the fringe of a highly delicate and rigidly controlled procedure which a bride-to-be had to master, or face social death. In the upper and middle classes the matter of introducing the right people *to* the right people and eliminating the undesirables was of the gravest importance, and applied not only to individuals, but to groups. Social-climbing families had to be kept at bay and they, in turn, were on guard against intrusion from people they considered to be lower than themselves, hangers-on who hoped to scale the ladder with the aid of their better cut coat-tails. One couldn't be too careful, and the model wife was keenly aware of it.

As for residents in the country, *Αγωγός* considered them to be in particular need of social guidance:

> Much misconstruction and unpleasant feeling arises in rural and provincial areas, from not knowing what is *expected* or necessary to be done on certain occasions ... besides, in a mercantile country like England people are continually rising in the world. Shopkeepers become merchants, and mechanics manufacturers; with the possession of wealth they acquire a taste for the luxuries of life, expensive furniture, and gorgeous plate; also numberless superfluities, with the use of which they are only imperfectly acquainted. But although their capacities for enjoyment increase, it rarely occurs that the polish of their manners keeps pace with the rapidity of their advancement ... *In all cases*, the observances of the Metropolis (as the seat of refinement) should be received as the standard of good breeding.

Such views were to continue throughout the century among those who believed that the stability of society depended on the observance of rigid principles of conduct.

Social rules regarding an impending marriage were explicit, and long before a young woman became a bride she was aware – especially if she had brothers – that when a man married, all his former acquaintanceships ended unless he intimated a desire to renew them by sending his own and his wife's card. Neglect to do so was a clear indication that no further association was desired. In explaining this to her daughter, a conscientious mother had no need of a reference book for it was well known and blandly accepted that a bachelor was seldom particular in his choice of companions. So long as he was amused, he could associate freely with those whose morals and habits later made them undesirable for introduction into the sanctity of his marriage. A bride should therefore not expect her own high moral standards to apply to the groom prior to the wedding.

In the whole carefully structured system of Society, introductions and 'calls' paid a vital part. *How to Behave – A Pocket Manual of Etiquette* (anonymous, Glasgow, *c*. 1850) also issued stern warnings on the undesirability of introducing everybody to everybody: ... 'the promiscuous presentations sometimes inflicted on us are anything but agreeable. You confer no favour on us ... by making us acquainted with one who we do not desire to know....'

This enlightened manual stressed that those guilty of such a *faux pas* put themselves in a highly unpleasant position, an introduction being regarded as a social endorsement and therefore making them responsible for the person introduced: '. . . .if he disgraces himself in any way, you share, to a greater or lesser degree, in his disgrace.'

Such a dire situation could have only one result – the dreaded 'cut', a snub used extensively and wholly damning, from which it could take years to recover, a disaster no conscientious bride could bear to contemplate. She therefore steeped herself in the etiquette of introducing and calling, and even in administering the cut herself should the occasion arise.

The basic rule for making introductions was simple: the lesser person was always presented to the greater, the inferior to the superior – providing that permission had been sought beforehand. Rank controlled everything, therefore the female newcomer had to be introduced to the older woman, the unmarried to the married. This enabled the 'right' people to choose whether to follow up the introduction or not, and whether or not to bestow further recognition. This was where the dreaded 'cut' came in.

Delivering it was an art in itself. On meeting in public, one crossed the road to avoid coming face to face with the undesirables. If an encounter was inescapable, one avoided catching the eye. Failing that, an ice-cold inclination of the head was enough to discourage any further presumption, indicating that though one acknowledged such people one did not 'know' them. But only the privileged could deliver this mark of disapproval. People not belonging to Society were not qualified to distinguish between the socially acceptable and the socially unacceptable. In this latter group came governesses, doctors and clergymen, all of whom were admitted into the home solely in their line of duty and never to be regarded as equals.

The practice of the cut was not considered cruel. It was used to protect one's status by emphasizing it – in particular, that of one's husband, the fostering of whose interests was the focus of a wife's duties. For him, she attended tedious parties, tiring bazaars, speech-making functions at which she had to stifle her yawns, and dull At Homes, for it was here that valuable contacts could be made. If fortunate enough to be invited, she and her husband ate heavy meals in the houses of people more elevated than themselves because such was the level of society to which they should aspire. She listened to political conversations which she was not even expected to understand, much less participate in, and cultivated people who were influential no matter how little she had in common with them or how greatly she disliked them. She had to know 'who was who' and who was not, what was 'done' and what was not, otherwise she would be no asset to her spouse.

Not all women found such a life frustrating. Some enjoyed it, recognizing the power it could give them to manipulate people. A successful hostess could ultimately preside over a salon patronized by the great and influential, eliminating those who did not qualify and drawing into the net only those who did. She might even become a member of that enviable coterie of women who ruled Society, women such as Lady Castlereagh and Lady Jersey. No dreams were too great for match-making mammas and ambitious daughters.

But to mix with the right people, first it was necessary to meet and win the approval of the right people, and this a bride could ensure not only by observing the social codes, but by assessing who would be useful in her husband's advancement (and therefore her own). It was then up to her to cultivate the desirable people with care and discretion, never pushing, never hurrying, and never putting a foot wrong.

'The woman behind the man' was no myth. She could be a valuable ally or a formidable foe. She could become an arbiter of fashion in more subtle ways than in dress. She could influence social acceptance or exclusion, and arouse envy in the hearts of wives who yearned for invitations to salons into which she was accepted.

CALLING

THE RULES FOR CALLING were simplified by the use of visiting cards, invented by the French and adopted in England around 1800. Earlier, the hall of every wealthy town house featured a slate on which the butler recorded the names of callers (a practice unnecessary in the country where they consisted mainly of neighbours or relatives). But now, in smart circles, there developed the snobbish practice of placing cards on a silver salver to catch the eye of other visitors – the more impressive names naturally displayed on top.

There were several essential rules to be learned about card-leaving:

(1) When making a formal call, a lady remained seated in her carriage while her groom took her card and handed it in. Her coachman performed this function only if accompanied by no other stable servant. Then came the anxious wait while butler, footman

or parlourmaid conveyed the card to his or her mistress, who then decided whether to receive the caller or not.

The correct attire of 'front' servants – those seen by visitors, as opposed to those who worked belowstairs – was of vital importance, indicating the status of the owners of the house. If the latter were of high social standing, butler and footmen would be immaculately liveried and parlourmaids immaculately uniformed. In households of lower social standing, a suitably attired maid or male servant would answer the door, but since visitors would be people of the same social rank, the right impression would still be conveyed – that the master or mistress knew how their servants should be dressed. This was a factor which model wives bore in mind at every level of society, not only when visiting but when receiving on At Home days. As a husband's standing rose, so must the front servants rise in rank and in uniform until, in time, only acceptable people presented their cards at the door.

In her *Manual of Etiquette or Social Forms, Manners, and Customs of Correct Society* (1896) Maude C. Cook pointed out that the correct usage of 'these magic bits of paste-board' could not be exaggerated. The important thing to remember was that the visiting card 'was meant to take the place of one's self'. The answer 'Not at home' therefore had to be accepted as a rejection, but possibly a temporary one. Everything depended on what happened next. If a reciprocal card was received, but not presented formally, it was a sign that there was no desire for the acquaintanceship to develop, and only the thick-skinned tried a second time. If, however, a formal call was returned with a formal call, the signs were good.

Etiquette ruled that a call should be returned with a call, a card with a card, within a week or, at the most, ten days.

(2) Card-leaving alone was not the same as making a formal call. For a first call it was wise simply to leave a card without enquiring whether the mistress of the house was at home, leaving her to take the next step.

(3) By the middle of the century it was accepted that a wife could deputize for her husband by leaving his card, and that the names of grown-up daughters, if accompanying their mother, could be printed on her card beneath her own. When a daughter had 'come out' and was therefore adult enough to pay calls without her mother, though usually accompanied by a female servant, she could use her mother's card, lightly crossing out the name and pencilling in her own.

Calling costume from *Harper's Bazar* 1897

(4)   A lady left her own card and two of her husband's, one for the mistress of the house and one for the master. A turned-down corner indicated that the card had been delivered in person, rather than by a servant, with the intention of calling again.

(5)   Formal calls were essential following 'ceremonial' events such as marriage or childbirth, also as acknowledgments of hospitality. For the latter, three days was the greatest permissible leeway following a ball, a reception, or an invitation to dine. If the host and hostess were members of the social hierarchy, the wise guest responded promptly or, at the very least, sent an elaborate letter of thanks delivered by a footman resplendent in immaculate livery. Giving the right impression was important.

(6)   With the exception of ceremonial occasions, calls should never be made on the off-chance, only on official At Home days. Days and times for these would be engraved on visiting cards. The newcomer to a district waited until she received such cards from her neighbours. Once received, it was good form to call. New acquaintances, met at the homes of 'acceptable' people, could be informed in this way of the 'At Home' days and times – for example, the second Wednesday or third Friday in the month, at three o'clock of an afternoon. Tea would be a ritual conducted with much formality.

Every nuance of this tricky business of making calls had to be understood by the aspiring model wife. She also had to be aware that though known as 'morning calls', they took place in the afternoon, strict hours being allocated to each type of call. 'Ceremonial' calls were made between the hours of three and four, semi-ceremonial between four and five, and intimate calls between five and six – but never on Sunday, the day reserved for close friends and relatives. Strict adherence to this practice wavered late in the century, when 'dining deep' became fashionable among people with a wide circle of friends. This meant visiting several houses in the course of an evening, but again, unless invited, never on Sunday.

Bachelors, however, *were* allowed to pay calls on Sundays. Some were regarded with compassion for having to undertake a duty which was essentially that of their female relatives, but most of them were secretly accused of assessing the prospects of eligible young ladies. Because they were always on their best behaviour, the practice was frequently dubbed as 'sewing seeds'.

Another very useful reason for leaving cards was to let it be known

Afternoon tea 1893

that the family was temporarily leaving the area, in which case P.P.C. – *pour prendre congé* – would be written on them. This had the advantage of offering a loophole on returning, a chance to form a new social set by deciding on whom to call now – and of breaking with those one was tired of, or who were no longer considered desirable acquaintances.

DINING

'THE DIRECTION OF A TABLE is no inconsiderate branch of a lady's concern,' an anonymous mother instructed her daughters, in a volume entitled *A New System of Domestic Cookery* by 'A Lady' (1819). This work was plainly written with the intention of turning them into model wives, for it covered all aspects of domesticity as well as cooking. It was splendidly illustrated with line engravings and was later 'Adapted to the Use of Private Families', still under the pseudonym of 'A Lady'. The author was subsequently identified as Mrs M. Rundell, a woman less fortunate than her successor, Mrs Beeton, who had a husband to publish her work and to launch a magazine, *The Englishwoman's Domestic Magazine* (1852), to exploit her writings further. Despite lacking these advantages Mrs Rundell's 1819 volume continued to be published throughout the years, culminating in a splendid edition as late as 1855 entitled *Modern Domestic Cookery*. This was based entirely on her original work and contained even more elaborate engravings.

Discerning women of the day were wont to say, 'Mrs Beeton's idea of economy is to throw a dozen eggs out of the window before making a cake; Mrs Rundell puts half a dozen back in the larder and makes a better one ...' But Mrs Rundell was concerned only with her daughters' graduation as expert housewives.

'It is not a multiplicity of things, but the choice, the dressing and the neat pleasing look of the whole, which gives respectability to her who presides,' she wrote. 'Perhaps there are few incidents in which the respectability of a man is more immediately felt than the style of dinner to which he accidentally may bring home a visitor ... if two or three dishes are well served, with the usual sauces, the table linen clean, the small sideboard neatly laid, and all that is necessary be at hand, the expectation of the husband and guest will be gratified.'

On the question of dinner parties the omnipotent *Αγωγός*, surprisingly, claimed to find it difficult to lay down hard and fast rules. 'Fashions,' she declared,

> are continually changing, even at the best of tables; and what is considered the height of good taste one year, is declared vulgar the next; besides which, certain houses and *sets* have certain customs, peculiar to that clique, and all who do not conform *exactly* to their methods are looked upon as vulgar persons, ignorant of good breeding. This is a mistake commonly fallen into by the 'little great' in the country, where the circle constituting '*society*' is necessarily so small that its members cannot fail to acquire the same habits, feelings, and observances. However, a few hints may not be thrown away, always recollecting people can only become ridiculous by attempting to be *too fine*. I am, of course, supposing my readers to be acquainted with the *decencies* of life.

Αγωγός clearly distinguished between the 'little great' and 'great little'. The former were long-standing 'County People', the descendants of patrician families, the squirearchy, with incomes of from £7,000 to £10,000 a year. By custom, these became parliamentary representatives of their county – 'persons who are of great *local influence* and importance on account of their descent and wealth, but who, notwithstanding, become insignificant and merely *units in the mass*, amidst the brilliant statesmen, the talent, the splendour of rank and fashion which adorn and elevate the metropolis.'

The 'great little', on the other hand, were 'that numerous class (however respectable), professional and mercantile, found in and about every country town; those merely "great little", who, without any other qualification than the possession of a few thousand pounds, constitute themselves the aristocracy of the place.'

Detestable as the snobbishness of *Αγωγός* now appears, her rules and guidelines were not only accepted but relied upon by inexperienced hostesses, especially when it came to giving dinner parties.

It had also to be remembered that well-bred people always arrived as nearly at the appointed dinner hour as they could. It was considered 'a very vulgar assumption of importance' to arrive half an hour behind time – 'besides the folly of allowing eight or ten hungry people such a tempting opportunity of discussing your foibles'.

> When members of the party have all assembled in the drawing room, the master or mistress of the house will point out which lady a gentleman is to take into the dining-room, according to some real or fancied standard of precedence, rank (if there be any rank), age, or general importance; that is, the married before the single, et cetera, et cetera; or they will show their tact by making companions those who are most likely to be agreeable to each other.

The lady was to be given the wall when descending the stairs, but if merely passing from one room to another, the man's right arm should be offered to her. It was stressed that the lady took precedence at all times over the gentleman, and to illustrate this *Αγωγός* quoted an apparently horrific social gaffe, describing how 'a person', when leading a Princess out of a room before her husband (who was accompanying a lady of lower rank), said, in an excess of politeness, '*Pardonnez que nous vous précédons* ...'; as the aghast *Αγωγός* explained, 'This person most embarrassingly forgot that it was the *Princess* and not *he* who led the way. A social *gaffe* never to be committed.'

The lady of the house always followed her guests to the dining room, and took the head of the table. The gentleman of the highest rank would be seated on her right, and the gentleman next in rank on her left, so that she would be supported by 'the two persons of the most consideration (who will assist her to carve)'. The gentleman of the house occupied the bottom of the table, and on each side of him sat the two ladies highest in rank.

When drawing up a seating plan it was not unknown for the most snobbish hostesses to take into account the number of servants employed by their respective guests. The financially well-off advertised their status by the size of their domestic staff, and the ignorant were always impressed by it.

The model wife paid meticulous attention to the niceties of table manners. Her guests would surely know that it was considered 'vulgar' to take fish or soup twice, thus leaving three parts of the company to stare at them while waiting for the next course, which was spoiling, to the annoyance of the mistress of the house. 'The selfish greediness, therefore, of so doing constitutes its vulgarity.'

Now to Mrs Rundell on the art of carving, which appears to have been the hostess's duty for at least part of the nineteenth century. The knife had to be light, of middling size and of a fine edge, for

Going in to dinner (The *Graphic* 1890)

strength was needed less than skill in handling it, but the first requirement was to give orders to the butcher 'to divide the joints in the bones of all joints which may then be easily cut into thin slices attached to the adjoining bones'. More clearly worded was the stipulation that 'the dish should not be too far off the carver, as it gives an awkward appearance'. Poise and grace were essential.

Carving fish was less daunting, though care not to break the flakes was stressed, particularly those in cod and fresh salmon which 'contribute much to the beauty of its appearance'. The heads of carp and fins of turbot were esteemed as delicacies, along with the roe, milt, or liver, which had to be equally divided between each person. Only the tail was rejected.

And here came the real gems of *Αγωγός*' advice:

Do not ask any lady to take wine, until you see she has *finished* her fish or soup ... but if either a lady or a gentleman be invited to take wine at table, they must *never refuse*; it is very *gauche* to do so. They need not drink half a glass, but merely taste of it.

At every respectable table you will find *silver* forks; being broader, they are in all respects more convenient than steel for fish or vegetables.

At family dinners, where the common household bread is used, it should never be cut less than an inch and a half thick. There is nothing more plebeian than *thin* bread at dinner.

NEVER *use your knife* to convey food to your mouth, *under any circumstances*; it is unnecessary, and glaringly vulgar. Feed yourself with a fork or spoon, *nothing* else – a knife is only used for cutting.

Fish does not require a knife, but should be divided by the aid of a piece of bread.

If you should carve and serve a joint, do not load a person's plate – it is vulgar. Also in serving soup, one ladleful to each plate is sufficient.

Making a noise in chewing or breathing hard in eating, are both unseemly habits, and ought to be eschewed.

Many people make a disgusting noise with their lips by inhaling their breath strongly whilst taking soup – a habit which should be carefully avoided.

You cannot use your knife, or fork, or teeth too quietly.

Do not pick your teeth *much* at table as, however satisfactory a practice to yourself, to witness it is not a pleasant thing.

And perhaps best of all:

Finger glasses, filled with *warm* water, come on with the dessert. Wet a corner of your napkin, and wipe your mouth, then rinse your fingers; but do not practice the *filthy* custom of gargling your mouth at table, albeit the usage prevails amongst the few, who think, *because* it is a foreign habit, it cannot be disgusting.

Ladies were not to dine with their gloves on, unless their hands 'were not fit to be seen'. But servants should wait at table wearing clean white gloves because 'there are few things more disagreeable than the thumb of a clumsy waiter in your plate.'

The rules of correct dining procedure were, however, even more extensive than *Αγωγός* indicated, and started with the question of invitations. These were accorded the same precedence as introductions, and formality demanded that they should be written and presented a fortnight in advance. Handbooks abounded for the instruction of footmen and butlers on the seating of guests, and so expert on the subject did these upper servants become that an inexperienced bride could wither beneath their scrutiny of her table plan. On this, and the processional order from reception room to dining room, the model wife could stand or fall.

In 1881, Burke published *A Book of Precedence*, outlining once and for all the grading of guests, which was primarily designed to help not only newly-fledged society hosts and hostesses but their footmen and butlers too. Despite the proliferation of handbooks on the subject, Burke's was accepted as the final word.

The hour for dining varied between town and country – country households, being less sophisticated, followed fashion less slavishly and certainly less speedily. Although in London, at the beginning of the nineteenth century, dining in the afternoon had preceded an evening's outing to the theatre or pleasure gardens, the hour became later when there was a gradual decline in public amusements for the upper classes. Private dinner parties and balls then became fashionable, and the hour of dining was delayed until evening. Formal clothes and correct procedure into the dining room became *de rigueur*, the pairing of guests being governed as meticulously as

The gentlemen, having been left to drink their port, join the ladies for coffee

the selection of the guests themselves – and always the stringent laws concerning introductions were carefully maintained.

With later dining also came new styles of entertaining. One was to dine *à la Russe*, first admitted as early as the 1820s. Prior to that, it had been the predominant custom for the host or hostess to carve at the table, with two major courses and accompanying dishes being placed on the table in sequence. But when dining *à la Russe*, a footman carved at a sideboard and his underling carried the plate to each guest in turn, and whereas previously the host had poured wine, or the guests had poured for each other, footmen now undertook this task also. These changes of custom meant increased staff and more elaborate dinner ware – and inevitably more social consciousness, more snobbishness, and more rivalry.

MOURNING

EVEN DEATH HAD ITS CODES OF ETIQUETTE, elaborate and filled with display. The importance of the deceased was judged by the length of time allocated to his mourning, as well as by the pomp of his funeral cortége. Special mourning carriages were brought out, drawn by black horses wearing tall black plumes; and the deepest 'widow's weeds' were essential for a mourning wife, to be worn throughout the First Mourning, which lasted a year and a day. They consisted of black clothes draped in black crepe, absolutely no ornamentation and a widow's cap and veil.

Second mourning followed for another twelve months, still wholly of black but with less crepe and without cap and veil, which could

Mourning costume for a young lady and an elderly lady, 1897

be replaced with a quiet black hat. Jet ornaments were now permitted, but no other kind. This relaxation was called 'slighting the mourning', not in any derogatory sense but to indicate that restrictions were slightly less stringent.

Half-mourning, which allowed the addition of grey or mauve to relieve the density of black, was permitted for the third year, but some widows remained in mourning for the rest of their lives, conscious that it carried certain social advantages. Advertising their loss and their unending devotion won both respect and admiration, and even acceptance into circles previously only aspired to – the circles of gracious ladies who knew how to behave and spent their time demonstrating it.

Near relatives were also drawn into the restrictive net of mourning etiquette. Parents and children mourned officially for a year, starting with deep mourning and discarding it by very slow degrees. For small children grey or black ribbons were allowed, and when white clothes were at last permissible they had to be trimmed with black. All other relatives mourned in descending order, the amount of black crepe depending on their rank in the family.

Nor did servants escape. When their master or mistress died they were supplied with mourning caps, gloves, black cravats or ties for the men and black work dresses for the women.

There was also the important matter of accessories, such as heavily black-edged writing paper with matching envelopes (the border could be narrower after the first year), black seals, black signet rings, and black-edged visiting cards. The truly devoted widow would have nothing but black floral decorations in her home; artificial flower makers did well out of this.

Mourning for Royalty was nationally observed. The streets were hung with black, windows were draped in it as were shop displays. Even Ascot fashions observed it. Not until Edward VII decreed that mourning should cease four months after the death of Queen Victoria in January 1901 did the rigid etiquette pertaining to death begin to relax. Many were shocked by his decision, fearing that the loosening of the established order of what was done and was not done might cause society to collapse.

Drums, Kettledrums & Dances

T HE DUTIFUL WIFE naturally wished to be as *au fait* with the right kind of entertaining as she was with all branches of etiquette. People of refinement began to withdraw from public places of pleasure during the early and middle part of the century, when it was no longer possible to rub shoulders with the great in the gardens of Ranelagh and Vauxhall, which became increasingly disreputable and were finally closed. Nor could tickets any longer be bought for the famous masquerade balls at Almack's club in King Street, St James's, where masks were supposed to conceal identities and unscrupulous women took the opportunity of annexing titled gentlemen who fondly imagined themselves to be incognito.

Disapproving dowagers and duchesses, concerned at the way in which these brazen social climbers ensnared their menfolk, firmly closed ranks, took over the running of Almack's balls, and effectively eliminated the undesirables by dictating laws to control admission, which became strictly private, by invitation only. Thus the respectable evening party was born.

Almack's Assembly Rooms 1821

Evening parties proved so successful that they finally fell into two categories – those with dancing, and those without. The latter ranked as a reception, commonly known as a 'kettledrum' but more casually referred to as a 'drum'. The former could be a modest 'dance', but was more usually a ball on the grand scale.

Invitations to either category were much sought after, and social success became marked by the number of engraved invitations displayed above the fireplace, where they often remained after events were over, to impress callers.

The sensible young wife inspected all invitations carefully and accepted the most desirable, including those for all-female drums, however small, where she was likely to meet women who would be socially advantageous to her or the wives of men who might promote her husband's career. Nor did she always turn up her nose at receptions where she might mix with people not *quite* out of the top drawer. After all, the vulgar little man who had trouble with his aitches might be a city tycoon currently making a fortune, or a wealthy industrialist who was likely to be so flattered by the charming attentions of a lady plainly accustomed to better circles than those he had risen from, that he would make a reciprocal gesture of gratitude to her husband ... an introduction to someone useful, a word in the ear of a rising politician, a few valuable tips on the stock exchange ... one never *knew*.

The highest level of reception included those given by the wives of cabinet ministers or ambassadors; at the opposite end of the scale were those boring little drums for a few elegant ladies in someone's drawing room very late in the afternoon – similar to an ordinary At Home except that one did not have to stay to the bitter end. Drums at any level were popular because guests could depart whenever they wished, nor was there any need to arrive on the dot, but an At Home invitation clearly stated 'from three o'clock to half past four', or whatever times the hostess chose.

An additional attraction of late evening drums was that they were naturally for both sexes. The hour of invitation for informal receptions was normally ten p.m.; for more formal ones, eleven.

People dressed superbly, even if intending to stay for only an hour before moving on to some rival party. The whole reason for being there was to see and be seen, to be able say that you had met such-and-such a person at such-and-such a house, the more imposing the better – especially if those to whom you related the event had not been invited.

Highly popular, and often much angled for, were receptions given for visiting 'lions', whose presence would be intimated on the card. 'To meet the well known opera singer, Signor So-and-So' or, better still, some visiting foreign Royal, however obscure, guaranteed one hundred per cent acceptance, and few guests would be bidding their hostess an early farewell.

The really grand kettledrums were those held in fine city mansions, and if the conscientious wife or match-making mamma could not stage a drum on an equal scale in her own home, she would persuade her husband to rent a better house for the occasion and he, equally conscious of the necessity to do everything in the right manner, would naturally concur. To owners of mansions in Park Lane and Mayfair such premises proved to be highly profitable.

For the important matter of drawing up the guest list, every hostess worth her salt would arm herself with a copy of the Red Book – otherwise Burke's *Peerage*, which listed the aristocracy in order of precedence and which, to this day, is still bound in red – because everyone she knew or hoped to know was named therein. It was perhaps audacious to send invitations to those with whom one was scarcely on bowing terms, but at least it helped to keep one's

Receptions given for visiting celebrities were popular, and enhanced the hostess's reputation

Too Early by James Tissot 1873

name before them and to demonstrate that one was entertaining in the right style – and the day might come when curiosity alone brought them to an evening party, from which they would depart so impressed by the hospitality, grace, and charm of the hostess that a reciprocal invitation would be sent. Or the praise of those who had attended would quickly spread, and those who had declined might then think again . . .

There were rules of etiquette even for evening parties, though compared with other social areas they were very elastic. No one was expected to arrive less than half an hour, or more than an hour-and-a-half, later than the specified time of invitation. Light refreshments, predominantly tea and non-alcoholic beverages with biscuits, sweetmeats and ices, would be available somewhere on the premises throughout the evening, served by upper servants and perhaps a hired waiter or two. Guests would be ushered to the refreshment rooms immediately on arrival, to sample the fare before greeting their hostess – even if they had already wined and dined.

Since no departure time was specified, guests could drift away when they chose, but even if they stayed for the supper, served around midnight, they could depart without taking formal leave of their hostess. Thus people could come and go as they pleased, proceeding to someone else's drum, then another and another throughout the night, taking such hospitality for granted and frequently comparing that of respective houses favourably or unfavourably. Knowing this, the socially-ambitious wife endured stress, anxiety, financial strain, anguish, fatigue and finally exhaustion which could render her prostrate for two or three days after the event, all of which was considered worthwhile if her most important guests lingered longer than she hoped for and went out of their way to compliment and thank her. With one successful drum she could 'arrive', and the casual manners of the guests be forgotten.

In spite of the comparative informality of such parties, there would have been no opportunity for the custom of gate crashing which developed in the 1920s. Invitations would have been inspected, guests individually greeted, and well trained servants would have barred the door to anyone lacking identification, or whose credentials were unsatisfactory.

More ambitious hostesses would give a 'dance' – particularly if launching a newly fledged daughter. This differed from a 'ball' not only in having fewer guests, fewer servants and musicians, but in the setting, the quantity of food, and the less elaborate quality of the decorations. A ball would cater for anything up to five hundred guests, making the dance seem modest indeed. Music at a dance would be provided by a trio or quartet, never more, and frequently by only a piano and violin (or even a solitary piano at genteel little gatherings.) By contrast, guests at a ball danced to music from a proper orchestra, the more famous the better. Decorations at a dance were simple and unostentatious; at a ball they were lavish and highly expensive. There was always the danger of a dance clashing with a more elaborate entertainment if by some mischance it should be held on the same night. The modest dance then had little hope of patronage and the loyalty of friends was well tested.

A newly-wed couple giving their first evening party would observe strict formalities in order to give the right impression. Not for them the come-and-go-as-you-please affair. They were staging this event to make themselves known, to be accepted, and to demonstrate their knowledge of correct behaviour. Therefore they would stand together to receive their guests while a butler or footman (hired for the evening if they could not yet afford their own) scanned the

The polka – from a music cover

invitations and announced the newcomers' names in stentorian tones. Since reception rooms in town houses were situated on the first floor, the hosts would be stationed at the head of the stairs, the footman or butler below; and with the echo of his voice following them the guests would slowly ascend, women lifting the hems of their billowing skirts to avoid stepping on them and perhaps to display the lovely sweep of them behind.

Gazing down over the banisters, visitors who had already been received would carefully note names and faces so that, with luck, they might manipulate an introduction to the more notable ones or get into conversation with them in the refreshment room. If they made the right impression, an 'official' introduction might well be granted later, after the right approaches had been made on their behalf in the correct way.

The first evening party held in the home of a newly married couple was a crucial test of a bride's talents as a hostess. All her husband had to do was be amiable to guests, but on her shoulders fell responsibility for everything, from organization, planning the supper menu, supervising the preparation of running refreshments if her cook wasn't wholly up to scratch, to calculating the amounts required for the numbers expected. She had also to plan and supervise the decorations, even arranging the flowers delivered from the florist at the last moment to preserve their freshness, unless she could afford one of the more expensive firms who sent young women to perform this service. She had to see that a space was cleared in the middle of the two first-floor rooms, normally divided by sliding doors but opened up for entertaining, with sofas and chairs ranged round the walls and the heaviest furniture removed entirely in case some of her guests wished to dance. She had to see that the servants were immaculately uniformed, that her husband's formal clothes were groomed and laid out for him if he lacked a valet, that posies or some enchanting small gift awaited every lady at the supper table, that the most important guest should be singled out for especial attention, and that the cost of everything did not exceed her budget – or, at least, not too heavily.

By the time she became a mother with a daughter ready to be launched on to the marriage market, a hostess took all this in her stride. By then the family had usually progressed to a larger house, which she made the most of by lighting up gardens and balconies with Japanese lanterns and placing tables and chairs in discreet nooks – for although chaperonage was strict it was well known that couples liked to slip outside occasionally. The hostess turned a blind eye ... particularly on the chaperones and wallflowers grouped in a corner, all silently praying that the gentlemen who seemed to prefer male conversation would break away from their clique around the door and notice them. A hostess could do little to help; it was up to her husband to steer the unwilling males in the right direction.

Her main interest was her own daughter, her greatest anxiety the projection of the girl's charms. To this end the girl would stand beside her mother at the top of the stairs to receive the guests, wearing her presentation gown if she had been to Court. Every detail of her toilette had been planned and supervised; her hair had been crimped and curled by her mother's maid, she had laid prone with a mask of cucumber between layers of muslin on her face, and she would have been compelled to sleep that afternoon so that no trace of tiredness marred her young features. Perfection was the goal if the aim of tonight's costly affair was to be fulfilled, and no effort had been spared in achieving it, nor would be spared in continuing to market her well.

If her parents' town house, fine as it might be, was still too small for a really big event, they would arrange for it to take place in one of those mansions which carried so much cachet, with a magnificent entrance hall and staircase, a splendid ballroom, and plenty of smaller reception rooms for refreshments, or merely for people to relax in. So much accommodation relieved overcrowding and prevented irritation which might drive guests away. Tension and anxiety thus allayed, serene in the knowledge that nothing could be faulted, the hostess was able to concentrate on the all-important observance of etiquette.

Young girl preparing for her first ball

Dancing always opened with the hostess or her elder daughter partnered by the gentleman of highest rank. The host would then dance with the most important lady. If it were a coming-out ball, the debutante daughter followed next, dutifully partnered by the highest-ranking bachelor. No other guests would step onto the floor until these courtesies had been observed.

Gentlemen guests were expected to dance at least once with all the daughters of the house. Another courtesy expected of them was that they should offer to escort their partners, after each dance, to one of the refreshment rooms where champagne, claret, and other wines were available. Only the most shy girl ever refused, for even if her partner subsequently abandoned her to seek another, she had at least been rescued from the humiliation of being a wallflower, as well as from her diligent guardian (who might herself be relieved to see her charge go, thus enabling her to report back to a hopeful mother that her dear girl had been sought in the dance). But to be left alone, sipping a solitary glass of wine and surrounded by laughing couples, could be equally humiliating, and if no one spared the girl a kind smile or a welcoming word, she would soon drift back to Chaperones' Corner.

It was a chaperone's duty to investigate the background and social standing of bachelors who came into the girl's orbit and skilfully to keep at bay those who did not pass muster. In this, the dance programme was a valuable aid. This folded piece of card, from which dangled a diminutive pencil attached to a tasselled cord, was introduced in the middle of the century and every young man seeking permission to dance with a young lady had to sign it along with his full name and rank. This provided an excellent springboard for the chaperone's investigation, skilled as she was in the art of social espionage. With this, his antecedents could be checked and his prospects assessed, but even if he met with approval the girl would not be allowed to dance more than three times with one partner, or she would be considered flighty. Nor was she allowed to 'sit out a dance' with a young man, or she would be considered fast. He had to return her to her chaperone, bow, and retreat. If, on investigation, he proved to be acceptable, an invitation of a discreet kind – such as to a dance being given on her behalf – could be issued.

Not surprisingly, lively young women would be hell-bent on eluding their vigilant guardians – or on making use of them if they wished to evade unwelcome overtures. These dragons could be a convenient refuge when needed, but an irksome fetter when not. And little did the conscientious chaperones know that their charges had their own names for particular events. A 'squash' was something one attended merely as a duty, and a socially eligible young man was a 'parti' (abbreviated from *bon-parti*), his opposite being a 'detrimental'.

Rules pertaining to chaperonage itself were severe. Married status was essential. An unmarried woman, even up to the age of thirty, could not be alone in a room with a male visitor, even in her own home, nor could she go anywhere with a man to whom she was not related unless a *married* gentlewoman or servant accompanied her. The only possible exception was a governess who, being of genteel birth, was known to be respectable and, because of her humble position, represented no matrimonial competition, but her lowliness made her wholly unsuitable as a chaperone at a sophisticated level. A person of such low rank could never be introduced to anyone, whereas a chaperone with a title would be presented by ambitious mothers not only with pride, but with triumph.

If a girl were lucky enough to be dancing when supper was announced, she would have a man to take her in. It was her partner's duty to escort her to the supper room – and very unpopular were men who avoided this particular dance and the possibility of being saddled for the next hour or two with a young lady lacking appeal.

The hostess always led the way to supper, again on the arm of the highest-ranking gentleman, with her daughter or daughters observing similar precedence and her husband again escorting the most important lady. Careful pre-arrangement would ensure that the debutante daughter was taken in by the most eligible young man.

In the supper room the experienced hostess presented a menu of surpassing good taste, served at tables decorated with flowers and lighted candles and sparkling with crystal and silver. The main table, always long and the most glittering of all, naturally accommodated the highest-ranking guests.

Apart from crystal dishes containing bonbons and delicious little things in aspic and a variety of patties, with other tasty things to nibble between courses (all of which would be cold, except soup served in individual cups), substantial dishes such as turkey, poultry, and game would be carved beforehand and tied up with ribbon, which had only to be untied for the sections to be taken out. Since even a supper on this scale was not on the level of a banquet (though the amount of food might correspond), footmen placed the dishes directly on the table, always facing a gentleman, who would then untie the bow and place portions on his partner's plate and his own. Good catering provided one dish for four people sitting opposite each other, so that the gentleman on each side could deal with it.

Vegetables and cheese were never included at suppers of this kind. Vegetables could stain a lady's dress, or the table linen, if served by

a man's inexperienced hand, and cheese was believed to foul a person's breath and was therefore considered vulgar.

Back in the ballroom a further demonstration of a hostess's expertise was the choice of dances, announced by a Master of Ceremonies as well as being listed on the dance programmes. The most popular were the quadrille, the polka – which sometimes replaced the galop – the lancers, the schottische, the waltz (spelled 'valse' on the dance programme) and the cotillion, which closed the ball.

If a hostess wished for a final accolade to mark a memorable evening party, she would wend her way among the weaving figures in the cotillion, graciously distributing farewell presents to both gentlemen and ladies. The dancers might stumble, but never let it be said that she herself put a foot wrong in any way.

PRESENTATION AT COURT

THE PEAK OF SOCIAL SUCCESS was to be presented at Court. Introduction to the reigning monarch was the ultimate aim of all who aspired to be accepted by Society. With a girl's 'coming out' she emerged from the schoolroom, lengthened her skirts, put up her hair, and was drilled in deportment because good carriage was essential if she were not to trip over backwards when bowing out of the Royal presence. If necessary, she was also subjected to strict elocution lessons so that she would at least sound as if she came out of the top drawer and not from some ill-spoken provincial corner of the country.

In this way she was prepared for the greatest moment of her life, which must surely lead to the next 'greatest' moment when she fulfilled her duty as a daughter and achieved a brilliant, or at least a satisfactory, marriage. If at the end of three 'Seasons' a girl had not acquired a husband, her chances were considered to be over. By thirty, an unwed woman was officially accepted as an Old Maid, and her disappointed mother would waste no more time on her daughter's future, turning her attentions instead to good causes. She had to do *some*thing to hide her shame; and by participating in charitable events she could at least satisfy her personal ambition to mix in higher circles, for such affairs were always patronized and sometimes even organized by the very best people. The failed daughter could tag along behind, if she wished, or stay at home. She could be useful for carrying parcels and serving at some worthy stall, but her mere presence could be an embarrassing reminder of failure.

But few of the newly emerging debutantes gave any thought to such a dire fate as becoming their mother's housekeeping prop and her 'comfort' in old age, or hostessing for a widowed father or unmarried brother, freedom from either of these latter positions only coming with a parent's demise or a brother's late marriage. In that event the unmarried daughter might be charitably received into the household of a relative who needed an educated, superior, unpaid housekeeper or governess.

Brighter prospects were available to one who was moneyed and venturesome, for she could travel and be dismissed as a female eccentric, but upbringing and discipline equipped very few for that.

The average girl could not hope for presentation at Court unless she could be sponsored by someone with an 'entrée', which meant a married woman who had herself been presented. Those born into the aristocracy, or what were known as country gentry and town gentry, would automatically qualify for presentation. This privilege was later extended, according to *Manners and Rules of Good Society* (1887), to include 'the wives and daughters of members of the legal, military, naval, clerical, medical and other professions, the wives and daughters of merchants, bankers, and members of the Stock Exchange, and persons engaged in commerce on a large scale. Although the word gentry is thus elastic, and although persons coming within the category might be fairly entitled to the privilege of attending Drawing Rooms, yet it is well understood that birth, wealth, associations and position give a *raison d'être* for such privileges.' This showed that as the century advanced such ranks as medical and clergy were becoming more socially acceptable, provided they had achieved some status in their professions, as were merchants and bankers providing they had made their pile.

The Royal Drawing Rooms were closed to such rogues and vagabonds as artists, writers, and members of the theatrical profession – the word 'profession' having an unfortunate but sometimes highly applicable connotation.

Many an ambitious mamma therefore had to seek a well-born sponsor to launch her daughter into the most elevated circle of all. Rumours that such sponsors could be financially acquired were firmly quashed, but it was an open secret that aristocratic connections were becoming commercially exploited and that introductions into the highest society could be obtained for a worthwhile sum; and since it was not unknown for society chaperones to advertise their services for a fee of £1000 a year, to cover a debutante's first twelve months on the social scene, it was feasible that for a considerably higher sum a lady courtier could wave the magic wand which conducted a girl into the royal presence. It was also widely known that members of the peerage accepted even more lavish gifts from socially ambitious Americans for the same service.

Presentations at Court always coincided with one of the Royal Drawing Rooms, held four times a year, and following this heady introduction the lady so honoured had to attend one Drawing Room annually and would receive an invitation to one State Ball each season. It was the peak of social recognition, the giddy heights of success, and its accomplishment was achieved in the most mundane way once the hurdle of sponsorship was overcome. The debutante herself had to apply to the Lord Chamberlain for two cards, on which she declared who she was, to whom she was related, and who intended to present her. Her sponsor had to endorse one of the cards, then both were returned to the Lord Chamberlain. With these, he could seek the royal approval. If successful, he would notify the debutante accordingly and name the elected date, whereupon she had to apply for two more cards. On these she provided the same information, taking them to the Palace on the great day, one to be handed in on arrival and the other just before entering the Presence Chamber.

Court requirements in the matter of dress were strict:

> The lady courtier must appear in full evening toilette, the corsage cut low to outline the shoulders, the sleeves extremely short. She must wear a Court train of three and a half to four yards long, white gloves, a white veil hanging from three plumes, which must be white if she is not in mourning, black if she is.

Only on health grounds could elbow-length sleeves and a slightly higher corsage be permitted, and to obtain consent for these variations a doctor's certificate had to be produced.

Beyond these royal stipulations the question of style and choice of materials was unlimited. For the most part youthful presentation gowns favoured white or delicate pastel tints, but a photograph of Elinor Glyn in full court dress (she was presented in May, 1896) testifies that there was no strict ruling on colour or material. Her tall white plumes and frothy white veil seem ill-matched with a gown of what appears to be heavy velvet, indeterminate in colour and adorned with mixed white and brown fur on sleeves and neck.

Jealous mothers zealously guarded the precious secret of their daughters' presentation gowns, and a discreet couturier would try to arrange fittings which would not clash with those of known friends. Indignant mammas coming face to face with each other on his doorstep could mean an end to the patronage of both.

Apart from the all-important gown, the tension and anxiety of fittings, and the trying on of headdresses complete with tiara and feathers, the weeks preceding a Court presentation became, for the debutante, a gruelling initiation into etiquette and procedure, into the art of climbing in and out of a carriage (preferably a State one if it could be begged or borrowed), curtseying, and walking out of a room backwards while manipulating train and veil, a fan and one long glove. Also to be rehearsed was the crucial moment of being received. If the debutante was a peeress in her own right, or the daughter of a peer, the Monarch would kiss her on the cheek or brow, but if she were a commoner it was the debutante's duty to kiss the royal hand. This required more careful rehearsing, bending her knee in a curtsey and extending her hand, palm down, while holding the pose. The royal hand would then be placed on top of hers to receive the humble salutation.

On the great day came the drive to Buckingham Palace, coming to a halt in the Mall in a long line of carriages all heading for the same goal. Although the Drawing Room was held early in the afternoon, the chain of carriages began to form hours before, causing an inevitable jam of vehicles and giving the public a chance to gawp at the occupants.

On entering the palace the debutante's first card was handed in, after which she deposited her wrap and received a mundane cloak-room ticket in exchange. She then crossed the Great Hall and inched her way up the Grand Staircase to the Corridor, in an endless queue crawling through ante-chamber after ante-chamber, a group at a time being ushered by Gentlemen-at-Arms.

She had been prepared for the precedence given to those more high-ranking than herself, but perhaps not for the subsequent jostling and shoving and jockeying for position, but she stood her ground, remaining as close as possible to her chaperone and resisting the lure of sofas into which she dare not sink for fear of creasing her gown and train or dislodging her long white veil. She had to bear the waiting with fortitude, carrying her train over her arm as she proceeded at a snail's pace toward the Presence Chamber – and, in the pressing crowd, possibly becoming separated from her

Preparing to enter the Presence Chamber (The *Graphic* 1895)

chaperone. When she eventually reached the entrance to the Picture Gallery, two Gentlemen-at-Arms used their wands to spread her train behind her.

She now removed her right glove and crossed to the door of the awe-inspiring room. Here she presented her second card, which was passed along a line of Court flunkeys until it reached the Lord Chamberlain, who read her name and details aloud as she approached the royal presence and made her obeisance, curtseying to any other members of the royal family who might be there, manipulating glove, train, veil and fan (or bouquet, as pictures from the *Graphic* of 1895 indicate), and never putting a foot wrong as she retreated backwards from the room.

After the hours of waiting, the greatest and most important introduction of her life was over in a matter of minutes. But she had 'arrived', she was accepted, she was admitted into the highest level of Society – and ahead lay her first Season, the first of a maximum of three during which she was expected to find a well-born husband. If she achieved that goal she would again be presented at Court, but this time by a female in-law who had already been received. Thus the seal was set on her much-envied marital status. Until then, she would continue to be chaperoned throughout the Season.

3 ✦ THE DILIGENT HOUSEWIFE

Man's work lasts till set of sun;
Woman's work is never done.

(Old proverb)

HAVING MASTERED THE COMPLEXITIES of social etiquette, the young bride had also to learn about the management of her household, on which Mrs Rundell had more practical advice to offer.

An inventory of furniture, linen, china, and all articles in the home had to be meticulously kept and everything in it checked twice a year. Tickets of parchment bearing the family name, numbered, and specifying which bed each belonged to, were to be sewn on every feather bed, bolster, pillow and blanket. Accounts were to be regularly kept, 'and not the smallest article omitted to be entered, and if balanced every week and month, the income and outgoings would be ascertained with facility'. Appropriate sums for different purposes were to be kept in separate purses 'such as for house, clothes, pocket, education of children, et cetera.'

It was particularly stressed that tradesmen should never be kept waiting for their money, not out of consideration or good manners, but because it could result in higher prices being charged in retaliation. Another danger in accumulating long bills was that articles never purchased could be cunningly added by the shopkeeper.

The good housewife was also expected to have an unerring knowledge of the current prices and quality of things, and of the best places at which to buy them – a practice still advisable today. The difference between then and now is that many a housewife had servants, over whom she was expected to exercise the strongest discipline. This applied particularly to the financial expenditure of her cook; if the unfortunate woman should exceed the weekly sum allocated to her, her 'public day' – her free one – should be forfeited.

The cook's expenditure on food was carefully controlled

Then there were domestic facts which every bride had learned at her mother's knee: that candles made in cool weather were best, and that it was the chandler's duty to tell his customers what the temperature had been at the time he made them, together with an indication of when the price was likely to rise so that they could lay in a stock. The same applied to soap. Both were the better for keeping eight or ten months, and 'would not injure for two years, if properly placed in the cool'.

The quality of notepaper, by which a hostess would be judged, also improved with keeping, and if bought in half or whole reams from large dealers would be much cheaper than bought by the quire. 'The surprising increase in the price of this article,' continued Mrs Rundell, 'may be accounted for by the additional duties demanded of it, and a larger consumption by the public'. In short, the masses were learning to read and write, the demand for paper increasing accordingly. This led to a monopoly in rags, used in its manufacture, and a consequent increase in price. Servants were instructed to keep a bag to hold all waste scraps of material 'from cuttings-out, et cetera', the sale of which, to a rag merchant, could supplement the housewife's purse. In some households such parsimony was resented, the proceeds being deemed the rightful perquisites of servants.

On the preservation of food, Mrs Rundell had strict rules. Every article of food had to be kept in the place best suited to its preservation because much waste could therefore be avoided. Vegetables should be kept on a stone floor if draughts could be excluded; meat in a cold, dry place, and sugar, sweetmeats, and salt similarly. Candles should be kept cold, but not damp, as should dried meats and hams. And 'every variety of seeds for puddings, saloop, rice, et cetera, had to be close covered to preserve them from insects', the worthy Mrs Rundell stressed, 'but that will not prevent it, if long kept'.

Straw on which apples were laid had to be absolutely dry, to prevent a musty taste. Large pears were hung up by the stalks, not touching each other. Fresh herbs such as basil, knotted marjoram, or thyme were used immediately but, being pungent, with discretion.

Soap could be saved by adding washing soda to the water; the soda was melted in a large jug and a quantity was then poured into washtubs and boiler; when the lather became weak, more was added. Soap was a precious commodity and was either bought or home-made in long blocks which were then cut with wire or twine and kept out of the air for two or three weeks, for if dried quickly the soap would crack and, when wet, break. Storing it on a shelf, with spaces between each piece, saved a full third in consumption.

Flour was an expensive commodity, and consequently starch, of which it was an ingredient, was also costly. According to Mrs Rundell's advice, 'The best flour will keep good in a dry warm room for some years; therefore when bread is cheap it may be bought to advantage, and covered close. Bread is so heavy an article of expense, that all waste should be guarded against. Cutting it in the room will do much to preserve it. And it should not be cut until a day old. Earthen pans and covers keep it best.'

Following the scarcity of flour in 1795 and 1800, the custom of slicing bread at sideboard or table was much adopted, thus making sure that servants made no extra inroads into this precious item. In many households the cook was compelled to exchange a ticket for every loaf of bread returned to the kitchen from the dining room, each cut loaf immediately being weighed and the amount recorded.

'And,' Mrs Rundell advised her daughters and all those private families who were deemed to need her help, 'though it is very disagreeable to suspect anyone's honesty, and perhaps mistakes have been unintentional, yet it is prudent to weigh meat, sugar, and all groceries when delivered, and compare with the charge. The butcher should be ordered to mark the weight with the meat, and the cook to file these checks, to be examined by her mistress when the weekly bill be presented.'

Trust in servants and shopkeepers seems to have been in short supply, and perhaps not without cause because connivance between domestics and tradesmen frequently gave rise to irate letters in the press. It was accepted that cooks were entitled to such perquisites as rabbit skins, dripping, candle stubs, old tea leaves, bones and the like, all of which were sold profitably to rag-and-bone merchants and others (and very unpopular were mistresses who sold their cast-off clothes to 'discreet ladies' wardrobe dealers' instead of passing them on to servants, who disposed of them as they wished).

Suspicions that new candles were melted down to add to the dripping, and that housekeepers or cooks entrusted with the ordering of household supplies received commission from traders, were rampant and possibly true. One irate lady voiced such sentiments in a letter to *The Times* protesting about the 'invidious perquisite system', declaring that 'the term "perquisite" is so comprehensive, so elastic and accommodating that it is made to embrace and signify almost everything in the various departments of the house.' Exaggerated or not, the claim was often substantiated by outraged employers who discovered that new liveries ordered for menservants annually (usually no less than two) were merely renovated by the crafty tailor but delivered, and charged, as new – commission discreetly entering the menservant's pockets.

The system of perquisites, the forerunner of present day 'perks', was something about which every bride was forewarned. An expert knowledge of such things would not only discourage dishonest servants, but earn their respect and encourage them to mend their ways.

The best way to preserve blankets from moths was to fold and lay them under feather beds that were in use, taking them out for shaking occasionally. This was better than using camphor balls. On no account were they to be stored on or beneath unused beds, for although these would be protected by holland covers the blankets would remain unused until needed, when not only a good airing but a good battle against the armies of occupation would be necessary.

Mrs Rundell's instructions regarding utensils were emphatic. If copper ones were used in the kitchen, the cook had to make sure that they were resurfaced when the least defect appeared, and should never on any account put aside any soups or gravies either in copper or metal receptacles, but only in stone or earthenware.

> Vegetables soon sour, and corrode metals and glazed red ware, by which a strong poison is produced. Some years ago, the death of several gentlemen was occasioned at Salt-hill, by the cook sending a ragout to the table which she had kept from the preceding day in a copper vessel badly tinned.

Vinegar could also corrode any glazed ware, since in those days glaze contained lead or arsenic. It was not until 1900 that British law stipulated only 10 per cent lead solubility for eating and cooking vessels, permitting greater amounts only for decorative articles. Today, wholly leadless glazes are widely used.

There were practical tips as well as warnings, some of which could be useful even in these days of refrigerators and freezers. In pre-refrigeration days a major problem was how to cool liquids in hot weather. The solution was to dip a cloth in cold water and wrap it round the container two or three times, then place in the sun. The process was repeated as often as necessary. The wet cloth absorbed the heat and converted it to evaporation, thus preventing it from reaching the contents.

Small coal wetted made the strongest fire for the back of the grate, but had to remain untouched until 'caked solid'. Cinders, too, were lightly wetted to give a greater degree of heat, and were better than coal for furnaces, smoothing irons, and ovens.

Jelly bags, and tapes used for tying up puddings, were to be scalded after use and then kept dry, to prevent an unpleasant flavour when next used.

If a cork was too large for a bottle, it was not to be trimmed down but soaked in boiling water for a few minutes to make it fit easily.

A little dry mustard sprinkled over the fingers after peeling onions, then rubbed between them before being washed away, would remove the smell, and a little vinegar kept boiling on the stove while strong-smelling vegetables were cooking would prevent the odour from spreading through the house.

To absorb damp from a cupboard (a condition much prevalent in those days) a small wooden box filled with lime would be placed on a shelf; this would keep the air both dry and sweet.

To clean glass or crystal articles such as decanters, crushed egg shells would be placed inside, then the article filled with cold water until three quarters full, shaken well, and allowed to stand. The contents would then be poured away and more crushed egg shells added, but this time with the addition of a few drops of vinegar in the water. If stains lingered, this new application would also be allowed to stand; otherwise, after shaking, it could be poured away.

And to prevent a sink pipe from freezing, common salt was poured over the sink drain at night. This served the additional function of dispelling grease.

4 ✍ THE REGIME BELOWSTAIRS
How the Other Half Lived . . .

I F THE BRIDE had been accustomed to servants all her life, becoming mistress of a household staff would hold few fears, but for one who had known only the services of a family 'general', or at the most a cook and housemaid, the supervision of a large domestic staff could be intimidating. It was often the custom for a bride to be greeted, on arrival at her husband's home, by the entire household staff lined up to welcome her (and, no doubt, to assess their new mistress). Such a reception could strike terror into the heart of a shy and inexperienced bride from a lower level of society. She would be faced with the nerve-wracking task of learning not only how to conduct herself as mistress of the household, but the right attitude to adopt toward each domestic. She would be expected to know the order of precedence belowstairs, so that on her visits to the kitchens she would never make the mistake of saying good-morning to someone of lower rank before those of a higher.

The housekeeper would naturally be acknowledged first, the lady's maid second (although the mistress may have been dressed by that particular servant on rising), then individual members of the staff according to grading, until reaching the lowest ranks of all – kitchenmaid, 'tweeny', scullery-maid, boot-boy or knife-boy, and washerwoman, though this last was frequently a village woman who came daily and, being confined to the wash-house to assist resident laundry-maids, might never come face to face with her employer.

The mistress who knew what was expected of her included the lowliest group in one comprehensive greeting and thereafter referred to them only through the medium of the housekeeper, thus tacitly acknowledging the woman's power and authority.

Ignorance of the rigid belowstairs and abovestairs etiquette could open chasms beneath a young wife's feet, into which she could stumble with ease and from which she would find it difficult to extricate herself. Sometimes the only way in which to re-establish her authority was to sack all the servants and start again, if she had the courage. If not, and if she wanted to earn the respect of servants whom time and tradition had made part of the place, she would behave in accordance with *her* place as surely as those beneath her behaved in accordance with theirs.

The average nineteenth-century household kept the average nineteenth-century housewife busy from morning till night, even with servants to help her, and if she couldn't match the best of them she failed not only in her duties, but in commanding their respect. Large families meant large houses, with endless rooms and endless stairs, and high ceilings ornamented with elaborate coves and cornices and intricate 'ceiling roses'. Housework was never finished and meals were perpetual, for apart from a large number of children many a family included ageing parents and relatives such as maiden aunts. Laundry day was a massive commitment which was not merely supervised, but often participated in, by the mistress. At such times a mother could be thankful to have her large brood taken off her hands and the nurse who cared for them was doubly blessed.

Mrs Beeton, whose *Book of Household Management* (1861) first appeared in serial form during 1859 in her husband Samuel Beeton's *Englishwoman's Domestic Magazine*, listed the requisite servants to be employed by people of modest means:

INCOME

About £1,000 a year: A cook, upper-housemaid, nursemaid, under-housemaid, and a male servant.

About £750: A cook, housemaid, nursemaid, and footboy.

About £500: A cook, housemaid, and nursemaid.

About £300: A maid-of-all-work and a nursemaid.

About £200 or £150: A maid-of-all-work and an occasional girl.

In the 1906 edition of Mrs Beeton's book, inflation had apparently taken its toll. The £1,000-a-year group could now only afford a cook, housemaid, and perhaps a manservant, while the staff of their less wealthy neighbours with £750–£500 a year had been reduced to a cook and a housemaid. At £300 a year the most a houseproud wife could afford was a mere 'general', (i.e. a general slavey to do everything, including cooking when necessary) while the unfortunate £200-a-year household had to get by with a young girl straight from workhouse or orphanage, who worked in return for 'keep' only. The £150-a-year group, if they were wise, no longer tried to compete in the social stakes.

Even so, the prestige of being among the servant-keeping classes was hard to relinquish, and examples of this desperate need to keep up appearances abound in nineteenth-century literature, memorably Anthony Trollope's curate in *The Last Chronicle of Barset*. Josiah Crawley sacrificed much to maintain a maid on an annual stipend of £130. The picture of his shabby house, broken furniture, and worn out carpets, possibly taken from real life, remains vivid; the Brontës would not be the only clerical parents to keep two maids on a stipend of £200 a year, deeming servants so indispensable that they transported them with their family of six when moving to Yorkshire.

Naturally, ambitious mothers hoped for better things for their daughters. After all, at any of the above financial levels mere tradesmen could be among the servant-keeping classes! In the mid nineteenth century, census returns showed that in rural towns approximately one household in six kept a 'living-in' maid and that around two-fifths were the households of grocers, plumbers, drapers and the like, none of whom would be invited to the table of a socially-conscious hostess.

To reign over a nobleman's household with its impressive fleet of servants was the ultimate ambition, but not all brides-to-be could hope for elevation into the peerage. For the most part they would have to be content with a 'good' marriage and a predominantly female domestic staff, since the tax on male servants, first imposed by Lord North in 1777 at a guinea a head (more for bachelor employers) to contribute to the cost of the American War of Independence, had led to the diminishing employment of men servants. There was even a tax on hair-powder for the wigs of footmen and coachmen, which remained in force until 1869. These taxes had later been supplemented by Pitt with a levy of two shillings and sixpence per annum on female servants. Women domestics, being therefore less costly than men, increased in number.

The tax on male servants eased toward the end of the century, although it did not finally disappear until the Finance Act of 1937. In the meantime, one male servant at least was considered essential in a city household, particularly in London where it was deemed undesirable for the lady of the house to walk abroad without a manservant walking some discreet steps behind her.

Only in the wealthiest establishments was a house steward employed. Compared with a housekeeper's manifold responsibilities a house steward could enjoy a very easy life. Sometimes his only duties were to take charge of the household accounts and oversee the dining room – never demeaning himself by serving at table, but supervising those who did. In establishments where a corps of manservants was kept, but no steward, these duties were undertaken by the butler, sometimes assisted by the under-butler, with footmen serving at table.

In the grandest houses there would be not only a house steward and chef, but butler and under-butler, valet, footmen, hall usher, pantry boy or boot boy who could double as page boy, odd job man, night watchman, coachman and stable boy, in addition to essential women servants. This list was modest compared with male retainers at country seats, where a groom of the chambers was a high-ranking and essential office and many more footmen and houseboys were required and where outdoor staff could include gardeners and under-gardeners, foresters, kennelmen, farriers, blacksmiths, coachmen, grooms and stable boys, plus lodge-keepers to guard entrances. The small garden of a town house could be tended by an odd-job man.

However, the average bride would not have to contend with a fleet of male servants as well as female, and the average mamma would be satisfied if her daughter acquired a staff of women only. Were the husband to advance in the world, the handling of menservants could come later. Meanwhile his young wife would learn that each domestic department was supervised by the servant most qualified in its particular function, with the housekeeper's eagle eye on all.

The housekeeper ranked as the most senior member of the staff, unless a steward was employed. By tradition, female domestics were interviewed and engaged by the housekeeper, and for the lady of the house to do so could provoke displeasure and open disapproval.

A good housekeeper missed nothing, nor did she neglect a single one of her own duties. The bunch of keys at her belt was her badge of office and the dreaded chink of them could strike terror into the hearts of servants idling at their work.

Every key was an essential part of her equipment, unlocking larders, still rooms, supply cupboards, pantries, wine cellars, china closets, linen cupboards, butler's pantry (where silver was kept and polished – by the butler, or footman if one were kept; by the housekeeper, assisted by housemaids, if not), and finally her own private sanctum, the housekeeper's room, where she dispensed tea after supper to the senior servants only. In some establishments the evening meal's main course was first carved in the kitchen by the housekeeper, then eaten in state in her sitting room in company with the butler, cook, and lady's maid, waited on by a housemaid; but for the most part only the nightly cup of tea (and sometimes a drop of something stronger) wound up the day for the senior staff, while the lower orders washed dishes, scrubbed the kitchen tables, brought in coals for the morning, polished boots for the entire household, and attended to any neglected jobs before tumbling into their beds.

The housekeeper

Early next morning the lower servants crept downstairs in bare or stockinged feet shortly after dawn, in peril of dismissal if they wakened the household. The kitchenmaid cleaned out the kitchen range, black-leading and polishing it where necessary, lit the fire and paid particular attention to the dampers, for woe betide her if cook arrived to find the ovens cold. The boot-boy replenished supplies of coal in all living rooms; he would attend to the bedrooms after they were vacated. He sorted out the household's boots and shoes, checked on their polishing, delivered them to bedroom doors as silently as possible, then returned to the kitchen to clean knives and to do whatever tasks were flung at him.

It was the housemaid's job to carry large cans of hot water upstairs for the hip baths of master and mistress. Bathrooms were virtually unknown and those that existed had to be similarly supplied until the advent of plumbing. In the 1850s even medium-sized houses still had no bathrooms – and 'medium-sized' included terraced houses of several floors, spacious suburban villas, or detached country houses with numerous bedrooms. Perhaps for this reason daily bathing, when it ceased to be regarded as injurious to health, was usually confined to babies, a weekly bath being considered sufficient for adults. And in less-well-off families with fewer servants adults had to share the same bath water, the youngest, traditionally, having to make do with soiled, tepid water.

In addition to carrying hot water up endless stairs to the family bedrooms, the housemaids were responsible for cleaning out grates, lighting fires, and cleaning and dusting the living rooms and stairs. Everything had to be completed before the family came down for breakfast, when the maids would proceed aloft to attend to the bedrooms. Meanwhile, the scullerymaid, after sweeping both scullery and kitchen floors, laid out everything in readiness for the cook, set the table in the servants' hall, fetched clean dishes from their racks and stacked them on the kitchen tables together with all requisites for the family's breakfast. These would be carried upstairs to the breakfast room by one of the housemaids; the lowest members of the domestic staff were never allowed abovestairs.

It was also the housemaid's duty to set the breakfast room table

and sideboard, light spirit lamps beneath hot plates and see that bread and other uncooked foods were ready and waiting.

In larger households, one of the kitchen maids – usually the one who had been there longest – cooked breakfast for the servants' hall, leaving cook to cater for those abovestairs.

No wise housekeeper would antagonize either the butler, if one were kept, or the lady's maid who, though often resented, was 'nearest to the mistress's ear' and could therefore be a treasured ally or a dangerous enemy. It was as well to curry favour with this most disliked member of the staff, if only for diplomacy's sake.

The housekeeper's personal responsibilities included the arrangement of bedrooms and their appointments – the supply of bedlinens, towels, toiletries, soap, candles, headed notepaper for senior members of the family who usually had writing desks in their private chambers, and the topping-up of ink wells – plus keeping wardrobes free of dust and re-lining drawers weekly. These tasks she also performed in visitors' rooms, which were allocated according to her mistress's choice; those of accompanying servants could be left to the housekeeper.

She was also in charge of the still room, where her tasks included making jam, cordial, and conserves; preserving fruits; candying lemon, orange, and citron peel; drying root ginger (or bottling the same in rich syrup); drying lavender to keep linen cupboards, wardrobes, and drawers fragrant, the making of potpourri, and sometimes rose water from dark red roses, for which it was essential to pick the fading blooms at precisely the right time. She also ground coffee and dried herbs, distilled herbal medicines and invalid wine, and invariably had her own pet recipe for cough mixtures and throat lozenges. She kept the first-aid cupboard well supplied and knew how to administer its contents in emergencies.

In many households the ordering of stores was the housekeeper's task. For this reason the conscientious mother instilled into her daughter the wisdom of keeping a personal eye on accounts, but should the unfortunate bride marry into a family where a housekeeper of long standing already shouldered this responsibility, relieving her of it could be not only embarrassing but might arouse the woman's ire and even precipitate her outraged departure.

This could come about for two reasons – either the insult was too great for an honest woman to accept, or the termination of a profitable sideline persuaded her to seek another post where she could continue to supplement her wages with deft manipulation. As the century advanced, and the suspicions of employers became widely voiced, caution persuaded more and more diligent mistresses to do their own household ordering and settling of bills, at the risk of incurring the housekeeper's displeasure.

Next to the housekeeper in the domestic hierarchy came the lady's maid, an unenviable yet frequently coveted post to which many a housemaid hoped to be promoted. The appeal of this position was wholly snobbish, for although it was not unknown for ladies' maids to become trusted friends of their mistresses, the position frequently carried no security, such as household servants could generally count on. The usefulness of a lady's maid often diminished as she aged, when she could be discharged with nothing more than the promise of a good reference, but few envious housemaids thought of this when hearing her referred to as 'Miss' So-and-So and observing the deference accorded her by the upper servants. No matter if this deference concealed resentment and mistrust; it was essential when someone was so close to the mistress of the house, someone likely to know intimate secrets; someone, moreover, who could whisper a favourable or unfavourable word in the mistress's ear.

To keep on the right side of the lady's maid was therefore circumspect. Not until she had outgrown her usefulness and was taking her exit through the servants' door, carrying her often modest possessions, could other staff reveal their feelings toward her by refusing to carry her bag up the area steps as, heretofore, she had expected parcels to be dealt with.

From the mistress's point of view, youth was considered essential in a lady's maid, for with it came stamina and, more often than not, a flair for fashion. The highest references, particularly regarding honesty, were essential for an employee who would be caring for furs and jewels and costly gowns. Also required was a modicum of education, soft speech, and good handwriting because many a note of acceptance or greeting would have to be penned on behalf of her mistress. Skill with the needle was necessary, and training in dressmaking and millinery a distinct asset. Few housemaids, therefore, were eligible, and ladies' maids were often recruited from higher social levels. The daughters of tradesmen and even of impoverished clergy were frequent applicants, but few realized the sadness of their lot until confronted with its end. Not many were so fortunate as to be pensioned off, or housed for life, a fact which never occurred to the envious housemaid who longed to step into the place of the lady's maid so that she could queen it over fellow domestics.

The lady's maid

It is difficult to make effective comparisons between domestic wages throughout the century because these varied not only in different parts of the country but between households, much depending on either the status or attitude of the employer and the skill of the employee. A lady's maid could rise to £40 or £50 a year, including her board and accommodation, as the century advanced. She could also receive gifts of fashionable clothes which her mistress had tired of. A lady's maid could be very well dressed indeed, but much depended on the generosity of her employer. A mistress who disposed of her wardrobe to private dealers would pass on to her maid only outworn garments which no dealer would look at, and sometimes no more than minor accessories long past their usefulness.

To a lowly scullerymaid the money earned by those above her could seem riches indeed. A housekeeper's salary was usually a well-kept secret. In some households it might excel that of the lady's maid's quite considerably, and in some be well below it. The cook, depending on her skill, could rise to a salary of £50 and upward as the century advanced, the 'good plain cook' naturally earning less than the 'professed' cook. For many upper servants, including governesses, nannies, valets and butlers, £50 seems to have become

The cook and her assistants

the average salary. A butler who undertook duties on a par with a house steward's could earn as much as £100. Footmens' wages varied between £25 and £50, the higher paid undertaking some of a butler's duties. A housemaid could eventually reach £25 a year, a parlour maid sometimes more, whereas a groom of the chambers or a house steward, being most senior of all, commanded as much as £100 to £150 annually.

The groom of the chambers, in the grandest homes, was general manager of the entire household. He occupied comfortable married quarters and frequently had his own servants.

By mid-century, and sometimes later, a nurserymaid who assisted and waited on the nurse, and took her charges for walks, could earn £20 to £30, a pageboy around £5, and for a charwoman or daily washerwoman, fourpence an hour remained the going rate.

Although it is popularly believed that the cook reigned supreme, in reality she came third in the domestic hierarchy, after the house-keeper and butler or steward, except in households where she com-bined the duties of cook-housekeeper. In such places a 'good, plain cook' usually fitted the bill, but in bigger establishments the 'pro-fessed' cook was essential, guaranteeing more skilled and soph-isticated cooking, sometimes only one degree less than that of a talented male chef. In that case her wages would naturally be higher.

By tradition, the cook was always given the courtesy title of 'Mrs', even if unmarried; the butler, although addressed by his surname by his employers, always received the prefix 'Mr' from other servants.

The model wife who also aimed to be the model mistress of her household would be at pains to establish her authority and to impress her staff by instructing them in matters which she considered neces-sary as additional knowledge. To this end various 'receipts' might be displayed on the kitchen wall, extracted from Mrs Rundell's or, later, Mrs Beeton's works.

To Clean Stone Stairs & Halls

Boil a pound of pipe-maker's clay with a quart of water, a quart of small-beer, and put in a bit of stone blue. Wash with this mixture and, when dry, rub the stones with flannel and brush.

To Clean Plate

Boil an ounce of prepared hartshorn-powder in a quart of water; while on the fire, put into it as much plate as the vessel will hold; let it boil a little, then take it out and drain it over the saucepan, and dry it before the fire.

Put in more, and serve the same, till you have done. Then put into the water some clean linen rags till all be soaked up. When dry, they will serve to clean the plate, and are the very best things to clean the brass locks and finger-plates of doors.

To Clean Paint

Never use a cloth, but take off the dust with a little long-haired brush, after blowing off the loose parts with the bellows. When soiled, dip a sponge or a bit of flannel into soda and water, wash it off quickly, and dry immediately, or the strength of the soda will eat off the colour.

To Preserve Gilding, and Clean It

It is not possible to prevent flies from staining the gilding without covering it; before which, blow off the light dust, and pass a feather or clean brush over it, then with strips of paper cover the frames, and do not remove till the flies are gone.

Linen takes off the gilding, and deadens its brightness; so it should therefore never be used for wiping it. Some means should be used to destroy the flies, as they injure furniture of every kind. Bottles hung about with sugar and vinegar, or beer, will attract them.

To Give a Fine Colour to Mahogany

Let the tables be washed perfectly clean with vinegar, having first taken out any ink stains there may be with spirit of salt; but it must be used with the greatest care, and only touch the part affected, and be instantly washed off.

Use the following liquid:– Into a pint of cold-drawn linseed oil, put four-pennyworth of alkanet-root, and two-pennyworth of rose-pink, in an earthen vessel; let it remain all night; then, stirring well, rub some of it all over the tables with a linen rag; when it has lain some time, rub it bright with linen cloths.

To Take Ink Out of Mahogany

Dilute half a teaspoonful of oil of vitriol with a large spoonful of water, and touch the part with a feather; watch it, for if it stays too long it will leave a white mark. It is therefore better to rub it quick, and repeat if not quite removed.

To Take Iron Stains Out of Marble

An equal quantity of fresh spirit of vitriol and lemon-juice being mixed in a bottle, shake it well; wet the spots, and in a few minutes rub with soft linen till they disappear.

To Take Rust Out of Steel

Cover the steel with sweet oil well rubbed on it, and in forty-eight hours use unslaked lime finely powdered, to rub until all the rust disappears.

To Preserve Smoothing Irons From Rust

Melt fresh *mutton*-suet, smear it over the iron while hot, then dust it well with unslaked lime pounded and tied up in muslin.

Fire-irons should be kept wrapped in baize, in a dry place, when not used.

To Clean the Backs of the Grate, the Inner Hearth, and the Fronts of Cast-Iron Stoves

Boil about a quarter of a pound of the best black-lead, with a pint of small beer, and a bit of soap the size of a walnut. When that is melted, dip a painter's brush, and wet the grate, having first brushed off all the soot and dust; then take a hard brush, and rub it till of a beautiful brightness.

To Clean Pewter Porter-Pots

Get the finest whiting, which is only sold in large cakes, the small being mixed with sand; mix a little of it powdered, with the least drop of sweel oil, and rub well, and wipe clean; then dust some dry whiting in a muslin bag over, and rub bright with dry leather. The last is to prevent rust, which the cook must be careful to guard against by wiping dry and putting by the fire when they come from the parlour; for if but once hung up without, the steam will rust the inside.

Fine Blacking for Shoes

Take four ounces of ivory black, three ounces of the coarsest sugar, a table-spoonful of sweet oil, and a pint of small beer; mix them slowly until cold.

No doubt servants were well acquainted with any household hints their mistress passed on, but valued their jobs too much to say so. There were few aspects of household management of which experienced servants were ignorant.

LEISURE AND PLEASURE BELOWSTAIRS

Today's widely-held idea that a servant's life was one of constant slavery was true in a limited number of households, but by no means all. Ill-treatment and ill-nourishment did not always pass unnoticed and the threat of public exposure in the courts, achieved in several notorious cases by conscientious Church societies and other vigilant bodies, made many an employer careful of how domestic staff were treated.

A stronger factor in the better treatment of servants was the industrial revolution, which offered tempting financial reward in factories and trades. Throughout the century domestic servants became increasingly independent. Since they were in constant demand, they could afford to pick and choose once they had gained good domestic experience, and a bad 'place' was often worth enduring for a few months in order to be able to qualify for a better one.

A good household, however, was worth remaining with, even if the upper servants ('the Upper Ten') patronized or verbally abused the lower ones ('the Lower Five'), for food could be abundant and of a better quality than many a maid or manservant had known previously. A good mistress provided her servants with three good meals a day, starting with a substantial breakfast, though costly items such as sugar and tea might be strictly rationed and supply cupboards kept locked. Sometimes an extra sum of money was paid weekly, to buy their own tea and sugar. But in many households such strictures were not imposed, particularly as 'the servant problem' increased with ever-widening industrialization. Domestic service had to be made more appealing, with guaranteed free time, and visitors allowed in the kitchen providing they were vetted and approved by the mistress or master of the house.

Even heavy drinking was tolerated by employers who couldn't afford to lose their servants. The heat from kitchen ovens, plus the lavish use of wines and spirits in cooking, created a thirst which was sometimes frequently slaked. A wise mistress learned to accept her cook's drunkenness with equanimity.

With similar equanimity, the most menial servants had to accept kitchen discipline. In the best regulated servants' hall this was strictly adhered to. In some households the mealtime procedure was severe, the under-servants marching into the servants' hall first, standing at their respective places at table until their seniors had arrived and seated themselves. Throughout the meal the juniors only spoke if spoken to by their betters. At all meals, male servants sat at one side of the table and female the other.

Sometimes cold beef or mutton or some other substantial dish was served for breakfast, with poultry or game or another joint at midday, plus pudding and cheese. In country houses grouse and pheasant were by no means unknown belowstairs and in many good

Light opera in the servants' hall (*Punch's Almanack* 1870)

establishments the evening meal might consist of four courses. After a dinner party abovestairs, this would sometimes be supplemented with leftover desserts.

At the other extreme, callous or parsimonious mistresses supplied only bread and cheese and then complained at the discontent of servants who were 'gone before one could say Jack Robinson!', but in large establishments where cost was not counted, a servant's life could be good. There might even be a piano belowstairs on which many an under-maid or boot boy had their first pianoforte lessons from one of the seniors and around which the staff could gather for a sing-song after the day's work.

Apart from the customary two weeks' annual holiday, sometimes only one week in lesser households, particularly in towns, there would be one regular evening off and a half-day on Sunday for the lower echelons, with a full day for the hierarchy. Menservants always had more free time than women. This they sometimes spent at local servants' clubs where they would discuss their respective employers over a tankard of ale.

Such opportunities were rare for female servants, except for the much-envied London nursarymaid who wheeled her charges to Kensington Gardens daily, to meet her counterparts from other households. Many a London nurserymaid would push the bassinette at a good brisk pace for a few miles to reach that mecca by the Round Pond. On returning, she would regale her fellow servants with the latest scandal from some noted or titled family.

As the century advanced, compassionate mistresses encouraged their maids to join Church organizations like the Girls' Friendly Society, which arranged social activities for working girls, enabling them to form friendships and take up various crafts. Some employers taught unschooled servants to read and write. But in poorer households few comforts would be found in the basement world, with kitchen quarters sparsely furnished, floors bare, recreation nil.

At great houses like Longleat and Welbeck Abbey, Christmas celebrations for the servants were held on a grand scale. Servants' halls were elaborately decorated, feasting was abundant and prolonged, and generous financial rewards were handed out. The servants' ball at Longleat was held in the dining room and was justly famed. To it were also invited local tradesmen and their families. The Marquis would open the ball with the housekeeper, and the Marchioness with the house steward. On Christmas morning all the under-maids were personally presented with the traditional gift of a new dress. But this celebration could not compare with the Twelfth Night Servants' Ball at Welbeck, for which a London orchestra was hired and the staff served by a fleet of waiters. Feasting was lavish and champagne flowed, enjoyed by well over a thousand guests, including not only the household staff but estate tenants and their wives, plus local tradesmen and their families.

In some of these great houses regular weekly events were arranged for the domestic staff. Servants at Longleat enjoyed twice-weekly dances in which the outdoor staff also joined. Music was provided by a hired musician and supper consisted of a buffet from kitchen and stillroom.

Inevitably, the servants of lesser households strongly envied those so fortunately placed.

5 ❧ In Sickness and in Health
The Ministering Angel

To the roles of diligent housewife and elegant hostess, the model wife added that of ministering angel, guardian of her household's health. Many ancient cures handed down from earlier generations were still in use in the nineteenth century, helping to reduce medical fees or even avert them.

> 'Tis better to hunt the fields for health unbought,
> Than fee the doctor for a nauseous draught,

was much-quoted among the wise, for it was well substantiated by historical fact.

Early in the seventeenth century the Countess of Chinchón, wife of the Spanish Governor of Peru, was cured of malaria by a preparation made with the bark of a South American tree subsequently named *Chinchona calisaya* after her. As a result of this remarkable cure, Jesuit priests sent a consignment of the bark to Europe, where it became known as Jesuits' Bark or Peruvian Bark. It is still used today as a source of quinine.

In the eighteenth century a Dr William Withering of Birmingham was told by an old woman, whom many dubbed a witch, that an infusion made of foxglove was good for dropsy and heart disease. Inevitably, she was ridiculed; but digitalis, a drug made from the foxglove plant, is now used in the treatment of heart disease.

Here are just a few Victorian 'old wives' cures':

To Take Away Freckles

Boil slowly for two hours, in a covered saucepan, five cupfuls of loose elder leaves to eight cupfuls of rainwater. Strain, then when cold wash the face with a cloth dipped in the liquor and allow it to dry.

To Cure Chilblains

In a teacup mix one dessertspoonful of mustard powder with two of liqueur brandy. When thoroughly mixed, stir in two teaspoonfuls of whisked white of egg, and immerse in the mixture a piece of folded gauze. At bedtime, place the soaked gauze around the chilblain (providing it is not broken); bandage over, and next morning the chilblain should have disappeared. If not, repeat once or twice.

To Cure a Boily Boy (or Girl)

Take some stale bread and boil it for one hour in an equal quantity of water. When it has become a paste make it into a poultice in some muslin and apply to the boil as hot as it can be borne, leave it for an hour, then replace with a second poultice, the practice to continue until cured.

To Remove Warts

Even the largest of warts can be removed painlessly without leaving a scar if treated as follows:

Steep a piece of raw beefsteak all night in a little tarragon vinegar, then cut as much from it as will amply cover the wart, tie it on the wart, or if on the forehead fasten it over with a tight bandage. Do this overnight and remove by day. In two weeks of this regular treatment the wart will die and peel off.

A simpler and less expensive recipe for removing these disfigurements came from gardens or hedgerows – the sap of milkweed applied frequently to the wart, leaving it uncovered, would prove effective in a matter of days, according to the size of the wart.

To Ease Toothache

A little laudanum mixed with a little essence of tarragon and applied on wool to the aching tooth or gum reduces pain.

Laudanum (tincture of opium) seems to have been freely available in those days, and was much used as a pain killer or to induce sleep.

To Cure the Rheumatics

The common nettle, *urtica pilulifera*, is said to have arrived in England with the Romans, who brought a plentiful supply of the plant with which to rub their bodies against the chill northern climate.

Later, whipping with nettles was practised to take away the tempers of naughty children – a method also highly recommended for rheumatism. To this day, nettle usage is strongly favoured as a cure. As tea, it is rivalled only by the celery seed.

> To make *Nettle Tea*, pour one quart of boiling water on six breakfast cupfuls of the leaves, and infuse for two hours. Drink when cold – the mixture is sufficiently hot by nature to require no additional heating. And so, added to mulled ale, is an infusion of chillies in boiling water.

Extract of Malt, for Coughs

Over half a bushel of pale ground malt pour as much hot (not boiling) water as will just cover it. In forty-eight hours, drain off the liquor entirely, but without squeezing the grains; put the former into a large saucepan, that there may be room to boil as quick as possible without boiling over; when it begins to thicken, stir constantly. It must be as thick as treacle. A dessert-spoonful thrice a day is prescribed.

Also much valued for fevers and colds was *Raspberry Vinegar*. For this, a pound of raspberries would be soaked for two days in a glass of white wine. The fruit would then be strained through a sieve and the liquor poured onto another pound of raspberries for a further two days. To every liquid pound of juice would be added two pounds of loaf sugar. The mixture would then be poured into a deep jar and placed in a pan of hot water. When the sugar had dissolved, scum would be removed, the vinegar bottled and sealed down when cold.

To Soothe Lumbago

First thing in the morning, and last thing at night, eat a lump of sugar on which two drops (no more) of juniper oil have been poured.

To Rout the Gout

Melt some beeswax and, when still liquid hot but not hot enough to burn, apply it on the affected place; cover with any non-absorbent

The Invalid, 1864

material. Leave for three quarters of an hour, by which time the pain should have gone.

Linseed was considered a cure for all ills and a poultice applied to a gouty foot, an aching back, or any other afflicted area, could prove effective, but it was essential to use *crushed* linseed, not linseed meal.

A Face Lotion for the Gentle Sex

When the strawberry is in flower, pick some of the leaves, add those of the violet and the leaves and flowers of tansy, the leaves from the plane tree, the flowers from the lime tree, and petals from red roses.

Now press into a teacup, packing to the rim each of the first three and mix with three unpressed teacupfuls of each of the last three.

Bring to the boil in a quart of rainwater, pour in one quart of freshly boiled milk, and after stirring well let it simmer slowly, under a lid, until one third diminished. Strain into warm dry bottles, and cork only when cool. Before retiring, wet a cloth with this lotion, wash the face with it, and let it dry into the skin.

To Cheer a Glum Heart

Gather petals of freshly-bloomed red roses and dry them in the sun with fresh violets, borage flowers and the flowers of anchusa in equal quantities. When thoroughly dry, mix well and preserve in a dry glass jar, well sealed. When feeling depressed, put four tablespoonfuls of dried flowers into a teapot, pour over them one breakfast cupful of boiling water, leave to infuse for ten minutes, then drink, sweetened with honey.

Illness, even of a serious nature, was nursed at home. Diseases such as cholera, typhus and scarlet fever were comparatively common, and long recuperation and careful nursing were necessary after the high fevers and subsequent weakness associated with them. The sickroom therefore demanded specific catering.

A Dr Ratcliff, renowned for his study of dietary food for the sick, offered many recipes, the most famous of which was for *Restorative Pork Jelly*. For this it was essential to have a leg of well-fed pork and, without slicing or cutting the meat, to beat it until the bone was broken, then to cover with three gallons of water and simmer over a gentle fire until the liquid was reduced to one gallon. The meat was then removed and half an ounce of mace, plus the same of nutmegs, was stewed in it for 'a reasonable time', after which the liquid was strained through a fine sieve. When cold, the fat was skimmed off, and a cup of the resultant jelly was served to the patient 'the first and last thing, and at noon', adding salt to taste.

And a recipe the good doctor described as 'a remarkably good thing for people who are weak' was for *Shank Jelly*. This required twelve shanks of mutton, to be soaked for four hours and then scrubbed and scoured until absolutely clean. They were then put in a saucepan with three blades of mace, an onion, twenty Jamaica peppers and thirty or forty black peppers, a bunch of sweet herbs, and a crust of bread well toasted. Three quarts of water were added, and the pan set on a hot hearth, covered close, and left to simmer gently for five hours; then the liquid was strained off and put in a cold place. A pound of beef could be added, for flavour.

For weak bowels there was the famous *Arrow-Root Jelly*. To half a pint of water was added a glass of sherry or brandy, grated nutmeg, and fine sugar. This was boiled up once, then mixed by degrees with a dessertspoonful of arrowroot previously 'rubbed smooth' with two spoonfuls of cold water, the whole then being returned to the saucepan and boiled for three minutes, constantly stirring.

There were many nourishing meat broths made from beef, mutton, veal, and chicken.

For *Calves' Feet Broth* a cupful of jelly made from boiled calves' feet was warmed with half a glass of sweet wine, a little water, and nutmeg, into which the yolk of an egg and a small lump of butter were then whisked without boiling.

Fish broth was considered highly nutritious and 'light of digestion', particularly when made from eels or tench:

Eel Broth

Clean half a pound of small eels, and set them on the fire with three pints of water, some parsley, one slice of onion, a few pepper-corns; let them simmer till the eels are broken, and the broth good. Add salt, and strain it off.

Tench Broth was made the same way.

Caudles were warm gruels containing spices, sugar, and wine. They were considered particularly good 'for women in child-bed'. *A Good Plain Caudle* was made from a smooth gruel of half-grits (husked but unground oats, or coarse oatmeal) boiled well, strained, and stirred occasionally until cold. When needed, sugar, wine, lemon peel and nutmeg were added, and sometimes a spoonful of brandy as well as the wine 'to tempt the patient'.

Recipes for caudles were many and varied, but all had the basic ingredients of oats, nutmeg, wine, brandy, or beer. *Cold Caudle*, for which spring water was considered essential, included the yolk of an egg, the juice of a small lemon, six spoonfuls of sweet wine, sugar to taste, and an ounce of syrup of lemons.

Mulled wine was frequently served to the sick. Some spice, such as cinnamon, was boiled in a little water until the flavour was considered right; to this was added an equal quantity of port, some sugar and nutmeg, all boiled together and served with toast.

Unheard of now, but highly esteemed in the nineteenth century, was *Saloop*. This was a hot drink made from salep, a nutritive substance extracted from the dried tubers of orchidaceous plants, purchased in powder form from an apothecary, or sassafras, the bark of a small North American tree. Some water, wine, lemon-peel, and sugar were all boiled together, then mixed with a small quantity of the salep or sassafras powder, well pounded and blended with a little water. After stirring, the mixture was boiled for a few minutes.

An interesting thing about saloop is that it was also sold as a cheap substitute for coffee at London street stalls, providing nourishment for those who were short of cash.

For invalids, *ass's milk* was considered to surpass cow's milk. It could be made artificially, but the real thing was much preferred.

Ancient instructions were that 'it should be milked into a glass that is kept warm by being in a basin of hot water . . . At first a teaspoonful of rum may be taken with it, but should only be put into the milk the moment it is swallowed.'

Preparing a nourishing broth for the sickroom

Artificial ass's milk was made by boiling together a quart of water, a quart of fresh cow's milk, an ounce of white sugar-candy, half an ounce of eringo-root, and half an ounce of conserve of roses, till the liquid was reduced to half its original amount. This was astringent, and had to be given to the patient with care.

An alternative was to boil two ounces of hartshorn-shavings, two ounces of pearl barley, two ounces of candied eringo-root, and one dozen snails that had been pounded lightly, in two quarts of water, until the amount was reduced to one quart. A measure of this was mixed with an equal quantity of fresh cow's milk and given to the patient twice daily.

Buttermilk was highly valued as a nutritious drink for the sick. According to the well-known instructions of Doctor Boerhaave, it should be drunk as frequently as possible and should 'form the whole of the patient's drink, and the food should be biscuits and rusks in every way and sort; ripe and dried fruits of various kinds when a decline is apprehended.' Baked and dried fruits, raisins in particular, were considered an excellent supper for invalids, with biscuits or cake, accompanied by Dr Boerhaave's sweet buttermilk.

Orgeat was another esteemed invalid food. For this two ounces of ground almonds were beaten with a tablespoonful of orange-flower water, and a bitter almond or two. To this paste was added a quart of milk and water, sweetened to taste. It was considered a fine drink 'for those who have a tender chest; and in the gout it is highly useful, and with the addition of half an ounce of gum arabic has been found to allay the painfulness of attendant heat. Half a glass of brandy may be added, if thought too cooling in the latter complaint, and the glass of orgeat may be put into a basin of warm water.'

Orgeat was apparently so greatly enjoyed that it was served when entertaining company – with additional brandy.

6 ❧ ON BECOMING A GOOD COOK
The Way to a Man's Heart

I F THE WAY TO A MAN'S HEART was through his stomach, the nineteenth century housewife certainly knew how to get there. In the days before refrigerators, frozen and pre-packed foods and labour-saving devices, the choice and preparation of food depended on what was seasonally available or could be preserved by smoking, salting, bottling or drying. The housewife's diligence in recording her catering skills demonstrated her pride in them. Her life seems to have been devoted to feeding her family, running her household, controlling the purse strings, bringing up her children, organizing her domestic staff and entertaining her guests.

In this world in which man was the breadwinner and woman graced his hearth and home (except in the case of the really poor) she would appear, to women of today, to have been his prisoner and his slave. Perhaps she was, and undoubtedly a lot of intelligent women chafed against eternal domesticity and sought escape in charitable work – history bears testimony to them – but there were also those who channelled their intelligence into creating an art of managing their kitchens.

Meals, by today's standards, were copious. According to Mrs Beeton, a 'plain family dinner' would consist usually of three courses, the main course often including two kinds of meat as well as vegetables. For a dinner party, four or five courses was normal, but each course would include several dishes – for example:

DINNER FOR 6 PERSONS (MARCH)

First Course
Oyster Soup
Boiled Salmon and dressed Cucumber

Entrées
Rissoles   Fricasseed Chicken

.

Second Course
Boiled Leg of Mutton
Roast Fowls, garnished with water-cresses
Caper sauce
Vegetables

.

Third Course
Charlotte aux Pommes   Orange Jelly   Lemon Cream
Soufflé of Arrowfoot   Sea-kale

.

Dessert

.

A hearty breakfast was considered essential. In addition to hot dishes of fish, steak, kidneys, bacon and eggs, sausages, etc., Mrs Beeton lists 'collared and potted meats or fish, cold game or poultry, veal-and-ham pies, game-and-rumpsteak pies ... as also cold ham, tongue, &c. &c.' as suitable cold dishes for the breakfast table

Surely it was in the latter half of the nineteenth century that the descriptive phrase 'a fine figure of a woman' was coined, for few sylphlike wives could have graced their husbands' tables in a period when thought was never given to dieting, but only to tables groaning with food. One hallmark of a wife's success was the lavishness of her menus.

These were the days when famous beauties were admired for their curves, and this attitude prevailed into the early twentieth century as buxom women like Lily Langtry, heavy on the hips and broad in the beam (and elsewhere), continued to be the toasts of society and the mistresses of kings and earls. With these ample and voluptuous ladies the model wife had to compete, and she did it by courting her husband's devotion and the admiration of his friends in the way she knew best – via her dining table.

Perhaps no other items in her lavish catering were more guaranteed to increase male corpulence and female bulk than her pies, puddings, and pastries. Every variety of fish, meat, fowl and game pie, encrusted with the richest pastry and in many cases cooked with the most generous ingredients and the finest wines, was served as extra courses or side dishes to supplement a meal, while delicacies

Kitchen range 1874 with exposed fire for open roasting; a Dutch oven with bottle jack is shown on the left

abounding in excessive calories (an unknown word) were dotted about the table to bridge gaps between helpings.

The most striking thing about recipes from the period is the lavish use of ingredients which, today, would be considered wildly extravagant. With so much to choose from, there was no excuse for a wife to lack expertise, and if she employed a cook she would win no respect if she did. It was therefore her duty to learn how a manifold number of dishes should be prepared, how ingredients should be chosen, for how long and by what method they should be cooked and, finally, how they should be presented at table.

CHOOSING AND PREPARING FISH

SINCE MOST MEALS BEGAN with a fish course, seafood was of prime importance. There was much imaginative use of both sea and freshwater fish, and a wide variety of both was available. The lower reaches of the river Thames, for example, yielded a plentiful supply of salmon and mackerel of the highest quality, and oysters were so commonplace that they were sold on street barrows alongside

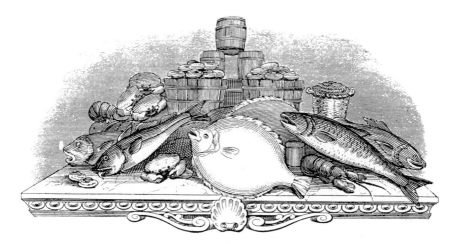

eels and mussels. The following advice on how and when to choose
fish came from Mrs Rundell's unique work, mentioned in chapter
one, which lists all kinds of fish including some, such as carp and
pike, that are rare today.

It was stressed that all fish should be firm, with red gills and bright
eyes and scales, when purchased.

CARP can live some time out of water and quality may therefore
diminish; it is best to kill them as soon as caught, or buy them as soon
as delivered to the fishmonger's slab. The same signs of freshness
attend them as attend all fish. To ask the fishmonger when they were
killed can only reveal ignorance of essential signs.

EELS – There is a greater difference in the goodness of eels than in
any other fish. The true silver-eel (so called from the bright colour of
the belly) is caught in the Thames. The Dutch eels sold at Billingsgate
are very bad; those caught in great floods are generally good, but in
ponds they have usually a strong rank flavour. They are always in
season, except the middle of summer.

GUDGEONS – They are chosen by the same rules as other fish. They
are taken from running streams about midsummer, and are to be had
for five or six months.

LOBSTERS – If they have not been long caught, the claws will have a
strong motion when you put your finger on the eyes and press. The
heaviest are the best, and it is preferable to boil them at home. When
buying ready-boiled, try whether their tails are stiff and pull up with
a spring; otherwise that part will be flabby. The Cock-lobster is known
by the narrow back part of his tail, and the two uppermost fins within
it are stiff and hard; but those of the hen are soft, and the tail broader.

The male, though generally smaller, has the highest flavour, the flesh is firmer, and the colour when boiled is a deeper red.

OYSTERS – There are several kinds. The Pyfleet, Colchester, and Milford, are much the best. The native Milton are fine, being white and fat; but others may be made to possess both these qualities in some degree by proper feeding. When alive and strong, the shell closes on the knife. They should be eaten as opened, the flavour becoming poor otherwise. The rock oyster is largest, but usually has a coarse flavour if eaten raw.

PIKE – The best are taken in rivers, the Thames ones being very fine. They are a very dry fish and are much indebted to stuffing and sauce.

TENCH – They are fine-flavoured fresh-water fish and should be killed and dressed as soon as caught. The tench has a slimy matter about it, the clearness and brightness of which show freshness. The season is July, August, and September.

ON PREPARING AND DRESSING FISH

'IF THE FISHMONGER DOES NOT CLEAN IT,' Mrs Rundell instructed, 'fish is seldom very nicely done; but those in great towns wash it beyond what is necessary for cleaning, and by perpetual watering diminish the flavour. When quite clean, if to be boiled, some salt and a little vinegar should be put into the water, to give the fish firmness; but cod, whiting, and haddock are far better if a little salted and kept a day; and if the weather is not very hot they will be good two days.'

The wise housewife was advised to purchase more than necessary for immediate needs and thereby get it cheaper. The surplus would be potted or pickled or, if sprinkled with salt and hung up, would be good for stewing the next day.

Large fish were best if cooked gently in a fish kettle.

Small fish, nicely fried, covered with egg and crumbs, were considered far more elegant than if served plain. Butter was not recommended for frying: 'it gives a bad colour; oil fries the finest for those who will tolerate the expense.' Much attention was paid to garnishing, using plenty of horseradish, parsley, and lemon. Fried parsley, thrown into hot fat straight from a bowl of clean water, and immediately taken out again, made a crisp, green garnish.

Instructions were also given for broiling fish on a gridiron 'on a very clear fire, that it may not taste smoky'.

Mrs Rundell commented that 'when well done, and with very good sauce, fish is more liked than almost any other dish. The liver and roes should be placed on the dish, so that the hostess may see them and serve a part to every one.'

Here are some of her more interesting fish recipes:

To Pot Salmon

Take a large piece, scale and wipe, but do not wash it: salt very well, let it lie till the salt is melted and drained from it, then season with beaten mace, cloves, and whole pepper: lay in a few bay-leaves, put it close into a pan, cover it over with butter, and bake it; when well done, drain it from the gravy, put it into the pots to keep, and when cold cover it with clarified butter.

In this manner you may do any firm fish.

To Dry Salmon

Cut the fish down the centre, take out the inside and roe. Rub the whole with common salt after scaling; let it hang 24 hours to drain. Pound three or four ounces of saltpetre, according to the size of the fish, two ounces of bay salt, and two ounces of coarse sugar; mix these well and rub into the salmon, then lay it on a large dish or tray for two days, then rub it well with common salt, and in 24 hours more it will be fit to dry. Wipe it well after draining. Hang it either in a wood chimney, or in a dry place, keeping it open with two small sticks.

Dried salmon is eaten broiled in its paper, and only just warmed through ... Or it may be boiled, especially the bit next the head.

(*Note*: Saltpetre is potassium nitrate or nitre, a white crystalline salty substance used not only medicinally and in preserving meat, but as a constituent of gunpowder.)

An Excellent Dish of Dried Salmon

Pull some into flakes; have ready some eggs boiled hard and chopped large; put both into half a pint of thin cream, and two or three ounces of butter rubbed with a tea-spoonful of flour; skim it, and stir till boiling hot; make a wall of mashed potatoes round the inner edge of a dish, and pour the above into it.

To Pickle Salmon

After scaling and cleaning, split the salmon and divide it into such pieces as you choose, lay it in the fish kettle to fill the bottom, and as much water as will cover it; to three quarts put a pint of vinegar, a handful of salt, twelve bay leaves, six blades of mace, and a quarter of an ounce of black pepper. When the salmon is boiled enough, drain it and put it on a clean cloth, then put more salmon into the kettle, and pour the liquor upon it, and so on till all is done. After this, if the pickle be not smartly flavoured with the vinegar and salt, add more, and boil it quick three quarters of an hour. When all is cold, pack the fish in something deep, and let there be enough of the pickle to plentifully cover. Preserve it from the air. The liquor must be drained from the fish, and occasionally boiled and skimmed.

Salmon Collared

Split such a part of the fish as may be sufficient to make a handsome roll, wash and wipe it, and having mixed salt, white pepper, pounded mace, and Jamaica pepper, in quantity to season it very high, rub it inside and out well. Then roll it tight and bandage it, put as much water and one third vinegar as will cover it, with bay leaves, salt, and both sorts of pepper. Cover close, and simmer till done enough. Drain and boil quick the liquor, and put on when cold. Serve with fennel. It is an elegant dish, and extremely good.

If salmon was a versatile fish in the hands of versatile cooks, the common cod was equally so. No part was discarded, especially the head. Some people boiled the cod whole, but a large head and shoulders contained all the fish it was considered proper to serve, because the thinner parts would be overdone and tasteless before the thicker were ready. The whole fish would be purchased when prices were low, and the lower half, salted and hung up, would reach perfection in one or two days. Or it could be salted and served with egg-sauce, potatoes, and parsnips.

Cod Sounds Boiled

Soak them in warm water half an hour, then scrape and clean; and if to be dressed white, boil them in milk and water; when tender, serve them in a napkin, with egg sauce. The salt must not be much soaked out, unless for fricassee.

Ingenious cooks even prepared cod sounds (a fish's swimming bladder) to look like chicken, described as 'a good maigre-day dish' – meaning, presumably, a good dish for a lean day, or when stymied for an appetizing meal.

Cod Sounds to Look Like Small Chickens

Wash three large sounds nicely and boil in milk and water, but not too tender; when cold, put a forcemeat of chopped oysters, crumbs of bread, a bit of butter, nutmeg, pepper, salt, and the yolks of two eggs; spread it thin over the sounds, and roll up each in the form of a chicken, skewering it; then lard them over as you would chickens, dust a little flour over, and roast them slowly. When done enough, pour over them a fine oyster-sauce. Serve for side or corner dish.

Currie of Cod

This should be made of sliced cod that has either been crimped or sprinkled a day, to make it firm. Fry it to a fine brown with onions, and stew it with a good white gravy, a little currie-powder, a bit of butter and flour, three or four spoonfuls of rich cream, salt, and Cayenne if the powder be not hot enough.

(Crimped cod – in which the flesh had been contracted by gashing, a customary practice with fresh fish to firm up the flesh by releasing excess water – was either boiled, broiled, or fried.)

To Dress Fresh Sturgeon

Sturgeon consists of various kinds of large anadromous fish which yield caviar (the roe) and from which isinglass is extracted for use in the preservation of eggs and other culinary purposes. In the nineteenth century it was much esteemed as a food and, like other fish now considered a luxury, was freely available in British waters and consequently inexpensive.

For dressing, it was cut in slices which were then rubbed with egg and sprinkled with breadcrumbs, parsley, pepper and salt, folded in paper and gently broiled. Butter, anchovy, and soy formed the sauce. The slices could be roasted on a larkspit, tied to a larger spit, and served with a good gravy, an anchovy, a squeeze of Seville orange or lemon, and a glass of sherry, or with sorrel and anchovy sauce.

Ingenious methods of disguising food – such as rabbit to taste like hare (see below) – were popular with nineteenth-century cooks. Not least was *An Excellent Imitation of Pickled Sturgeon*. For this a large turkey was needed, but not old. It was picked carefully, singed, cleaned, boned and washed, and tied across with mat string thoroughly cleansed. It was then boiled in a pan containing a quart of water, a quart of vinegar, a quart of dry white wine, and a very large handful of salt, all previously boiled together and well skimmed. When sufficiently done, the strings were tightened and the turkey placed on a dish with a two-pound weight on top. The liquor was then reboiled for half an hour. When both were cold, the turkey was plunged into the liquor again. By this method it kept well for some months and, many claimed, 'ate more delicately' than sturgeon. It was usually served with vinegar, oil, and sugar, and sent to the table elaborately garnished with fennel.

The Thames and other inland rivers and ponds yielded a plentiful supply of carp, which became as commonplace as eel and cod.

Stewing was a popular way of cooking carp. After scaling and cleaning, carefully saving the roe and liver, the fish was simmered in a rich beef gravy, with an onion, eight cloves, a dessertspoonful of Jamaica pepper, the same of black, and port or cider equal to a fourth part of the gravy. When nearly done two finely chopped anchovies were added, together with a dessertspoonful of made mustard, some fine walnut ketchup, and a knob of butter rolled in flour. The gravy was allowed to boil a few minutes. The carp was then served with snippets of fried bread, fried roe and liver, and a good deal of horse-radish and lemon.

Carp was also stuffed and baked with herbs, seasonings and port wine.

Other recipes for fish included:

Trout à la Genevoise

Clean the fish well; put it into your stewpan, adding half Champagne and Moselle, or Rhenish, or Sherry wine. Season with pepper, salt, an onion, a few cloves stuck in it, and a small bunch of parsley and thyme; put in a crust of French bread; set it on a quick fire. When the fish is done, take the bread out, bruise it, and then thicken the sauce with it; add flour and a little butter, and let it boil up. See that your sauce is of a proper thickness. Lay your fish on the dish, and pour the sauce over it. Serve it with sliced lemon and fried bread.

Potted mackerel were baked in a pan with spice, bay-leaves, and some butter. When cold, they were to be laid in a potting-pot, and covered with butter.

Pickled Mackerel, Called Caveach

Clean and divide them, then cut each side into three, or, leaving them undivided, cut each into five or six pieces. To six large mackerel take near an ounce of pepper, two nutmegs, a little mace, four cloves and a handful of salt, all in the finest powder; mix and, making holes in each bit of fish, thrust the seasoning into them and rub each piece with some of it. Fry them brown in oil; let them stand till cold, then put into a stone jar and cover with vinegar. If to keep long, pour oil on the top. Done thus, they may be preserved for months.

To Bake Pike

Scale it, and open as near the throat as you can, then stuff with the following ingredients: grated bread, herbs, anchovies, oysters, suet, salt, pepper, mace, half a pint of cream, four yolks of eggs; mix all over the fire until it thickens, then put it into the fish and sew it up; butter should be put over it in little bits; bake it. Serve sauce of gravy, butter, and anchovy. *Note*: if, in serving the pike, the back and belly are slit up, and each slice drawn gently downward, there will be fewer bones.

To Dry Haddock

Choose of two or three pounds in weight: take out the gills, eyes, and entrails, and remove the blood from the backbone. Wipe dry, then put salt into the bodies and eyes. Lay them on a board for a night; then hang in a dry place, and after three or four days they will be fit to eat. Skin and rub them with egg, and strew crumbs over them. Lay them before the fire, and baste with butter until brown enough. Serve with egg-sauce.

Whitings, if large, are excellent this way, and will prove an accommodation in the country where there is no regular supply of fish.

Eels were very popular. Small ones could be coated in egg and breadcrumbs and fried, or boiled and served in their liquor with butter and chopped parsley.

Spitchcock Eels

Take one or two large eels, leave the skin on, cut them into pieces of three inches long, open them on the belly-side, and clean nicely; wipe dry, then wet with beaten egg and sprinkle both sides with chopped parsley, pepper, salt, a very little sage, and a bit of mace pounded fine and mixed with the seasoning. Rub the gridiron with a bit of suet and broil the fish to a fine colour. Serve with anchovy and butter for sauce.

Collared Eel

Bone a large eel, but do not skin it; mix pepper, salt, mace, allspice, and a clove or two, in the finest powder, and rub over the whole inside; roll it tight, and bind with a coarse tape. Boil in salt and water till done, then add vinegar, and when cold keep the collar in pickle. Serve it either whole or in slices. Chopped sage, parsley, a little thyme and knotted marjoram, mixed with spices, much improve the taste.

Similar to the eel, and cooked in much the same way, was the *Lamprey*, an unattractive fish to look at, but much relished through-out history (so much so that King Henry I is reputed to have died of a surfeit of them).

Herrings were fried, broiled or baked with seasonings, and were also smoked over a barrel of sawdust. As with other fish, vinegar and small beer were often used when baking.

To Pot Lobsters

Half-boil them, pick out the meat, cut it into small bits, season with mace, white pepper, nutmeg, and salt; press close into a pot, and cover with butter; bake half an hour; put the spawn in. When cold take the lobster out, and put it into the pots with a little of the butter. Beat the other butter in a mortar with some of the spawn, then mix that coloured butter with as much as will be sufficient to cover the pots, and strain it. Cayenne may be added, if approved.

Currie of Lobster or Prawns

Take them from the shells, and lay into a pan with a small piece of mace, three or four spoonfuls of veal gravy, and four of cream; rub smooth one or two teaspoonfuls of currie-powder, a teaspoonful of flour, and an ounce of butter; simmer an hour; squeeze half a lemon in, and add salt.

Hot Crab

Pick the meat out of the crab, clear the shell from the head, then put the meat with a little nutmeg, salt, pepper, a bit of butter, crumbs of bread, and three spoonfuls of vinegar, into the shell again, and set it before the fire. You may brown it with a salamander.

Dry toast should be served to spread it upon.

In the days when oysters were sold on street barrows they were considered a tasty but by no means luxurious dish. Consequently there were many ways of cooking them, but first the young bride had to learn how to fatten them up for table by feeding them for, like lobsters, they were still alive when bought. The method was to put them into a deep bath of water and to wash them by brushing with a birch besom. Then they were laid bottom downwards in a pan and sprinkled with flour or oatmeal and a large amount of salt, after which they were covered again with water. This was done every day until they were considered to be fat enough for cooking and eating; they could then be stewed, boiled or scalloped, fried in butter as a garnish for boiled fish, or used to make a sauce with butter and lemon juice and a little cream for special occasions.

Pickled Oysters

Wash four dozen of the largest oysters you can get, in their own liquor, wipe them dry, strain the liquor off, adding to it a dessertspoonful of pepper, two blades of mace, a tablespoonful of salt, if the liquor be not very salt, three of white wine, and four of vinegar. Simmer the oysters for a few minutes in the liquor, then put them in small jars, and boil the pickle up, skim it, and when cold, pour over the oysters: cover close.

CHOOSING AND PREPARING MEATS

A FADED HOUSEKEEPING BOOK of 1835 contained an unknown woman's observations on purchasing, keeping, and dressing meat. From her instructions on how to send dishes to the table it seems likely that she was a cook in a good household or a very knowledgeable housewife who recorded her comments for the benefit of those serving under her. She emphasized that the best of any produce went farthest and was the most nourishing, that rounds of beef, fillet of veal, and leg of mutton were the most costly but, being more solid meat, were good value, but she also pointed out that inferior joints could be dressed palatably and their nourishment improved by the addition of good ingredients in gravies and sauces.

No butcher could have bettered her judgment of meat. Woe betide him if he failed to take out the long pipe running by the bone in loins, or the kernels from beef, since both were apt to taint the flesh. She also knew how to recognize bruises in rumps and edgebones of beef, and knew that they were caused by blows administered by drovers driving cattle to market, 'for the part that has been struck always taints'.

Dripping, she insisted, would baste everything as efficiently as butter, except fowls and game; and for kitchen pies, nothing else was to be used. Suet from beef, veal, or mutton was good for puddings, or to clarify, but the fat of a neck or loin of mutton made a far lighter pudding than ordinary suet.

Instructions regarding meat delivered in warm weather were explicit. It should be thoroughly examined and if flies had touched it, that part was to be cut off and the remaining joint well washed. In the height of summer it was wise to let meat which had been bought for salting lie for an hour in very cold water, then it was to be wiped dry and the salt rubbed thoroughly into every part. It was then to be turned over every day and treated with renewed applications of salt. It would be ready for the table in three or four days. Weather permitting, meat would 'eat much better' for hanging two or three days before being salted.

Bones were never to be wasted. Shank-bones of mutton, after soaking and brushing, were to be added to gravies or soups to give richness. Roast-beef bones, or shank bones of ham, made fine pea soup 'and should be boiled with the peas the day before eaten, that the fat may be taken off'.

A particular concern of Mrs Rundell's was the loss sustained in some families by 'the spoiling of meat':

> The best way to keep what is to be eaten unsalted is ... to examine it well, wipe it every day, and put some pieces of charcoal over it. If meat is brought from a distance in warm weather, the butcher should be ordered to cover it close, and bring it early in the morning; but even then, if it is kept on the road while he serves the customers who live nearest to him, it will very likely be fly-blown. This happens often in the country.

Large households required large joints of meat; a ham of twenty pounds or a beef joint of ten pounds was not unusual. Meat was often boiled: 'If for boiling, the colour will be better for soaking; but if for roasting, dry it. Boiling in a well-floured cloth will make meat white.' Large joints could be roasted on a spit: 'Meat should be much basted; and when nearly done, floured to make it look frothed. The spit should never be run through the best parts, or a black stain appears on the meat. Salting meat before it is put to roast draws out the gravy: it should then be only sprinkled when almost done ... A piece of writing paper should be twisted round the bone at the knuckle of a leg or shoulder of lamb, mutton, or venison, when roasted, before they are served.'

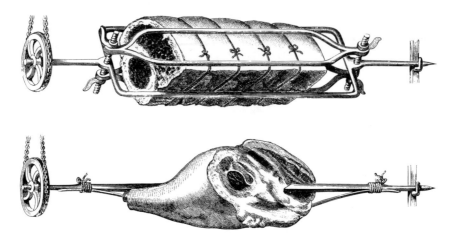

The roast beef of Old England was as firm a favourite in the nineteenth century as it has ever been, closely rivalled by venison, and the head of an ox was considered particularly delicious. The model wife would not hesitate to smell the meat before purchase, and she knew that if the eyes were sunk the head was not fresh and therefore not worth buying. She knew how to judge a young animal by the texture of the flesh and the condition of the meat by the colour of the fat, and that tender pork has a thin rind. She was reminded that, when buying veal, 'the whitest is not the most juicy, having been made so by frequent bleeding and having had whiting to lick'. (A doubtful practice of the time was to give calves a lump of shoe-whitening to lick, to lighten the flesh.)

There were many recipes for preserving meat by salting and pickling, such as:

To salt Beef red; which is extremely good to eat fresh from the Pickle, or to hang to dry

Choose a piece of beef with as little bone as you can (the flank is best), sprinkle it, and let it drain a day; then rub it with common salt, saltpetre, and bay-salt, but only a small proportion of the saltpetre. You may add a few grains of cochineal, finely powdered. Rub the pickle every day into the meat for a week, then turn it.

It will be excellent in eight days. In sixteen, drain away the pickle. Let it be smoked at the oven-mouth when heated with wood, or send it to the baker's. A few days will smoke it.

Beefsteaks were sometimes served with oyster sauce, and oysters could be added to a steak and kidney pudding.

The palates from the mouths of cattle were considered a great delicacy, and this was a popular recipe:

Beef Palates

Simmer them in water several hours, till they will peel, then cut the palates into slices, or leave them whole, as you choose; and stew them in a rich gravy till as tender as possible. Before you serve, season them with Cayenne, salt, and ketchup. If the gravy was drawn clear, add some butter and flour.

If to be served white, boil them in milk, and stew them in a fricassee-sauce; adding cream, butter, flour, and mushroom-powder, and a little pounded mace.

Nothing was wasted. In Mrs Rundell's *A New System of Domestic Cookery* there is a recipe for *Roast Tongue and Udder* ('a tasty dish', served with currant-jelly sauce) in which the salted tongue and 'a fine young udder with some fat to it' were boiled till tender and then tied together and roasted. Ox or calf's head was boiled until the meat could be taken off to make into a fricassee or hash, or added to soup. The brains were boiled and then mixed with melted butter, chopped sage, pepper and salt. Marrow bones were boiled and the marrow extracted to serve on dry toast.

Here is a brief selection of other contemporary recipes for beef and veal, from the same source:

Rolled Beef That Equals Hare

Take the inside of a large sirloin, soak it in a glass of port wine and a glass of vinegar mixed, for forty-eight hours; have ready a very fine stuffing, and bind it up tight. Roast it on a hanging-spit and baste with a glass of port wine, the same quantity of vinegar, and a tea-spoonful of pounded allspice. Larding it improves the look and flavour: serve with a rich gravy in the dish; currant jelly and melted butter, in tureens.

An Excellent Way of Doing Tongues to Eat Cold

Season with common salt and saltpetre, brown sugar, a little bay-salt, pepper, cloves, mace, and allspice, in fine powder, for a fortnight: then take away the pickle, put the tongue into a small pan, and lay some butter on it; cover it with brown crust, and bake slowly till so tender that a straw would go through it.

The thin part of tongue, when hung up to dry, grates like hung beef, and also makes a fine addition to the flavour of omlets.

Veal Collops

Cut long thin collops, beat them well, and lay on them a piece of thin bacon of the same size, and spread highly seasoned forcemeat on that, also a little garlick and Cayenne. Roll them up tight, about the size of two fingers, but no more than two or three inches long; put a very small skewer to fasten each firmly, rubb egg over; fry them of a fine brown, and pour a rich brown gravy over.

(*Note*: Collop is a term, little used today, for a slice of meat. In Biblical language it also applied to a fold of skin in a fat person or animal. It is also an obsolete term for an egg fried with bacon.)

Mock Turtle

Bespeak a calf's head with the skin on, cut it in half, and clean it well; then half boil it, take all the meat off in square bits, breaks the bones of the head, and boil them in some veal and beef broth to add to the richness. Fry some shallot in butter, and dredge in the flour enough to thicken the gravy; stir this into the browning, and give it one or two boils; skim it carefully, and then put in the head; put in also a pint of Madeira wine, and simmer till the meat is quite tender.

About ten minutes before you serve, put in some basil, tarragon, chives, parsley, Cayenne pepper, and salt, to your taste; also two spoonfuls of mushroom-ketchup, and one of soy. Squeeze the juice of a lemon into the tureen, and pour the soup upon it. Serve with forcemeat-balls and small eggs.

Mutton was popular in Victorian cookery. It kept better than lamb, due to its closer, drier texture, and there were special rules for cutting a carcass and dressing the joints, which varied from city to city. It was recommended that mutton for roasting should be hung as long as it would keep, the hind-quarter especially, but not so long as to taint, 'for whatever fashion may authorize, putrid juice ought not to be taken into the stomach'.

One way of preserving it was as *Mutton Ham*:

Choose a fine grained leg of wether mutton of twelve to fourteen pounds weight; let it be cut ham-shape, and hung for two days. Then put into a stew pan half a pound of bay salt, the same of common salt, two ounces of saltpetre, and half a pound of coarse sugar, all in powder; mix, and make it quite hot, then rub it well into the ham. Let it be turned in the liquor every day; at the end of four days take it out, dry it, and hang it up in wood smoke a week. It is to be used in slices, with stewed cabbage, mashed potatoes or eggs.

Among the many recipes for mutton and lamb the following are of interest:

Steaks of Mutton or Lamb, with Cucumber

Quarter the cucumbers, and lay them into a deep dish, sprinkle them with salt, and pour vinegar over them. Fry the chops of a fine brown, and put them into a stew-pan; drain the cucumbers, and put over the steaks; add some sliced onions, pepper, and salt; pour hot water or weak broth on them; stew and skim well.

China Chilo

Mince a pint basin of undressed neck of mutton, or leg, and some of the fat; put it with two onions, a lettuce, a pint of green peas, a tea-spoonful of salt, a tea-spoonful of pepper, four spoonfuls of water and two or three ounces of clarified butter, into a stew-pan closely covered. Simmer two hours, and serve in the middle of a dish of boiled dry rice. If Cayenne is approved, add a little.

Lamb's Sweetbreads

Blanch them, and put them a little while into cold water. Then put them into a stew-pan with a ladleful of broth, some pepper and salt, a small bunch of small onions, and a blade of mace; stir in a bit of butter and flour, and stew half an hour. Have ready two or three eggs well beaten in cream, with a little minced parsley and a few grates of nutmeg. Put in some boiled asparagus-tops to the other things. Do not let it boil after the cream is in, but make it hot, and stir it well all the while. Take great care it does not curdle. Young French beans or peas may be added, first boiled of a beautiful colour.

Much advice was given by Mrs Rundell and other experts on the subject of pork and bacon, including instructions for cutting up the carcass of a bacon-hog (a larger and older pig than a 'porker') and the use of every part of the animal including the feet and ears.

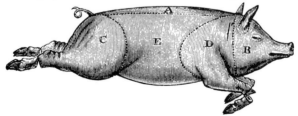

Country wives, who were accustomed to the home-slaughtering of pigs, felt no qualms about carving up the head of a newly-killed animal, nor did they shrink from removing the guts and stuffing them to make sausages. After cleaning and soaking to produce greater elasticity, the guts would be filled with lean and fat meat chopped together and seasoned with sage, pepper, salt and two or three berries of allspice. The skin was then tied in lengths of eight or nine inches and the festoons of sausages would be 'hung high to dry' from the kitchen ceiling, along with hams and a variety of joints and game. Different regions had their individual recipes for sausages.

There was also a recipe for *An Excellent Sausage to eat Cold*, made as follows:

> Season fat and lean pork with some salt, saltpetre, black pepper, and allspice, all in a fine powder, and rub into the meat; the sixth day cut it small, and mix with it some shred shallot or garlick, as fine as possible. Have ready an ox-gut that has been scoured, salted, and soaked well, and fill it with the above stuffing; tie up the ends, and hang it to smoke as you would hams, but first wrap it in a fold or two of old muslin. It must be high dried. Some eat it without boiling, but others like it boiled first.

But perhaps this is the most delicious-sounding sausage recipe:

White Hog's Puddings

When the skins have been soaked and cleaned as before directed, rinse and soak them all night in rose-water, and put into them the following filling:

Mix half a pound of blanched almonds cut into seven or eight bits each, with a pound of grated bread, two pounds of marrow or suet, a pound of currants, some beaten cinnamon, clove, mace, and nutmeg, a quart of cream, the yolks of six and whites of two eggs, a little orange-flower water, a little fine Lisbon sugar, and some lemon-peel and citron sliced, and half fill the skins.

To know whether sweet enough, warm a little in a pannikin. In boiling, much care must be taken to prevent the puddings from bursting. Prick them with a small fork as they rise, and boil them in milk and water. Lay them on a table-cloth until cold.

The roasting of pork appears to have varied little since the nineteenth century, though sucking pig was a popular dish and no model wife, nor any cook worth her salt, would roast a sucking pig any way but on a spit, or fail to serve it slit down the back and garnished with the ears and the two jaws – first delicately removing the upper part of the head down to the snout. First, however, it had to be scalded whole immediately after slaughtering:

To Scald a Sucking Pig

The moment the pig is killed, put it into cold water for a few minutes; then rub it over with a little resin beaten extremely small, and put it into a pail of scalding water half a minute; take it out, lay it on a table, and pull off the hair as quickly as possible; if any part does not come off, put it in the pail again. When quite clean, wash it well with warm water, and then in two or three cold waters, that no flavour of the resin may remain.

Take off all the feet at the first joint; make a slit down the belly, and take out the entrails; put the liver, heart, and lights, to the feet. Wash the pig well in cold water, dry it thoroughly, and fold it in a wet cloth to keep it from the air.

Swathed thus, it was hung until required.

The pettitoes, or trotters, were to be boiled with the liver and the heart, very gently, in a small amount of water; they were then split and, with the meat of heart and liver chopped fine, were simmered in a little water until tender. The mince of heart and liver was thickened by boiling with a knob of butter mixed with flour, a spoonful of cream, and seasoning to taste, and then poured over snippets of bread, with the feet placed on top.

Tremendous importance was attached to a hog's head, which was prepared and cooked with infinite care. After splitting the head, the brains and ears were removed and sprinkled with common salt for a day. After draining, common salt and saltpetre were added and left for three days. Meanwhile, the broken head was skinned, salted and soaked in a small quantity of water for two days, after which it was washed and boiled with a seasoning of pepper, salt, and a little mace or some allspice berries, until all bones were loosened. After removing these, the remaining meat was chopped up.

The tongue was also skinned, and both skins saved. The skin from the head was put into a small pan, and the prepared contents of the head were then put in, the skin from the tongue pulled over and the whole thing pressed down. When cold, it made a kind of brawn which was very much favoured.

A porker's head, stuffed with sage and breadcrumbs, could also be roasted 'on a string or a hanging jack'.

Ears were as great a delicacy as the head and trotters, with a multitude of recipes devoted to them. Here is a popular one:

To Force Hog's Ears

Parboil two pairs of ears, or take some that have been soused: make a

forcemeat of an anchovy, some sage, parsley, a quarter of a pound of
suet chopped, bread-crumbs, pepper, and only a little salt. Mix all
these with the yolks of two eggs; raise the skin of the upper side of
the ears, and stuff them with the above. Fry the ears in fresh butter,
of a fine colour; then pour away the fat, and drain them; make ready
half a pint of rich gravy, with a glass of fine sherry, three tea-spoonfuls
of made mustard, a little bit of flour and butter, a small onion whole,
and a little pepper or Cayenne. Put this with the ears into a stew-pan,
and cover it close; stew it gently for half an hour, shaking the pan
often. When done enough, take out the onion, place the ears carefully
in a dish, and pour the sauce over them. If a larger amount is wanted,
the meat from two pettitoes may be added to the above.

Pig's Harslet

[This is probably the origin of the 'haslet' we buy today.]
Wash and dry some liver, sweetbreads, and fat and lean bits of pork,
beating the latter with a rolling-pin to make it tender; season with
pepper, salt, sage, and a little onion shred fine; when mixed, put all
into a cawl, and fasten it up tight with a needle and thread. Roast it
on a hanging jack, or by a string.

Serve in slices with parsley for a fry, or with a sauce of port-wine
and water, and mustard, just boiled up.

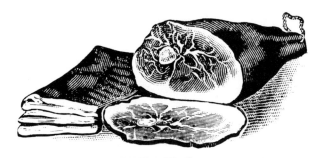

Hams were cured for three or four weeks before being smoked for
ten days, hanging in the kitchen above a wood fire, sometimes sewn
up in hessian. The flavour depended on the ingredients of the
'cure' – for a highly flavoured ham, beer, treacle, and spices such as
coriander, juniper berries and allspice were added to the normal
mixture of saltpetre, bay salt and sugar.

Bacon was cured in a similar way and then either smoked, or dried
by hanging in the kitchen. A good housewife always produced her
own bacon.

POULTRY, GAME, ET CETERA

IN ADDITION to the game birds and animals eaten today, plovers, larks, landrails and other small birds were also enjoyed. Poultry and game birds were bought unplucked and with heads and feet intact. Advice for judging their condition and preparing them for the table was covered in some detail by Mrs Rundell.

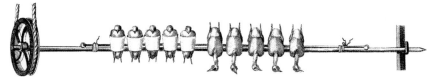

Recipes for cooking poultry and game were similar to those of today, but small birds were roasted on a bird-spit, or long skewer, basted with butter; woodcock, snipe, quail and plover were cooked without drawing and served on toast. Pigeons were to be eaten fresh, either roasted or stewed (sometimes with cabbage) but they could also be pickled or served in jelly:

To Pickle Pigeons

Bone them; turn the inside out, and lard it. Season with a little allspice and salt, in a fine powder, then turn the inside once more within, and tie the neck and rump with thread. Put them into boiling water; let them boil a minute or two to plump; take them out, and dry them well; then put them boiling hot into the pickle, which must be made of equal quantities of white wine and white wine vinegar, with white pepper and allspice, sliced ginger and nutmeg, and two or three bay-leaves. When it boils up, put the pigeons in. If they are small, a quarter of an hour will do them, but they will take twenty minutes if large. Then take them out, wipe them, and let them cool. Store them in a *stone* jar, tied down with a bladder to keep out the air.

Instead of larding, put in some a stuffing made of hard yolks of eggs and marrow in equal quantities, with sweet herbs, pepper, salt and mace.

Pigeons in Jelly

Save some of the liquor in which a knuckle of veal has been boiled, or boil a calf's head or a neat's foot; put the broth into a pan with a blade of mace, a bunch of sweet herbs, some white pepper, lemon-peel, a slice of lean bacon, and the pigeons. Bake them, and let them stand to be cold. Season them as you like, before baking. When done, take them out of the liquor, cover close to preserve the colour, and clear the jelly by boiling with the whites of two eggs; then strain it through a thick cloth dipped in boiling water, and put into a sieve. The fat must be perfectly removed, before it be cleared. Put the roughly chopped jelly over and round them.

(*Note*: A 'neat' is any bovine animal; also, collectively, cattle. A cowherd was frequently referred to as a neatherd and, similarly, a cattle shed as a neat-house. Neat's-leather was, of course, ox-hide.)

To Keep Game, et cetera

Game ought not to be thrown away even when it has been kept a very long time, for when it seems to be spoiled with age, it may often be made fit for eating by nicely cleaning it, and washing with vinegar and water. If there is a danger of birds not keeping, then draw, crop, and pick [i.e. pluck] them, wash in two or three waters, and rub them with salt. Have ready a large saucepan of boiling water, and plunge them into it one by one; drawing them up and down by the legs, that the water may pass through them. Let them stay five or six minutes, then hang them up in a cold place. When drained, salt and pepper the insides well.

Lumps of charcoal put about birds and meat will preserve them from taint, and restore what is spoiling.

When buying venison, the sweetness of the meat could be ascertained by running a sharp narrow knife into the shoulder or haunch 'and the scent will tell you. Few people like it when it has much of *hautgoût*'. (This method was also recommended for hams.)

A method for keeping venison was to wash it with milk and water until very clean and then dry thoroughly with clean cloths, and dust pounded ginger over every part, 'a good preventive against the fly'. Pepper could be used in the same way. It could then be hung for a fortnight. Before cooking, the meat was washed in a little lukewarm water and dried.

Hares were preferred well hung, and 'even when the cook fancies them past eating, may be in the highest perfection'. If eaten when fresh-killed and paunched in the field, they were considered less good. 'The hare keeps longer, and eats much better, if not opened for four or five days.'

An old hare should be kept as long as possible, if to be roasted. The scent should be strong. It should be well soaked before cooking.

To Jug an Old Hare

After cleaning and skinning, cut it up, and season it with pepper, salt, allspice, pounded mace, and a little nutmeg. Put it into a jar with an onion, a clove or two, a bunch of sweet herbs, a piece of coarse beef, and the carcase-bones over all. Tie the jar down with a bladder, and leather or strong paper, and put it into a saucepan of water up to the neck, but no higher. Keep the water boiling five hours. When it is to be served, boil the gravy up with a piece of butter and flour; and if the meat gets cold, warm it in this, but do not boil.

To Make a Rabbit Taste Like Hare

Choose one that is young, but full grown; hang it in the skin three or four days, then skin it; and lay it, without washing, in a seasoning of black pepper and allspice in a very fine powder, a glass of port wine, and the same quantity of vinegar. Baste it occasionally for forty hours, then stuff it, and roast it as a hare, and with the same sauce. Do not wash off the liquor that it was soaked in.

SOUPS, SAUCES, AND VINEGARS

In making gravy or stock there was no substitute for fresh meat, purchased specifically for that purpose. The gravy was put by in stone utensils on the tiled slabs of a cold larder big enough to walk into and to chill a person equally.

Gravy-meat was intended for immediate use, but if delay was unavoidable it was seasoned well and fried lightly, thus preserving it for two days, but no more. Gravy was always best when made with uncooked meat juices.

When it was necessary to delay the serving of soups or gravies they were re-stored in freshly scalded pans, particularly vegetable soups which were apt to turn sour sooner than those containing only pure meat juices.

Long slow boiling was essential to extract the full flavour of ingredients, and soups were considered best if made a day early, provided they were kept as above. The finest results came from meat placed in the bottom of the pan, with the herbs and various roots stewed separately in butter, then added. Water was always poured onto the meat, the meat never added to the water, and any juices emerging from the meat, prior to cooking, had to be almost dried up before water was poured in. Sediment of left-over gravies that had gone cold were never to be used, nourishment having been lost.

When onions were strong, a turnip was boiled with them to make them mild. Truffles and morels (a kind of mushroom) were used for thickening and to enhance flavour, half an ounce of each being carefully washed, simmered for a few minutes, then boiled with the mixture until tender. A good lump of butter mixed with flour would also be boiled with the soup, to add richness and texture.

Always indispensable to the good housewife was a clear jelly of cow-heels, which kept well for weeks and greatly improved all soups and gravies.

To create individual recipes was a matter of pride. The wife of an inn-keeper in Bow was famed for what became known as her Pepper-Pot, which she served, very impressively for a tavern, in a tureen. This soup was widely copied until, perhaps goaded by competition, she yielded up her recipe:

A Pepper-pot, to be Served in a Tureen

To three quarts of water put vegetables according to the season; in summer, peas, lettuce, and spinach; in winter, carrots, turnips, celery; and onions in both. Cut small, and stew with two pounds of neck of mutton, or a fowl, and one pound of pickled pork, till quite tender.

On first boiling, skim. Half an hour before serving, add a lobster or crab, cleared from bones. Season with salt and Cayenne. A small quantity of rice should be put in with the meat, or suet dumplings if favoured.

Pepper-pot could be made of various things, but the secret was to cook equal proportions of fish, flesh, fowl, vegetables, and pulses well seasoned with Cayenne pepper.

Varieties of soup and broth, whether of meat, vegetable, or fish, were unending. Partridge and lobster soups were as commonplace as carrot, onion, spinach, old peas (gray) and new peas (green), giblets, macaroni, leek, ox-rump, hare, eel, skate, crawfish, prawn, and oyster. Of the last, there were two popular varieties available to the most limited purses. Oysters were bought and used by the hundred, as the following recipe shows:

Oyster Mouth Soup

Make a rich mutton broth, with two large onions, three blades of mace, and black pepper. When strained, pour it on a hundred and fifty oysters, without the beards, and a bit of butter rolled in flour. Simmer gently a quarter of an hour, and serve.

Eggs were also used in plain *Oyster Soup*, in a number which many a housewife today would consider extravagant:

To two quarts of fish stock put the yolks of ten hard eggs, and the hard part of two quarts of oysters, both ground together in a mortar. Simmer all for half an hour, then strain it off, and put it and the oysters (cleared of the beards, and nicely washed) into the soup. Simmer for five minutes; have ready the yolks of six raw eggs, well beaten, and add them. Stir it well in one direction only, on the side of the fire, until it is thick and smooth, but do not let it boil.

Another popular fish soup was *Crawfish or Prawn Soup*. For this it was necessary to boil six whiting and a large eel (or the eel and half a thornback), with as much water as would cover. It was then skimmed and a whole pepper added, together with some mace, ginger, parsley, an onion, a little thyme, and three cloves. These were boiled to a mash. After that fifty crawfish, or a hundred prawns, would be carefully picked, and the shells pounded and mixed with a bread roll after they had been boiled with a little water, vinegar, salt, and herbs. The shells were then put into a sieve and the liquor poured over them into the first batch of soup, which was then poured clear of all sediment. A chopped lobster and a quart of good beef gravy were added, also the tails of the craw-fish or the prawns, and some flour and butter, plus seasoning to taste.

The much-appreciated hare was also relished as a soup:

Hare Soup

Take an old hare that is good for nothing else, cut it into pieces, and put to it a pound and a half of lean beef, two or three shank-bones of mutton well cleaned, a slice of lean bacon or ham, an onion, and a bunch of sweet herbs; pour on it two quarts of boiling water; cover the jar into which you put these with bladder and paper, and set it in a kettle of water. Simmer till the hare is stewed to pieces; strain off the liquor, and give it one boil-up with an anchovy cut into pieces, and add a spoonful of soy, a little Cayenne, and salt. A few fine forcemeat balls, fried of a good brown, should be served in the tureen.

The next recipe hailed from Hesse in Germany, becoming very popular in England:

Hessian Soup and Ragout

Clean the root of a neat's [i.e. ox] tongue very nicely, and half an ox's head, with salt and water, and soak them afterwards in water only. Then stew them in five or six quarts of water, till tolerably tender. Let the soup stand to be cold; take off the fat, which will make good paste for hot meat-pies, and will do to baste. Put to the soup a pint of split peas, or a quart of whole ones, twelve carrots, six turnips, six potatoes, six large onions, a bunch of sweet herbs, and two heads of celery. Simmer them without the meat, till the vegetables are done enough to pulp with the peas through a sieve, and the soup will then be about the thickness of cream.

Season it with pepper, salt, mace, allspice, a clove or two, and a little Cayenne, all in a fine powder. If the peas are bad, the soup may not be thick enough; then boil in it a slice of bread, and put it through the colander, or add a little rice-flour, mixing it by degrees.

For the Ragout: Cut the nicest part of the head, the kernels, and part of the fat of the root of the tongue, into small thick pieces. Rub these with seasoning, as for Hessian Soup, as you put them to a quart of the liquor kept out for that purpose before the vegetables were added; flour well, and simmer them till nicely tender. Then put a little mushroom and walnut ketchup, a little soy, a glass of port wine, and a teaspoonful of made mustard, and boil all up together before serving. If for company, add small eggs and forcemeat balls.

This way furnishes an excellent soup and a ragout at a small expense, and they are not common. The other part will warm for the family.

Another cost-cutting recipe was for *Gravy to Make Mutton Eat Like Venison*: A very stale woodcock or snipe, cut in pieces (after first taking out the bag from the entrails) was simmered with as much unseasoned meat-gravy as required, then strained and served.

But perhaps the real prize should be awarded to the following recipe – or to the cook who invented it:

Portable Soup

Boil one or two knuckles of veal, one or two shins of beef, and three pounds of ordinary beef, in as much water only as will cover them. Take the marrow out of the bones; put any sort of spice you like, and three large onions. When the meat is done to rags, strain it off, and put it into a *very* cold place. When cold, take off the cake of fat (which will make crusts for servants' pies), put the soup into a double-bottomed saucepan, and set it on a pretty quick fire, but do not let it burn. It must boil fast and uncovered, and be stirred constantly for eight hours.

Put it into a pan, and let it stand in a cold place a day [while the cook, exhausted after eight hours stirring, snatched some rest?] then pour it into a round china soup-dish, and set it in a stew-pan of boiling water on a stove, and let it boil, and be now and then stirred, till the soup is thick and ropy; then it is done enough. Pour it into the little round part at the bottom of cups and basins turned upside down, to form cakes, and when cold, turn them out onto flannel to dry.

Keep them in tin canisters. When they are to be used, melt them in boiling water, and if you wish the flavour of herbs, or anything else, boil it first, strain off the water, and melt the soup in it.

This is very convenient in the country, or at sea, where fresh meat is not always at hand; as by this means a basin of soup may be made in five minutes.

Could that recipe be the origin of our packaged stock cubes?

The nineteenth-century wife usually kept a large stock of home-made sauces. Apart from the common-or-garden mint, parsley, and vinaigrette sauces, she had many special ones for specific dishes, all widely used. Home-made mushroom ketchup, brewed from fresh mushrooms and spices in September and October, and stored in sealed jars, was an invaluable flavouring ingredient in many of her recipes.

One housewife even recorded for posterity *A good Sauce to hide the bad colour of Fowls*, which indicates that she was hard-pressed economically and therefore had to settle for inferior meat. Even so, it is likely that she would have improved the quality by careful cooking in vinegar, water, and lemon, completing the illusion with a sauce which not only disguised the colour but added a delicious flavour. To make her 'sauce-camouflage' she diced the chicken livers with slices of lemon, parsley that had been scalded and six hard eggs. To these she added salt, mixed them with butter, covered it with water and boiled the mixture once, and poured it over the fowls.

The water in which fowl, veal or rabbit had been cooked was reserved as the basis for *A White Sauce For Fricassee of Fowls, Rabbits, White Meat, Fish, or Vegetables.* To it was added the feet and necks of chickens, raw or dressed veal, and any other scraps of uneaten meat, stewed with a bit of lemon peel, some sliced onion, some white peppercorns, a little pounded mace or nutmeg, and a bunch of sweet herbs, then strained. A little good cream, a piece of butter, and a *little* flour, plus salt to taste, were added with a squeeze of lemon after the sauce was taken off the fire, shaking it well. 'Yolk of egg is often used in fricassee, but if you have any cream it is better, for the former is apt to curdle.'

For a slightly more extravagant *Sauce For An Old Fowl* a teacupful of port wine was simmered for ten minutes with the same quantity of good meat gravy, a small shallot, a little pepper, salt, a grating of nutmeg and a bit of mace. After adding a piece of butter and a little flour, the mixture was given one 'boil-up' and poured through the birds, for as a general rule an old fowl was not stuffed.

There were also sauces suitable for both fish and meat, one of which was:

An Excellent Sauce For Carp Or Boiled Turkey

Rub half a pound of butter with a tea-spoonful of flour, put to it a *little* water, melt it, and add near a quarter of a pint of thick cream, and half an anchovy chopped fine, but not washed; set it over the fire, and as it boils up add a large spoonful of real India soy. If that does not give a fine colour, put a little more. Turn it into the sauce-tureen, and put some salt and half a lemon; stir it well, to hinder it from curdling.

Liver Sauce served with either rabbits or fowls, was made by dicing the boiled livers from both, then boiling them in melted butter, with very little pepper and salt and some parsley.

Green Sauce for Green Geese Or Ducklings, mandatory at any well-served table, was made by mixing a pint of sorrel juice with a glass of white wine and some gooseberries, scalded by pouring boiling water over them and promptly pouring it off again. To this, sugar and a small amount of butter was added, and the whole mixture then brought to the boil.

Nothing was ever wasted, not even parsley that had gone to seed, for the seeds became an essential ingredient in *Parsley Sauce When No Parsley Leaves Are To Be Had*. A little parsley seed, tied in a bit of clean muslin, was boiled for ten minutes in water. Some butter was then melted in the water and a little boiled, minced spinach added to look like parsley.

Sauce Robart was considered essential for rumps or steaks.

> Put a piece of butter, the size of an egg, into a saucepan, set it over the fire, and when browning, throw in a handful of sliced onions cut small; fry them brown, but do not let them burn; add half a spoonful of flour, shake the onions in it, and give it another fry; then put four spoonfuls of gravy, and some pepper and salt, and boil it gently for ten minutes; skim off the fat, add a tea-spoonful of made mustard, a spoonful of vinegar, and the juice of half a lemon. Boil it all, and pour it round the steaks. They should be of a fine yellow brown, and garnished with fried parsley and lemon.

For hot or cold roast beef, the much revered *Benton Sauce* was made with fresh grated horseradish, a little made mustard, some pounded white sugar, and four large spoonfuls of vinegar – served in a 'saucer'. (In the nineteenth century a sauce boat was frequently called a 'saucer'.)

Carrier Sauce for Mutton consisted of six shallots chopped very fine and boiled with a gill of gravy, a spoonful of vinegar, some pepper and salt. No more than that, but try it next time you cook mutton and discover the difference in flavour.

Ham Sauce was a more laborious process in the initial stage:

> When a ham is almost done with, pick all the meat clean from the bone, leaving out any rusty part; beat the meat and the bone to a mash in a mortar until fine ground, place into a saucepan with three spoonfuls of gravy; set it over a slow fire, and stir it all the time, or it will stick to the bottom. When it has been on some time, put to it a small bundle of sweet herbs, some pepper, and half a pint of beef-gravy; cover it up, and let it stew over a gentle fire. When it has a

good flavour of the herbs, strain off the gravy. A little of this is an improvement to all gravies.

There were endless fish sauces – shrimp, anchovy, lobster, crab and, of course, oyster, but a particularly delectable one was labelled simply *A Very Fine Sauce*:

> Chop twenty-four anchovies not washed, and ten shallots, and scrape three spoonfuls of horse-radish to which add ten blades of mace, twelve cloves, two sliced lemons, half a pint of anchovy liquor, a quart of hock or Rhenish wine, and a pint of water. Boil down to a quart in quantity, and then strain. When cold, put to it three large spoonfuls of walnut ketchup, and store in small bottles, well corked.

Vinegar was considered a vital necessity in the household of those days, and the model wife wasn't worth her salt if it was not home-produced. It was customary to make it by the barrel-load.

Sugar Vinegar To every gallon of water was added two pounds of the coarsest sugar; after boiling and skimming thoroughly, one quart of cold water was added for every gallon of hot. When cool, a 'toaster' spread with yeast was put in and the mixture stirred frequently for nine days, after which it was barrelled and set in a spot which attracted the maximum amount of sun, the bung-hole plugged with a fragment of slate. Sugar vinegar was always made in March, and took six months to mature. When sufficiently sour, it was bottled, or drawn straight from the cask with a wooden spigot and faucet.

(*Note*: Research in archives and among brewery and winemaking authorities has failed to come up with any definition of 'toaster', but it is believed to be an archaic form of 'toast' since culinary records confirm that a piece of hard toast was often spread with yeast and added to the filled casks to assist fermentation. As the toast disintegrated, so the yeast dispersed.)

Gooseberry Vinegar For this, spring water was essential. First it was boiled in a large wooden tub and, when cold, a quart of bruised gooseberries was added for every three quarts of liquid. The mixture was left for sixty hours, with frequent stirrings; it was then strained through a hair bag, and to each gallon of liquor was added a pound of the coarsest sugar. All this went into a barrel, again with a 'toaster' spread with yeast, and the bung-hole was sealed with slate.

The greater the quantity of sugar and fruit, the stronger the vinegar.

Cucumber Vinegar demanded a less laborious procedure. Fifteen large cucumbers, pared and sliced, were put into a stone jar with three pints of ordinary vinegar, four large sliced onions, two or three shallots, a little garlic, two large spoonfuls of salt, three teaspoonfuls of pepper, and a half teaspoonful of Cayenne. This mixture had to stand for only four days, after which it was given a boil-up and, when cold, strained and then filtered through paper into small bottles, to be stored for use with salad or meat.

Wines were frequently home-made and the remaining fruit pulp was put to good use in the making of *Wine Vinegar*. One of the most popular ingredients was the left-over pulp from raisin wine. This was stacked in a pile to heat, which it did of its own volition, and to every hundredweight was added fifteen gallons of water, the cask and yeast being dealt with as before.

Because vinegar was also deemed to be an item on which manu-facturers made a vast profit, a barrel or two was always in course of preparation, the type varying according to the season. If no fruit pulp was available, sugar vinegar would bridge the gap. The import-ant thing was never to let the casks be empty, and thus grow musty.

FOR THAT DESIRABLY CURVACEOUS FIGURE

AFTER A FIRST COURSE of soup and fish, a choice of entrées, and a main or 'second' course of various roast meats with vegetables, the grand finale of the dinner party would be a selection of rich, delicious and extravagant puddings, tarts, creams and custards – followed by dessert and ices. Guests were expected to do more than justice to these lavish creations, for even if greed was secretly frowned upon, it could also be accepted as a compliment – a sign of appreciation that pleased the hostesss and a mark of approval that satisfied her husband.

The model wife did him proud but, being a model wife, she had many economical secrets. The fact that some of her delectable puddings contained a few spoonfuls of fresh small beer, or bottled malt liquor, or one of yeast, as a substitute for eggs was never known beyond her kitchen walls. In winter, snow was also an excellent substitute for eggs, either in puddings or pancakes, two large spoonfuls of it taking the place of one egg. Snow obligingly fell at a time of the year when eggs were most expensive, and it could be taken up from any clean spot in the garden or street even before it was wanted, without losing its virtue, though the sooner it was used the better.

In other respects, economy went by the board. Even the everyday *Almond Pudding* contained a whole pound of sweet almonds, supplemented by a lesser quantity of bitter ones, half a pound of butter, eight eggs, four spoonfuls of cream warmed with the butter, a dollop of brandy, a touch of nutmeg, and a goodly amount of sugar. When served, more butter, more sugar, plus wine, crowned each helping. This, and the following recipes, were among Mrs Rundell's examples of everyday family fare.

Dutch Pudding, or Souster

Melt one pound of butter in half a pint of milk; mix into it two pounds of flour, eight eggs, four spoonfuls of yeast; add one pound of currants, and a quarter of a pound of sugar sifted.

This is a very good pudding hot, and equally so as a cake when cold. If for the latter, caraway seeds may be used instead of currants. An hour will bake it in a quick oven.

German Puddings or Puffs

Melt three ounces of butter in a pint of cream; let it stand till nearly cold; then mix two ounces of fine flour, and two ounces of sugar, four yolks and two whites of eggs, and a little rose or orange-flower water. Bake in little cups buttered, half an hour. They should be served the moment they are done, and only when going to be eaten, or they will not be light. Turn out of the cups and top with white wine and sugar.

Few puddings lacked wine or brandy, even the homely College Pudding had a generous glass of brandy mixed with the batter. Only wine, however, was needed for:

Quaking Pudding

Scald a quart of cream; when almost cold, put to it four eggs well beaten, a spoonful and a half of flour, some nutmegs and sugar; tie it close in a buttered cloth; boil it an hour, and turn it out with care, lest it should crack. Serve with melted butter, wine, and sugar.

Puits d'Amour

[This was one of those small fillers to be dotted about the table.]

Cut a fine rich puff-paste rolled thin, with tin shapes made on purpose, one size less than another, in a pyramidical form, and lay them so; then bake in a moderate oven, that the paste may be done sufficiently, but very pale. When done, spread brandy-butter between layers and lay different coloured sweetmeats on the edges.

A Tansey

Beat seven eggs, yolks and whites separately; add a pint of cream, near the same of spinach-juice, and a little tansey-juice gained by pounding, in a stone mortar, a quarter of a pound of rich biscuits, sugar to taste, a glass of white wine, and some nutmeg. Set all in a saucepan over the fire, just to thicken, then put it into a dish, lined with paste to turn out, and bake it.

If for company, double or treble the quantities according to number.

An Excellent Sweet Potato Pudding

Take eight ounces of boiled potatoes, six ounces of butter, sweetmeats, and almonds, the yolks and whites of three eggs, a quarter of a pint of cream, three spoonfuls of white wine, a morsel of salt, the juice and rind of a lemon; beat all to froth; sugar to taste, and bake it.

Flummery

Put three large handfuls of very small white oatmeal to steep a day and night in cold water; then pour it off clear, and add as much more water, and let it stand the same time. Strain it through a fine hair sieve, and boil it till it be thick, stirring it well all the time. When first strained, put to it one large spoonful of white sugar, and two of orange-flower water. Pour it into shallow dishes, and serve to eat with wine, cider, cream and sugar. It is very good.

Creams of varied kinds were a stock favourite in the nineteenth century, not the least of which were –

Brandy Cream

Boil two dozen sweet almonds blanched, together with bitter almonds pounded, as many as desired, in a little milk. When cold, add the yolks of five eggs beaten well in a little cream, sweeten, and put to it two glasses of the best brandy; and when well mixed, pour into it a quart of thin cream; set it over the fire, but do not let it boil; stir one way till it thickens, then pour into cups or low glasses.

Ratafia Cream

Boil three or four laurel, peach, or nectarine leaves, in a full pint of cream; strain it; and when cold, add the yolks of three eggs beaten and strained, sugar, and a large spoonful of brandy stirred quick into it. Scald till thick, stirring all the time.

There was an endless variety of such creams – Almond, White Lemon, Chocolate, Codlin, Imperial, Raspberry, Pistachio, Caramel, and even:

Spinach Cream

Beat the yolks of eight eggs with a wooden spoon or a whisk; sweeten them a good deal; and put to them a stick of cinnamon, a pint of rich cream, three quarters of a pint of new milk; stir it well; then add a quarter of a pint of spinach-juice; set it over a gentle stove, and stir it one way constantly till it is thick. Put into a dish some Naples or other biscuits, or preserved orange in long slices, and pour the mixture over them. It is to be eaten cold, and is a dish either for supper, or for a second course.

Many a household prided itself on its syllabubs. A hostess could become famous for her individual recipes and it was not unknown for local syllabubs to be called after their creator, though a greater number brought renown to their places of origin.

For *Staffordshire Syllabub* a pint of cider and a glass of brandy, sugar and nutmeg, were put into a bowl, and milk was added; but to give the true Staffordshire taste, the trick was to warm the milk and pour it from a large tea-pot from some height above.

Somerset Syllabub consisted of a pint of port, a pint of sherry or other white wine, sugar to taste, and milk, to fill a large bowl; after twenty minutes it was covered with 'clouted' cream and decorated with grated nutmeg, powdered cinnamon, and nonpareil biscuits.

A good, reliable, family recipe was *Everlasting, or Solid Syllabub*, for which a quart of thick raw cream, one pound of refined sugar, and a pint and a half of fine raisin wine were mixed in a deep pan with the grated peel and the juice of three lemons, and beaten or whisked for half an hour. The mixture was then drained through a sieve lined with thin muslin, till next day. This would keep, in a cool place, for ten days, and was to be served in glasses.

IN DAIRY AND BREWERY

COUNTRY WIVES FREQUENTLY EXCELLED as model wives, and not the least of their skills was in the dairy and brewery. If the house lacked a proper dairy, the scullery would contain a churn in which to make butter from milk supplied by a local farmer. What was left in the churn after making butter was known as 'butter milk' (or 'sour milk' in Scotland) and was used in breadmaking. The butter churn was a wooden tub containing paddles or beaters rotated by a handle. It was sometimes small enough to stand on a table.

In larger houses, with well equipped dairies, rules for dairy work were strict. In winter, milk would be emptied into clean pans the moment it was brought in, but not until it had cooled in summer. White glazed ware was preferred to unglazed red because the latter was porous and could not be thoroughly scalded. Utensils, shelves, dressers and floor had to be kept spotlessly clean. Shutters were essential in summer for the sake of coolness, and the hanging of meat in the dairy was strictly forbidden because it would taint the milk.

Rich families who moved to their town houses for the Season, taking additional servants with them to supplement the resident town staff and leaving behind an essential quota to deal with essential maintenance, would receive weekly supplies of home-made cheeses, butter, wines and beverages, together with fruit and vegetables from kitchen garden and orchard. All would be expertly packed and, after the coming of the railways, sent by rail, or by carrier's cart if within easy reach of London. Thus the mistress of the house need not concern herself with London prices or make do with food which was not strictly fresh.

When the family was absent it was a dairy-maid's task to prepare for winter storage, keeping a strict account in her dairy book. Butter was stored in pots, each marked with the weight it contained. She preserved eggs in isinglass and again recorded the number. She also recorded the amount of cheese, milk, cream, eggs, and poultry consumed weekly in the servants' hall, and the number of poultry reared, for many of the larger establishments had their own poultry and dairy farms.

One of her main occupations was the making of cheese. For this, milk was poured into a large tub, having previously been warmed but not over-heated, for if too hot the cheese would be tough. Rennet was then added, the vessel covered, and the preparation left to stand until thickly curdled. The curd was then broken with a skimming tool, or lightly by hand, the cover replaced, and the mixture left to separate until ready to be placed in a vat lined with cheese-cloth. The vat had holes in the sides and the base, through which the whey would drain. When it was filled the cheese-cloth would be drawn smoothly from all sides, covering the cheese entirely. When finally drained, the cheese would be set aside to mature.

Cream cheese was made last of all because it used up the last of the milk (commonly called 'strippings'). To five quarts were added two teaspoonfuls of rennet and when the curd formed it would be briefly and delicately broken with a skimming tool. After standing for two hours it would then be placed in a sieve lined with cheese-cloth and left to drain. The final curd would be crumbled very slightly with the fingers, covered loosely with the cheese-cloth, and put into a vat with a two pound weight on top. After standing for twelve hours the choose-cloth would be tightened round it and the cheese turned over daily, from one board to another, until dry. It was preserved with a covering of nettles or clean dock leaves and put between two pewter plates to ripen. In warm weather it would be ready in three weeks.

Sage cheese, for which Derbyshire became famous, was a firm favourite. For this, the tops of young sage would be bruised in a mortar along with spinach leaves. The juice would then be strained off and, with the rennet, added to the milk. The procedure was then the same, except that pressing was necessary for eight to ten hours.

Although home brewing was undertaken by senior servants in wealthy households, an efficient wife was familiar with every phase and with every term. She knew that the wort was the malt infusion before fermentation, that on average, and particularly in the brewing of ales (mainly for staff consumption in wealthy households, but often enjoyed by the family as well) the vent-peg should not be removed from the cask for three or four months, that bottles should be scrupulously clean and well dried, and that corks should be of the best quality.

She also knew the function of every tool and utensil in a well equipped home brewery, from the coppers for boiling infusions (these coppers had to be thoroughly cleaned before use and again afterward) to the mash tuns and fermenting tuns, the funnels and mallets and spigots, the faucets and the wooden bushel measures, the grist mills and thermometers, the saccharometers for measuring sugar and the big, wide wooden trays for cooling. She knew which size skimmer and rouser to use and when to use them. Rousers were for stirring up the mash, and the requisite shape and size depended on the stage the infusion had reached. A commonly used rouser was fairly large and closely resembled a lacrosse racquet.

Apart from special beers such as nettle and dandelion, which could be extremely potent, a variety of wines was also made, the system being very much the same as today. Favourite wines in most families were raspberry, blackcurrant, cowslip, and elder. The last, with a quart of brandy added to eight gallons of liquor, could be very potent when fully matured.

Raisin wine was another household standby. In addition to eight pounds of fresh Smyrna raisins, it required a full bottle of brandy to a gallon of spring-water. A conscientious housewife kept a cask exclusively for raisin wine and bottled off one year's brew just in time to make the next which, allowing for six months of infusion, made the wine eighteen months old when ready for drinking. *Raisin wine with cider* demanded a whole gallon of the best brandy to two hundredweight of Malaga raisins which had had a prolonged soaking in a hogshead of good cider and been allowed to stand for six months before being casked and the brandy added.

Sack mead, made from hops and honey, with a quart of brandy to every thirteen-gallon cask (and kept for a year to mature) was as well known to nineteenth-century households as *Norfolk Punch*, which required twenty quarts of French brandy in which to soak the peel of thirty lemons and thirty oranges, pared so thinly that not a fragment of white pith remained. This was left to infuse for twelve hours before adding thirty quarts of water that had first been boiled. Two quarts of fresh milk were finally added. This punch would keep for many years and improved with age.

There was also a milk punch commonly known as *Verder*. For this the fruit of six oranges and six lemons were squeezed onto two pounds of sugar, and the peels steeped in a bottle of brandy for twenty-four hours. Then the peels, plus the brandy, were added to the fruit and sugar, onto which four quarts of water and one quart of boiling milk had been poured. Straining through a jelly bag followed.

Apart from home-made wines, the stocking of the cellar with vintage wines was the husband's choice, for which the model wife would take care to praise him.

7 ❧ THE FASHION SCENE

FIRST HALF OF THE CENTURY

While the world lasts, fashion will
continue to lead it by the nose.

(William Cowper)

ALTHOUGH DOMESTICITY FIGURED LARGELY in the average nineteenth-century woman's life, by no means was it the only thing she thought about. Dress was of major interest to both sexes, especially in Society circles, and the century was to see a constant flow of new fashions. Styles changed more frequently than in any previous period and, thanks to contemporary fashion journals and the arrival of photography around 1850, all these changes have been recorded.

Many styles hailed from Europe. Illustrations of Paris modes had been freely available since the 1770s, but the Napoleonic wars deprived English women of the latest French styles. The arrival of fashion magazines was therefore a godsend and did much to supersede the fashion plates previously guarded so jealously by dressmakers. Soon even the less moneyed housewife could get her dressmaker to copy the latest London modes and, since in 1813 a few shillings could purchase a fashionable muslin gown, it was soon being said that the only distinction left between mistress and maid was that one wore a cap. This distinction ceased when caps returned for general use in the 1820s.

The nineteenth century tends to be regarded as the Victorian era – which certainly encompassed the greater part of it – but the Regency lasted from 1810 until 1820, and Victoria did not come to the throne until 1837. From the start of the century fashion was an obsession, led by the Prince of Wales and his roistering set with whom society women felt it necessary to compete. Although recalled by romantics as the age of elegance and ease, the Regency period was in fact one of a decaying aristocracy threatened by an enemy overseas and by revolutionary ideas at home. Rioting in the streets became commonplace and Society's desperate attempts to blind itself to reality by ever-increasing self-indulgence led, inevitably, to unashamed sexuality. This was quite blatantly reflected in feminine clothes.

In 1810, when the classical style in dress was approaching its peak, the *Universal Magazine* commented that the female form, after an eclipse of many centuries, was reappearing. The style, influenced by the classical revival that had started in the late eighteenth century, derived from Greek statuary and, to emphasize the draped and clinging effect, gowns were made of the thinnest materials cut on vertical lines and plain stuffs with little or no ornamentation. Jane Austen's sedate characters, in their Empire dresses, exemplified respectable country folk who undoubtedly existed, but the Beau Monde, in striking contrast, indulged a taste for semi-nudity and looser morals. At balls, the *ton* would wear their flimsy, often semi-transparent gowns well dampened to make them cling even more to the almost naked body beneath. Stays had gone, petticoats had gone, and even day wear was flimsy enough to see through. This fashion, observed a correspondent in *The Satirist*, 1807, was 'very levelling', quoting as an example a shop girl 'who in point of nakedness might have vied with any duchess in the land ... the very Abigails have divested themselves of every petticoat in order that the footman or the valet may discover the outline of their secret beauties through a transparent calico'.

In contrast, the *Universal Magazine*'s correspondent continued to defend the classical fashion in women's clothes, refuting the allegation that discarding bodily support beneath was injurious to health and declaring that the whalebone case in which 'females of every age, shape, and size used to be trussed' must have been the cause of many physical distortions. On the whole, the magazine approved of the new freedom in dress, at the same time deploring the fact that in its wake had come a new freedom of manners accompanied by 'a boldness of look and scantiness of apparel', but conceding that the changes which had taken place in dress did favour ease and convenience. Nevertheless, hoops remained obligatory for Court dress until 1820.

This year heralded a style dubbed the Gothic, in which emphasis was on the shape of the dress rather than the shape of the body. Those in favour of the classical style considered the Gothic hideous and, in the Gothic period, the classical was thought indecent.

Both attitudes were hard on the average, respectable woman, who longed above all to be fashionable, but who remained modest and retained her stays. To suit the flowing classical style, stays, when worn, were overlong and tightly laced. Newspapers of the period abound with advertisements proclaiming that 'long stays are adapted to give the wearer the true Grecian form'. The difficulty in walking in such extended cages resulted in mincing steps which, in sedate middle-class circles, came to epitomize good breeding.

A transformation in hair-styles had been slowly coming about for some years prior to the French Revolution, but it was the powder tax of 1795 which began to restore feminine (and masculine) heads to their natural colour. This change continued into the nineteenth century, starting with the younger members of a family but very soon, for economic reasons, their elders following suit. As a result, taste veered toward the natural and the 'crop' came into fashion, the short curly haircut of the Regency period. This put an end to the towering, powdered, and frequently unclean hairdressing prevalent in the eighteenth century. One cropped hair-style, called 'à la Titus' featured deliberately ragged ends. The Brutus crop was similar, but shorter, and the hair could be close-curled all over the head, a style favoured by Lady Caroline Lamb.

ABOVE An extreme example of neo-classical dress; French 1802

RIGHT Pelisse worn with straw bonnet 1825

Women were so relieved to be rid of the hot, heavy wigs, which made the scalp itch and the natural hair matted and uncomfortable, that many wrote about it ecstatically, lauding their own looks. In *The Journals of Mrs Calvert* (1805) this self-satisfied lady boasted of having a famous hair-cutter 'to make a smart crop of me ... I really do not look within ten years as old as I am, with my hair cut short'.

An alternative hair-style, considered by many women to be just as youthful, consisted of the hair combed half back and gathered in a bunch of curls on the crown, or in classical coils towards the back, with the front hair brought forward and arranged in ringlets round the face and forehead.

The century opened with two essentially English fashions. One was the chemise dress for women, already in vogue in the 1790s and moderately based on the classical style but now with bodice and skirt cut separately. The other was ankle-length trousers for men.

If it is thought that male influence had nothing to do with feminine fashion in the nineteenth century, Beau Brummell gives the lie to that. Brummell, a member of the Prince Regent's clique, The Dandies, and a leader of fashion, was fanatical about cleanliness and grooming, hitherto largely ignored even by people of rank. He voiced his disgust if women failed to match up to his standards of cleanliness and, thus humiliated, they became more fastidious, defying the prevailing belief that bathing the body was a risk to health.

Around 1812 to 1814, English women finally discarded the high-bosomed, clinging classical dresses. By 1820 corsets were back and skirts began to widen again over stiff petticoats. Drawers reaching to below the knee were worn for walking, together with little ankle boots. But when communication with France was renewed, English ladies found that the high waist still dominated French fashions and that their own normal waistlines were ridiculed. Promptly, England reverted to the classical style, only to have the tables turned when the French revived the natural waistline and made their English cousins feel dowdy once again.

By 1824 close-belted waists were the vogue, with widening skirts, drooping shoulders and puff sleeves, topped by enormous hats be-decked with flowers and feathers. In 1827–9 came the introduction of gigot sleeves, tight from wrist to elbow and ballooning above. Less modest ladies wore an almost plunging décolletage even for morning wear. For evening, necklines were alway décolleté. Another popular new mode in 1829 was the beret sleeve, a very wide circular affair aping the beret headdress. It could be double or double-bouffant, and the shape was reinforced with whalebone. Both puffed and beret sleeves were usually covered with transparent over-sleeves of tulle or muslin.

Turbans were sometimes worn indoors – the influence of Lord Byron, whose writings about his Turkish travels had awakened a taste for Eastern fashions. The turban was much worn by older women, the young ones favouring a lace cap indoors, tied beneath the chin. This was also the period of the coal-scuttle bonnet, first mentioned in the fashion journals of 1815. For another forty years all types of bonnets reigned supreme for outdoor wear.

By 1820 the pelisse was in fashion, an outdoor garment following the outline of the dress, including the shape of the sleeve. It was frequently made with multiple capes, elaborately trimmed with chevrons. The hem was wadded to improve the hang of the garment. Sometimes it featured a double or triple pelerine (a wide, flat collar spreading over the shoulders) and a fur border with matching muff.

Shawls were always a popular accessory, due to their simplicity and manifold uses. A square of material was easy to store and could be worn in many ways. The beautiful colours and soft fabrics of Indian shawls were highly flattering. These were imported into England until factories in Norwich and Paisley imitated them.

Day caps for indoor wear were small at first, usually bonnet-shaped, tied under the chin, and known as cornettes. They were sometimes pointed at the back of the crown. The cornette was also popular for evening, as was the turban. Early in the century a vast variety of evening headgear was worn, prompting the *Ipswich Journal* to comment, in 1805, on 'white satin hats with ruby and plum-coloured linings, with beautiful pearl and diamond crescents and feathers ...'. There was also the much-favoured lace evening cap with a hole at the back through which hair could cascade in curls.

For the first ten years of the century hats were predominantly small, but from 1804 to 1808 they widened, and featured crowns of Spanish style. The capote, a bonnet with a soft crown, sometimes puffed out, had a stiff brim which projected round the face and was worn with or without ribbon tied beneath the chin. Unique to this period was the calash, a folding hood ringed with whalebone, or sometimes cane. It was designed expressly to cover a cap or bonnet when travelling. On arrival it would be folded and stowed away in a bag for the return journey.

A distinctly provocative fashion, worn for either day or evening, was a short lace eye veil, rivalled only by the 'chin veil' which hung loose from the crown of the head to the chin.

Stockings were of woven cotton, angola (a thread made from wool of the angora goat), or silk. They came in black, white, and a variety of colours, pink being most popular. In 1809 silk stockings with cotton feet and fashionable clox (or clocks) were widely advertised. Garters were tied below the knee, leaving the stocking loose above – and surely uncomfortable. In 1803, when the classical style was in vogue, the *Chester Chronicle* remarked that the only sign of modesty in the current ladies' fashions was the pink dye in their stockings, making their legs appear to blush for the total absence of petticoats. And as for garters, the *Ipswich Journal* reported that 'The German waltze has become so general as to render the ladies' garters an object of consideration in regard to elegance and variety.' Lace stockings were worn with sandal slippers, criss-crossed laces being tied round the ankles.

In the 1820s, corsets and bustles were essential to sustain the shape of the dress, and tight lacing became excessive, due to the new fashion for a plumper figure. In 1825 Harriette Wilson, an expert on feminine appeal, wrote in *Paris Lions and London Tigers* that 'Mrs Nesbit's corsets give the most natural *en bon point* of any I saw,' which was a fine advertisement for Mrs Nesbit, the corset maker.

There were other artificial aids to beauty. Rouge continued to be popular and some women still followed the eighteenth-century custom of stuffing cork 'plumpers' in their cheeks to make their faces look rounder and fatter. But the greatest emphasis was on immense sleeves to diminish the apparent size of waists which had to appear as small as humanly (or inhumanly) possible. Stays were so tightly laced that a tradesman of 1828 recorded how his daughters were 'unable to stand, sit, or walk as women used to do. To expect one of them to stoop would be absurd. My daughter Margaret made the experiment the other day; her stays gave way with a tremendous explosion and down she fell and I thought she had snapped in two.'

By 1827 hats had become bigger and bigger, and the fashion continued. They were made of satin, transparent gauze, straw (Leghorn or Dunstable), chip, silk and crepe, all loaded with trimmings of flowers, feathers, and yards of wide ribbon in multitudinous colours. For evening the turban still remained in favour, along with the beret which, from this date, became excessively large – very like a big tam-o'shanter. This was trimmed with ribbons, feathers, and flowers, and worn at an exaggerated angle.

Bonnets followed the fashion in hats, the brims widening just slightly earlier. A soft frill called a bavolet, attached to the back of the bonnet and curtaining the neck, appeared in 1828 and remained fashionable right into the 1860s. Bonnets also sported *mentonnières* or 'chin stays'. These were quillings or goffers, pieces of tulle or lace shaped into quill-like folds and inserted into the bonnet strings so that they formed a white frill below the chin when tied.

Hair was now arranged in tight curls on the forehead and temples, with the back hair sometimes brought up in a draped chignon and sometimes left in loose ringlets, the latter mainly for evening wear. The centre parting was often retained. The Apollo Knot appeared in 1824, mainly for evening wear though some women sported it by day and were consequently considered flamboyant. It was formed by a loop or loops of plaited hair added to the natural hair, fixed upright on top of the head and allowed to merge with the chignon or fall as it wished. Two or three loops, and sometimes more, were decorated with bird-of-paradise feathers, flowers, jewelled combs, and glauvina pins. These pins, sometimes called 'Swiss bodkins', were long skewers with metallic heads, often with ornamental chains dangling from them.

Bonnets and enormous sleeves 1830

By the mid-thirties fabrics had become heavier and the weight of clothes likewise. The model wives of rich industrialists would wear elaborate turn-outs designed to advertise their husbands' successes.

By the 1840s the ethereal shawls of Eastern flavour which had covered transparently clad shoulders were now draped over thick-bodiced dresses with billowing skirts. They were quickly succeeded by a variety of capes and mantles.

A new fashion in 1833 was the pointed waist, but the round waist with buckled belt was, on the whole, more popular. The gigot sleeve became immense, supported with a stiff lining or a pad stuffed with down. Closely rivalling it was the imbecile, or *à la folle* sleeve, wider still and only slightly narrowed toward a tight-fitting cuff at the waist. There was also the Donna Maria sleeve, full to the elbow and then tight to the wrist, and the Marino Falieri, so named after Byron's hero – a large sleeve billowing to the wrist.

In the summer of 1836 big sleeves suddenly collapsed, heralding the bishop sleeve with vertical pleats at the shoulder, flowing fully and limply to wrist gatherings and a tight cuff, and the *en bouffant* or *en sabot* sleeve which was tight, with puffed-out expansions at intervals to the elbow, and sometimes as far as the wrist. In 1837 came the Victoria sleeve, with a large puff at the elbow, but tight above and below. A tight sleeve with frills above the elbow was introduced at the end of the decade.

In 1836 the general outline became narrower and the décolletage semi-low, but the slimmer outline was frowned on by *World of Fashion*, which remarked that nothing could be more unbecoming than the present tight apparel when worn by 'a lath and plaster damsel, all skin and bone', which indicates that the buxom woman was still in high favour.

A revival of this time for outdoor wear was the redingote, a version of the former pelisse which followed the line of the dress, but now with a flat back, and with lapels or pleats at the front hanging from the shoulders to the waist to form a point.

For evening, the extreme décolleté was back, the waist of the bodice sometimes pointed both at front and rear, with single boning down centre front. Sleeves carried multiple bouffants and elaborate trimmings of all kinds, with lace and ribbon predominant. After 1836 a short train could be added to the skirt.

Corsets now became demi-corsets for morning wear, but for social wear they remained very long and very tightly laced. Over this framework came the bustle (commonly called the 'false bottom') which was either a crescent-shaped cushion or a tier of stiff frills, both being tied about the waist under the dress.

Dress materials were muslins, jaconet, batiste, gingham, challis, washing foulards, merino, sarcenet, cashmere, mousseline-de-laine, and a large range of chintzes and silks and wools. Very popular were printed floral designs and convoluted mixtures of delicate colours. Checks were used extensively for walking dresses, coats, and riding or sporting clothes.

Evening wear saw painted and printed foulards, all of English make, also *gros de Naples* and heavy flowered silks, satins, and velvets, plus organdie, crepe, or muslin over satin slips. In 1835 the Spitalfields silk industry revived flowered brocades and toward the close of the decade chine silk (the forerunner of crepe-de-chine) leapt in popularity. After 1836, colours became more subdued.

Peculiar to this period was the 'breakfast dress', worn for luncheon.

Outdoor garments remained virtually unchanged, except for the revival of the 'Witzchoura mantle', now minus a cape and with the addition of vast hanging sleeves. This was a winter garment, often lined with fur. There was also the Polish mantle, caped and knee-length, and the mantlet, made like half a shawl and shaped to the neck with sometimes the addition of a hood or very small cape. The burnouse, a large mantlet with a large hood, was for evening wear.

Hats, in fact headwear of all kinds, diminished in size from the middle of the decade, with emphasis on demureness. About this time the beret disappeared, but the turban still persisted, occasionally decorated with a plume. It was rivalled by the evening hat, made of crepe or silk and turned up from the face, with ostrich feathers and/or ribbons waving from it. To increase its attraction, it was worn at a rakish angle. The *petit bord* sported a narrow halo brim and was worn on the back of the head. By 1838 this had become known as a 'toque'.

For evening, young women decorated their hair with artificial flowers and fruit, sprays of currants or bunches of grapes, plus jewellery, feathers, and bows, not to mention the *ferronnière*, a narrow gold or silver band, sometimes bejewelled, worn low across the forehead. This was both a day and evening accessory.

For hair-styles during the 1830s the centre parting remained, but the hair was always brought smoothly down to the temples and then arranged either with tight curls over the temples and ears, in plaits encircling the ears, or in plain tresses covering them and then coiled into a fairly high bun or 'knot' at the back. Alternatively the back hair was twisted on top of the head, subsiding to the back of it by the end of 1840.

The use of rouge now ceased to be fashionable. A frail, pallid appearance was deemed romantic, so much so that in 1839 a woman writer declared that 'the number of languid, listless and inert young ladies who now recline upon sofas is a melancholy spectacle; it is but rarely that we meet with a really healthy woman.'

Tight lacing remained unchanged. In the years between 1840 and 1850, the 'Victorian Gothic' fashion reached its pinnacle, but the excessively tight, long-waisted stays and layers of burdensome underclothes restricted physical activity and caused many young women to go into a decline. This was not deplored; it was even considered a social asset, a testimony to their gentle breeding. A volume entitled *The Girls' Book of Diversions* appeared at this time, with instructions on 'How To Faint', stressing that the modes of fainting should all be as different as possible and could be made not only diverting, but appealing.

Then the waistline became very low but remained tightly laced and restricting. Shoulders drooped, sleeves became tight or semi-tight, and skirts very full. Bodice and skirt were usually in one piece, but a novel idea was to have both a day and evening bodice of the same material to wear with the same skirt, each one being lightly tacked to the skirt to prevent it from slipping out of the waistband. In 1846, this fashion was often coupled with the jacket bodice, to be followed in 1848 with the princess robe, a garment with no seam at the waist and a heavily gored skirt.

Also in 1846 the gilet corsage became popular. This aped a man's waistcoat and was either joined to the skirt or separate, as was the jacket bodice.

Skirts were long enough to touch the toes, with the material gathered into the waist by small tubular pleats, drawn close, known as organ pleating.

Important innovations at this time included a skirt-lining made partly of horsehair and known as 'crinoline'. This maintained the shape of the skirt and was much used when it became even larger in 1848. Later, the name was applied to the hooped petticoat. Other new ideas were the braiding of hems to protect them against wear, large pockets instead of the earlier placket holes, and small watch-pockets concealed in waistbands. Double skirts became common for summer wear, the upper one ending near the knee.

Day dresses consisted mainly of the pelisse-robe or redingote, the round dress, and the peignoir. Earlier, the redingote had been an outdoor garment worn for promenading and the pelisse-robe a dress for morning or afternoon wear, but by 1847 the two styles were

A low waistline and sloping shoulders 1844

almost indistinguishable and the term 'pelisse-robe' died out.

The bertha, for evening wear, was a deep collar of lace frills, with ribbon and other fancy decorations covering the sleeves. In conjunction with the pointed waist for evening, which became longer and sharper after 1846, the bertha was a throwback to the mid seventeenth century.

A knee-length overskirt, sometimes left open in front, was looped up with festoons of ribbon and flowers. For evening two or more overskirts, each reducing in length, were fashionable variations.

Fabrics, by day, were merino, alpaca, striped silks (known as 'Pekins'), levantine, foulard, chine silk, grenadine, taffeta (often plaided or broched), barège, organdie, tarlatan and gingham; for evening, shot silk, figured silk, moiré, velvet, organdie, tarlatan, barège, terry velvet, broché silks, glacé silks, and grosgrain. Primary colours were considered very bad taste, delicate ones the reverse. All-over patterns on printed materials could be in mixed colours, but never loud, and stripes had to be narrow, never wide.

New styles for outdoors were, in the main, variations on former garments, re-named. The shawl persisted, often in varying sizes consisting of large squares with elaborate fringed borders, Paisley being particularly popular. Shawl materials were predominantly glacé or figured silks, embroidered organdie, chine crepe, or fringed foulard for summer. Afternoon and evening shawls were made of silks and satins, lace, gauze, muslin, or any other gossamer material. Winter still saw cashmere, but with woven or printed designs, particularly pine-pattern. By 1849–50 the long shawl was in vogue, measuring six feet by four. The long shawl cost one and a half to two guineas, the short shawl, around seven shillings and sixpence.

There were many variations on the cloak or mantle, but the two garments eventually became synonymous. Both hung loose from the neck and were knee-length; sometimes with loose sleeves and sometimes with armhole slits. The paletot, a mantle with three capes and slits for the arms, bore no resemblance to the masculine garment of the same name. The mantlet had changed little, but now usually resembled a larger-size pelerine, the front panels being broad and long and frequently trimmed with frills. The pelerine was now mainly a shoulder cape, but sometimes reached the waist; the feather-pelerine was made at home of farmyard feathers individually stitched onto a canvas ground, lined with silk; the feathers formed decorative patterns, reminiscent of Maori robes, but smaller.

'Pardessus' was the comprehensive name for any sleeved, three-quarter length outdoor garment; variations included the *sortie-de-bal*, an unwaisted evening coat with bell sleeves, later renamed an 'evening cloak'; and the pelisse-mantle, a long cloak with a waist-length cape.

The enthusiasm for beauty aids continued undiminished. Artificial busts were much sought after. *The Lady's Newspaper* of 1848 advertised 'the registered bust improver of an air-proof material, an improvement on the pads of wool and cotton hitherto used', and *The Handbook of the Toilet* deplored the use of 'lemon bosoms and many other means of creating fictitious charms'. And it would be interesting to know the ingredients of 'Hubert's Roseate Powder' which claimed, in 1847, to 'stand pre-eminent for the removal of superfluous hair on face, neck, and arms of beauty'. Legs, never being revealed, could apparently remain hairy.

SECOND HALF OF THE CENTURY

Skirts hitched up on spreading frame,
Petticoats as bright as flame,
Dandy high-heeled boots proclaim
Fast Young Ladies.

(Music Hall song, 1860)

THE YEAR 1850 LAUNCHED ENGLAND into a period of enormous commercial prosperity. This produced a new branch of society – the *nouveaux riches* – whose fashion indulgences were frowned on by a publication called *Ask Mamma*. In 1858 it named extravagance in dress as one of the current vices, adding that distinction between the upper and middle classes was now difficult to recognize and pointing out that this passion for dress was not exclusive to the upper and middle levels of society, but had even spread to the 'lower orders', so much so that:

> This speedy influx of fashion and abundance of cheap tawdry finery has well-nigh destroyed the primitive simplicity of country churches. The housemaid now dresses better – finer, at all events – than her mistress did twenty years ago, and it is almost impossible to recognise working people when in their Sunday dresses. Gauze bonnets, marabout feathers, lace scarves and silk gowns usurp the place of straw and cotton print, while lace-fringed kerchiefs are flourished by those whose parents scarcely knew what a pocket handkerchief was.

Ask Mamma also remarked that 'your lady's maid must now have her crinoline and it has even become essential to factory girls', all of which proves that the snobbishness typified by *Αγωγός* nearly twenty-five years earlier was still prevalent.

Chief fashion features at the opening of the second half of the century were the broadening of the Gothic outline and the ever-widening skirt. Drooping shoulders and tight bodices persisted, though corseting relaxed slightly and the waist, while still small, was not so strangulating.

Early in 1856 the hooped crinoline arrived. This was necessary to support the vast skirt, and was made in various ways, usually with ever-widening rings of whalebone, soon replaced by steel. The top rings of the hoop were left open to enable the wearer to step into it before tying it at the front. *The Times*, in July 1857, reported that a firm in Sheffield had taken an order for 40 tons of rolled steel for crinoline construction.

The size and width of crinolines varied, some becoming so enormous that contemporary cartoons depicted gentlemen straining to kiss ladies' hands and totally failing to bridge the distance, and in 1856 Lady E. Spencer-Stanhope wrote in her 'Letter-bag': 'I only wish you could have seen the dress of Lady Wallace. Last night she absolutely could not sit down in an armchair till she had lifted her hoop over the arm on both sides.' The point of absurdity was reached with a creation made of vulcanized indiarubber tubes, in place of the steel hoops, which were inflated by blowing hard through another, detachable, tube and then sealed. Alas, too many punctures led to too many embarrassing moments, and the ambitious project failed.

However, it is plain from photographs of the times that many women never wore cages, relying only on masses of petticoats to achieve the billowing effect, which sometimes achieved a width around the hem of from twelve to fifteen feet.

A revolutionary landmark was the chain-stitch sewing machine, introduced by Singer around 1850, with the lock-stitch hard on its heels. This led to a new innovation – the ready-made dress. In 1851

The ever-widening crinoline – a cartoon by George Cruickshank 1851

the sensational Mrs Amelia Bloomer, an ardent advocate of women's emancipation, arrived from America to launch her frilled trousers, worn under a loose tunic, which became known as 'bloomers'. For a while this scandalous style caught on with a few venturesome females, but the fashion magazines urged that anything so unladylike should be shunned even though the climbing of stiles in a crinoline was virtually impossible – '. . . and if in so attempting a lady suffers much from the comments of vulgar little boys it would be better, in a high wind, to remain indoors'.

Poor Mrs Bloomer stood little chance, despite the eulogizing of one doting mother over 'my lovely daughter Constantia in the full-blown costume of a Bloomer . . .'. Constantia's daring outfit included a silver-buttoned vest with a flowing jacket above a lavender-coloured tunic and white trousers. With this she wore a cambric collarette and crimson silk necktie, coupled with a richly figured shirt with mock diamond buttons scattered freely down the front, and very fetching she probably looked; but alas for Constantia, the fashion for women's trousers was killed overnight by an East End publican who clad his barmaids in similar outfits and reduced the mode to ridicule. The news spread across London and people flocked eastwards for the laugh, which was good for the publican's business, but not for Mrs Bloomer's.

A style also considered a little 'fast' was the gilet (waistcoat), shaped to the figure and worn with an open jacket-bodice shaped to the waist and flared into twin basques. The jacket-bodice came in two styles: the basquin, with short basques, and the caraco, with long ones reaching over the hips. Either style could have a 'V' opening at the neck, edged with revers or a turn-down collar, or be closed and finished with a small white collar, and both were hooked or buttoned as far as the waist but not below. Buttons came in gilt, pearl, mosaic, or stone. Some jackets were made with false waistcoat fronts attached to the garment.

Open sleeves were highly fashionable up to the end of 1860. *Engageantes* (washable half-sleeves, usually white, worn beneath open sleeves) were mandatory with this style. There was also the bell sleeve, narrow at the shoulder but flaring to a bell shape from elbow to wrist, and the much favoured pagoda sleeve, tight at the shoulder then expanding to a wide opening at the wrist, sometimes with a long front slit, and dipping at the back.

Other fashionable sleeves were the Amadis and the Gabrielle. The first was close-pleated at the armhole, but the pleats were hidden beneath an epaulette, from where the sleeve was tight-fitting all the way to a deep cuff at the wrist. The second featured a tier of puffs the whole length of the arm. Epaulettes were frequently worn with both these and the bishop sleeve. A decorative bow, called a 'jockey', was a fashionable gimmick adorning both shoulder and wrist.

Plain skirts were unusual. Most had multiple flounces, or were made in double or treble layers, decreasing in length from hem to waist. Except for summer, skirts were always lined. Short trains began to appear around 1860.

Bodices for evening wear were tight-fitting with a deep point at the waist-front, and back fastenings. The décolletage was off the shoulders and elaborately trimmed, or worn with a deep bertha also lavishly decorated. Sleeves for evening wear were short and straight, or 'en bouffant' ending well above the elbow.

Dress materials for day wear produced nothing new, but silks increased and were much used in varieties of moiré, poplin, glacé, taffeta, and foulard, closely rivalled by satin, velvet, organdie, batiste, barège, muslins, delaine, merino, and grenadine. For evening, silks were richer, as were brocades, velvets, tarlatans, organdies and muslins, with guipure and blonde lace in abundance.

Small turn-down collars, usually white, were *de rigueur* with high necked day dresses, while muslin and lace-trimmed fichus were considered essential with open 'V' necks. The ends of the fichu crossed at waist level.

Outdoor garments commanded much attention. The mantle remained fashionable, and was now very full and three-quarter-length, shaped to the waist in front but loose behind. The shawl-mantle or cloak fitted round the neck, then flowed almost to hemline. A new touch was the drawn-up sides with two long panels trailing down the front. The Talma-mantle was a full cloak with a hood, or a deep tasselled collar worn flat. In 1854 the Talma had become shorter and thenceforth was occasionally called the *rotonde*. Popular for travelling on either long or short trips was the very wide Highland cloak with a capuchin hood.

Bonnets were as indispensable as ever, especially for church-going, when hats were unacceptable. A new bonnet style, featuring the bavolet, was large and stiffened with buckram, sometimes trimmed with a ribbon bow with long ends trailing down the back. Undersides of brims were trimmed with lace, tulle, ribbons and flowers, with broad ribbon tied beneath the chin. As the 1850s progressed the bonnet became smaller and continued to shrink for the rest of the decade until it was worn, to much ridicule, almost on the back of the head. This necessitated the use of a velvet bandeau over the front of the head to prevent it from falling off.

Hats for country wear were of plain, supple straws, with moderate crowns and brims. In 1854 a copy of the man's 'round hat' appeared. This was mushroom shaped, with a wide brim and low flat crown, trimmed with ribbon with floating ends at the back. The hat had to be tied beneath the chin to keep it in place; sometimes a front string was attached, to enable the wearer to hold onto it during high winds. It was nicknamed the 'seaside hat' because it was chiefly worn there.

The years 1860–70 were not only 'an age of extraordinary wealth and of corresponding luxury' (according to Mrs Lynn Linton, an essayist of the time) but had the unique distinction of heralding a hitherto unknown financial inflation, with a corresponding increase in the cost of living. There were growing complaints about feminine extravagance and, as if in defiance, fashion decreed bold masses of colour in startling and sometimes violent contrasts. The newly-arrived aniline dyes, especially magenta, encouraged this.

Also encouraged was the reduction in bulk in the skirt. This led to the decline of the crinoline and the renewal of the back bustle, with the skirt cut to hang straight at the front and spread out behind. Pannier dresses, with huge 'overpuffs' draped over the hips, became popular because, without the aid of a crinoline, they provided width and emphasized the small waist. A sensational walking dress could be hitched up with hidden cords to give women a freedom of movement previously unknown in this century. Other skirts for walking were short enough to show the ankles. The exposure of feet and ankles inevitably led to a boom in the boot and shoe industry, producing a greater variety of styles – including the 'dandy high-heeled boots' of the popular song; they were worn with stockings in all colours and patterns and a profusion of fancy clox.

Young women discarded the bonnet in favour of the hat, and the use of make-up also emphasized the changing outlook. Even some respectable Englishwomen began to paint their faces and tint their eyelids. False hair was freely advertised, and used.

But, alas, tight lacing returned, resulting in billowing skirts and the revival of a substructure. Around 1870 the crinoline reappeared to support a pyramid or funnel-shaped skirt with an enormously wide base. Eighteen feet around the hem was not unknown, but hips were less full due to gored side panels. Skirts had small trains for afternoon and evening wear. Separate bodices and skirts became à

Outdoor wear: *left* street dress with fichu 1868, *right* two types of paletot 1871

la mode, but not necessarily matching. The Garibaldi shirt, seized on by young women in 1863, and worn with a contrasting skirt, was popularly scarlet and braided in black, with matching front buttons. A black Tudor hat with scarlet feather and scarlet snood, plus scarlet stockings, completed the outfit.

Jackets included the casaque, tight-fitting with wide sleeves, and the corsage postilion (1862), buttoned down the front and with two short basques at the back, which later covered the top of the skirt at the back and became known as the Balmoral bodice.

Outdoor garments continued to be cloaks and mantles, but there was also the camail, a long circular cloak without sleeves. The paletot continued as an overcoat, either loose or shaped to the figure, single or double-breasted, three-quarter length or short. The redingote-paletot, resembling a princess dress with revers and buttoned down the front from neck to ankle, was popular. The zouave jacket was short and loose, cut square at the front; braid trim was considered very much 'the thing' for this. For winter use, the short sealskin jacket became the vogue.

The year 1867 saw the launching of a sensational fashion journal from America – *Harper's Bazar*. It reigned supreme until 1898, when it was edged out by a number of new and more sophisticated periodicals, including *Vogue*. (Not until William Randolph Hearst

took over *Harper's* in 1913 did this magazine regain its eminence.)
Another notable event of 1867 was the International Exhibition in
Paris. American businessmen and industrialists flocked to it, taking
their womenfolk with them. Needless to say, these wives and daughters returned home with trunkloads of French fashions, many of
which can still be seen in costume collections in the USA, testifying
to the care lavished upon them.

It is likely that many of these clothes were of English inspiration,
for in the years immediately preceding the exhibition an English
designer named Charles Frederick Worth, working in Paris, launched the 'mannequin parade', a hitherto unheard of display of gowns
on live models, for the inspection of prospective customers. This
was the birth of the French couture. By 1867 Worth had become as
fastidious about his selection of clients as he was about his materials,
trimmings and accessories. It became the ultimate social accolade to
be dressed by a man who designed and made clothes for royalty. But
he was not alone in focusing attention on the English style; the
marriage in 1863 of the Prince of Wales (later King Edward VII)
to the lovely Danish princess Alexandra had attracted world-wide
attention and the London fashion scene came in for its fair share.

During the 1860s, headwear became as lavish as dress, and the
music hall song of 1860 immortalized it:

> The Wide-Awake our heads adorn,
>   Fast young Ladies;
> Feathers in our hats are worn,
>   Fast young Ladies.

This was the era of Mary Stuart hats dipping to a point over the
forehead, perched saucily and with flowing plumes; of spoon bonnets
which the young hoped disapproving elders would accept in place of
hats for Sabbath wear (few did); and of Empire bonnets with large
bows beneath the chin ending in wide flowing ribbons, plus matching
ribbons sailing from the back, commonly called 'follow-me-lads'.
There was also a very small and enchanting hat called a 'puff bonnet',
resembling nothing so much as an inverted, lace-and-flower-be-
decked saucer with a long ribbon-and-lace loop framing the face
and hanging loosely beneath the chin; and, from 1864, the glengarry
cap and pork pie hat.

Another was the Tyrolese hat, covered in silk or velvet, with a
flower-pot crown and narrow brim rolled upwards. In the 1870s

tall-crowned hats appeared, reminiscent of a coachman's, with upstanding ostrich feathers. High crowns won the name 'three storeys and a basement' (1886), but there were also small straw or chip hats with lower flower-pot crowns and narrow rolled-up brims, and sailor hats with low crowns and stiff brims, and 'wide-awakes' with low crowns and wide limp brims.

The angle at which headgear was worn was inevitably influenced by hair styles. The chignon dominated this decade, forcing hats to a forward tilt, but the evening coiffure favoured curls. Sometimes the side hair would be brushed back and then puffed out above or over the ears, pads frequently being used to maintain the shape, or it would be plaited and looped around them, the ends always being linked to the chignon behind. This was usually increased in size by the use of false hair for evening, but enclosed in a net by day. From being worn low on the neck, the chignon finally reached the crown of the head. For evening, massed curls fell over it and an odd ringlet or two strayed negligently from beneath. Ready-made chignons were widely used, as were false hair and toupees. In 1869 *Punch* reported that the sale of false hair had increased by 400 per cent in the last twelve years.

In 1868 *The Englishwoman's Domestic Magazine* reported that at a recent public assembly every other woman seemed to be wearing false hair, and was also painted, with eyebrows and eyelashes coloured. And about the same time *Punch* declared that the latest fashion whim was to be black-haired and bronze complexioned, pearl powder being discarded in favour of 'golden powder', with no more yellow or auburn hair 'even if nature intended it so'.

Artificial aids to beauty were frowned on by many, but disapproval was ignored by the more adventurous who wished to be ultra-fashionable. False bosoms had long been worn, and in 1860 a newspaper announcement of a provisional patent for 'an improved inflated undulating artificial bust' which, when blown up, would 'produce the form required', was heralded with delight.

In 1873 that revered magazine, *The Queen*, wrote that women now expected their husbands to tolerate 'their costly and incessant change of fashion, their powder and cosmetics, their monstrous erections of dyed and false hair, their padded figures, every rounded line made by milliners' [meaning dressmakers] 'and none by nature.'

Certainly this latter part of the nineteenth century was a fashionable woman's heyday, styles changing so rapidly that one seemed to be out of fashion before the next came in. Woollens and brocades would be mixed with satins and velvets in one ensemble, excessively trimmed. In 1875 the bustle disappeared and gowns became shaped to the hips with fullness below. Sometimes a large bow would be placed half-way down the back of the skirt. Dresses were tied back tightly under the back fullness, to flatten the front, a style which must have been very trying to a stout figure, especially by 1878 when dresses had become sheathlike.

The 1870s were marked by over-elaboration of trimming, even on accessories such as scarves, collars, and cuffs. A 'scarf drapery' across a skirt would be loaded with pleats and frills, buttons and bows. Flounces were gathered, fluted, box-pleated or knife-pleated, and even crowned with 'stand-up' flounces in reverse. There were velvet bands, ruchings, tassels, 'waterfalls' of lace, chenille decorations, passementerie, tinsels, spangles, jet, paste jewellery, and gauging. Bugle beads, rainbow beads, and moonlight beads added weight to everything. Amid the mixture of materials and colours, fashion-confusion reigned.

Only one outfit remained unadorned – the high-necked blouse and single skirt, which might be flounced but was always made without an overskirt. This was known as a 'house dress' and the model wife would wear it in the morning.

The jacket-bodice now had short basques or a 'spreading corsage postilion', or occasionally long basques forming an over-skirt. The cuirasse bodice was a tight, corset-shaped affair hugging the hips and dipping to a front point; sometimes it sported a panel of contrasting material down the front, called a plastron. Russian or French blouses appeared in 1877, and the Norfolk jacket the same year, based on the male version but worn as a bodice ending at the hips, usually accompanying a pleated skirt ending in a train.

The Dolly Varden dress, named after Dicken's heroine in *Barnaby Rudge*, appeared in 1871. It had a bodice and overskirt joined at the waist, the overskirt being short in front and long but bunched out behind, in the style of the late eighteenth-century polonaise, and was made in chintz or cretonne, with the underskirt brightly coloured. It was worn with a bergère hat, which inevitably became known as the 'Dolly Varden'.

Lily Langtry, the 'Jersey Lily', mistress of Edward VII, set another fashion in 1879 – the Jersey or Guernsey dress, made of fine wool or knitted silk. It clung to the figure down to mid-thigh, where it was swathed round the knees in a deep sash. Beneath it a kilted skirt, usually of serge or, in winter, of flannel, was either pulled on

Summer suit with deep flounces, lace and bows, and with tucked bodice and frilled neckline and cuffs 1873

over the head or fastened, as invisibly as possible, down the back. Many of these 'jerseys' were boned down the back, and were actually worn for tennis.

Then came the tea gown, a development from the *robe de chambre*. Being a loose garment, it had one great, even merciful, asset – corsets could be abandoned. Later, it was adorned with a fichu front and even with a 'Watteau sac back' sweeping into a train. Moralists declared that the tea gown encouraged 'free and easy morals' and pointed the way to degeneracy. Made in muslin, silks, satin or sateen, the tea gown was exclusively for married women; young ladies were not allowed to wear it.

Hard on the heels of this apparently licentious mode came the Aesthetic Movement, whose influence produced a feminine type hitherto unknown. She was 'wan, superb-browed, with a throat like Juno', according to an admirer who saw an 'aesthetic lady' at a soirée. This sensational woman wore a loose yellow garment with gold Egyptian ornaments round her neck and arms, and held tiger-lilies in her hands. The Aesthetic Movement was partially inspired by the Pre-Raphaelite Brotherhood, a group of artists and poets formed in London in 1848, among whom were Dante Gabriel Rosetti, Holman Hunt, and John Everett Millais. Their aim was to produce work in the spirit which generally imbued art before the time of Raphael.

This movement for artistic reform spread to fashions in clothes, furnishings, and manners. Millais's painting of Ophelia had a strong influence and encouraged the type of 'aesthetic lady' mentioned above. The famous Regent Street shop opened by Arthur Lazenby Liberty on 15 May 1875, and grandly named East India House, catered for the new fashions. Liberty imported silks from the east and printed them with oriental patterns, including Mysore silk woven by hand in India and shipped in the raw state to be dyed in England 'by a permanent process especially for Liberty & Co.' Authentic Indian designs were obtained from the authorities of the new Indian Museum, and then hand-printed by the wood-block process. Liberty fabrics draped easily and adapted well to the Greek influence so favoured by the Pre-Raphaelites, with its natural, flowing line and freedom of movement, but the dress was tight-fitting underneath, with the top drapery swathed deceptively in limp materials. This style became known as the Pre-Raphaelite when someone commented that all the women at a party looked wan and untidy, 'like figures in Pre-Raphaelite pictures, with unkempt hair.' Favourite colours were dull green or yellow, deep red, or peacock blue.

The most memorable thing about the decade 1880–1890 was the unpleasant practice of adorning clothes with dead animals, real or faked. Shoulders displayed birds perched in nests which were also inhabited by beetles, centipedes, spiders, flies, caterpillars, and a host of other insects. Rats, mice, snakes, lizards, scorpions and various birds or beasts of prey were considered highly ornamental, many of them artificial, but some actually stuffed by taxidermists. A magazine of the time commented on a ball gown decorated with cascades of dead mice and a report of an auction sale quoted thirty thousand humming birds sold in one afternoon.

Despite condemnation, both by the public and in the press, the fashion persisted, until mercifully eclipsed by a passion for drapery, which became so tightly sheathed that women could only take hobbled footsteps. Between 1880 and 1890 the large bustle returned. From 1885 to 1888 it projected like a shelf, and half-hoops of steel were inserted into the back of the skirt, adding so much weight that women eventually found it unbearable, and the large bustle went out of fashion in 1889, heralding a final decade in which the desire for freedom vied with a reluctance to lose the male attention won by cloying femininity.

Parisian fashions exploited this seemingly helpless femininity, but England had more advanced ideas which resulted in a mixed assortment of frills and furbelows on the bodice of a dress and stark plainness in the skirt. The practicality of such a skirt was mainly attributable to the increase in outdoor exercise, particularly to the bicycle. English tailor-mades led the world for morning wear, and the influence was reflected in clothes designed for sport.

Also in this decade the waterproof, dust-cloak, ulster or travelling wrap appeared. All were names for the same garment, a long neck-to-foot coat shaped at the waist or tightened with a half-belt. Some even bore the hint of a train, and some had hoods or two or three capes called 'three-deckers'.

In the final ten years of the century a large variety of skirts were mainly fitted over the hips, to fall either in a bell shape, or straight to the knee, then spreading widely, or they were pleated or flounced. The umbrella skirt was cut on the cross with a stiffened hem, and the tight-fitting eel skirt had seven gores with all except the front one cut on the cross.

Hair styles were less becoming, the front hair mainly worn in a curly fringe, produced with the aid of curl-papers until 1896 when it was commonly waved with heated irons and brushed high from the

LEFT The return of the bustle: walking dress and evening dress 1883
RIGHT The slimmer skirt of the 1890s – a mid-season gown from Paris 1898

forehead. The back hair was then coiled low, or worn in a higher 'Greek' style, or with a flat bun in the nape of the neck or atop the head. 'Buns' were twisted over hair frames to add volume. The 'teapot handle' or 'door knocker' style, with a loop projecting from a coil high at the back of the head, became fashionable in 1896.

UNDERWEAR, SPORTSWEAR AND ACCESSORIES

A PART FROM STAYS AND CORSETS, and the varying layers of petticoats, the basic garments beneath all nineteenth-century ensembles was a chemise; this covered the naked form from neck or shoulders to well below the knee (becoming shorter later) and absorbed perspiration, thus protecting the remaining clothing. Drawers, reaching to below the knee, were worn from about 1806, but the legs were not joined at the crotch until the middle of the century. From the mid 1870s the chemise and drawers were com-bined as combinations. A camisole or under-bodice was worn over the corset in the latter half of the century.

In addition to innumerable dresses – day dresses, street dresses, walking dresses, afternoon and evening dresses, in fact dresses for every possible occasion – a rich woman's wardrobe, from the 1860s, could also include 'sporting costumes' which seemed to have little bearing on the sports for which they were designed. The American journal, *Harper's Bazar*, featured several 'tennis gowns' between 1867 and 1898, with flowing skirts and layered petticoats, billowing leg-o'mutton sleeves and sometimes bolero jackets with sleeves ballooning to the elbow and finishing in tight-fitting embroidered or lace sleeves to the wrist; or they could comprise a fashionable and highly decorated polonaise over equally festooned underskirts. Whatever the style, it was worn with hats varying between straw boaters and elaborate bonnets. Frilled and embroidered 'tennis aprons', with bibs and tuckers adorned with much crewel work and broderie anglaise all round, were featured in 1881; lace-trimmed headgear completed the impression of an overdressed parlourmaid.

Such clothes permitted no really energetic activity. The same applied to the 'yachting costumes' illustrated in the same magazine, especially those by the famous Paris-based designer, Worth, whose 'seaside toilette' scarcely permitted the wearer to do more than sit in a wicker armchair overlooking the sea, encased in flowing skirts crowned with tiers of ornamental capes, not to mention a befrilled parasol and a lace-bedecked hat adorned with stuffed birds, seagulls providing a truly nautical touch.

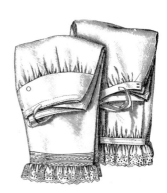

Chemise, combinations and drawers 1890s

For golf, again little concession was made to physical freedom, except that skirts could finish at booted ankles and hats could be smaller – predominantly boaters, or toques trimmed with upstanding quill feathers or cockades of pleated gros-grain. There was even a flowing 'golfing cloak' of thick wool which could be anchored to the shoulders with encircling straps. 'Golf, our late British importation in the way of games, is becoming naturalized very fast,' read the *Harper's* caption, adding that the golfing cloak was 'in favor as a steamer wrap and for long journeys by rail'.

But an 1889 illustration captioned 'The Ladies Class at the Fencers' Club' indicates that American ladies were certainly venturesome in launching some sporting fashions. 'Some two years ago a number of ladies who had witnessed the grace and dexterity of their male friends, in an exhibition of fencing given by the Fencers' Club, thought they also would be benefited by such exercise. In practising, the ladies wear an ordinary tennis dress and flat-soled shoes, no corset, an easy-fitting blouse or jersey. A wire mask protects the face, a padded buckskin *plastron* is worn over the chest, and a buckskin gauntlet saves the hand from any chance scratches or thrusts.' The picture shows two unmasked and ungauntleted ladies with swords crossed, clad in full flowing skirts with draped sashes trailing down almost to the hemline.

More daring was *Harper's* gymnasium costume, comprising a full cotton tunic handsomely belted, with befrilled high neck, long bouffant sleeves frilled at the wrists, and knickerbockers frilled below the knee, the whole ensemble completed with slippers thrice bound at the ankles, like ballet shoes.

The taste for exercise, encouraged by the new freedom-of-movement walking dresses, was further indulged by the advent in 1866 of a swimming costume made of thick brown Holland or dark blue serge, advertised as offering 'perfect liberty of action without exposing the figure'. It consisted of a body and loose trousers cut in one. In this garment a lady would be conveyed to the water's edge in an enclosed horse-drawn conveyance, down the steps of which she could descend straight into the water without observation or embarrassment. Later the bathing costume developed into a form of combinations made in lighter materials, with frills round ankles and armholes; some were made in stockinette in one piece, with a detachable short skirt over knickerbockers.

The influence of the plainer skirts of the 1890s and of English tailoring was reflected in clothes designed for specific sports – such

ABOVE *Left and centre* Golfing outfit and gymnasium suit 1896; *right* tennis dress 1893; from *Harper's Bazar*

RIGHT Flannel bathing suit and hat 1881

as tennis, skating, riding, archery, shooting, tricycling, boating, and particularly walking tours. When cycling became popular in the 1890s, the more adventurous women cyclists wore baggy knickerbockers reaching to below the knee, sometimes called 'bloomers' after Mrs Bloomer's earlier pantaloons.

Gloves were a highly important item in a lady's wardrobe, for only in her home was she ever seen without them, and even there she might wear mittens in cold weather. She had gloves for day wear and evening wear; gloves for winter, spring, and summer; gloves of cotton and wool, of silk and lace, of doeskin and leather; gloves with gauntlets and gloves which fastened neatly at the wrist; short gloves, long gloves, and mid-length gloves. All of them were carefully tended, for not only did gloves keep the hands clean, they were an elegant fashion accessory.

Rules for glove-wearing were well heeded. Formal town wear required kid or doeskin in summer; calf skin, preferably double sewn, in winter. Less formally, gloves of silk or lace had to harmonize with dresses in the summer. Wool was permissible for winter wear in the country; in town, muffs of fur or velvet or feathers protected hands in thinner gloves.

Even the colour was decreed. At the start of the century, buff or yellow was the rule for short day gloves fastened with a single button, and the desired shade could be achieved by dyeing jaded white gloves with well-diluted saffron. By mid century brighter colours could be worn, with scalloped wrists. Then fashion lengthened gloves until, by the 1870s, they came well over the wrists, reaching above the elbow in the eighties for wearing with short sleeves.

Long evening gloves were *de rigueur* with décolleté evening gowns, usually white but sometimes pastel coloured, often embroidered or lace-trimmed, usually of kid but often of material to match the gown. Net mittens, which had been fashionable for social events up to 1840, were back in fashion in the eighties but very much longer, and in harmonizing colours and fabrics. These won approval because removing one's gloves entirely at the supper table bordered on vulgarity, but mittens left the fingers free and the arms elegantly covered.

Bags and reticules were preceded by hanging pockets beneath full skirts, reached through concealed side slits; but with the advent of slimmer dresses early in the century this convenient way of carrying personal possessions was impractical, and so evolved the purse or handbag. Most were made in the same material as the gown and attached to the belt, but later styles, which could be either suspended from the belt or carried, featured silk, satin, velvet or fur, and were often highly decorated with embroidery or beads. A novel Victorian purse was made from a long tube of knitted or crocheted silk, tassellated at the ends, with sliding metal rings to close a centre slit. From the middle of the century leather was used for small purses to be contained in a handbag, but leather handbags did not come into general use until the 1880s. Muff bags, introduced in the same period, had a section into which the hands could be slipped.

Fur was the favourite material for muffs, which were carried throughout the century. In the 1840s and 1850s they were long, lined with silk and padded with horsehair or wadding. For the next twenty years they were small, but in the 1880s they increased in size and popularity and were made of such inexpensive materials that a popular magazine, *The Woman's World*, wrote in 1889 that 'now-a-days even the poor little "slavey" has her muff made of dyed rabbit-skin or cat's fur, and it is merely the length of the purse that decides what fur is to be worn.'

Lace was used prolifically, not only in trimmings but in the creation of ball gowns and evening gowns; sometimes even for afternoon gowns, though a real lady avoided looking too ostentatious at such an hour. Honiton lace became popular for bridal wear, for those who could afford it; the fashion was set by Queen Victoria, and was followed in 1863 by Princess Alexandra, whose white satin wedding petticoat was trimmed with lavish flounces of Honiton lace to match her veil and train.

Feathers were popular throughout the century for trimming hats, bonnets, parasols, muffs, mantles and fans. At the start of the 1800s birds-of-paradise were the favourite, being eclipsed by the ostrich after 1850. Large ostrich feather fans remained fashionable until well into the 1920s, and the feather boa has made continuous comebacks. Originally, both were exclusive fashions among the rich because their upkeep was so costly. Hair ornaments could also consist of an aigrette of feathers and gemstones.

At the start of Victoria's reign, fans were out of fashion, but they returned in the 1840s and continued in popularity throughout the century. Most were imported from France or the Far East, in a variety of materials: painted vellum, paper, or lace, with ribs of ivory or carved wood. In the 1870s feathered fans became fashionable, and in the 1880s silk, satin, or ostrich feathers adorned very large ones. Plain ivory fans became popular because they were easier to clean than fragile materials; an American method was to rub gently with fine glass-paper, then to polish with powdered pumice-stone.

Victorians considered a tan unbecoming, so the aim of Victorian women was to achieve a 'peaches and cream' complexion. This made the use of a parasol essential. At the start of the century the parasol was small, covered in material to match a gown, or in plain, printed or figured silk to harmonize with it. Lace parasols came into fashion in the 1850s and 1860s. Larger parasols, with heavier handles, were introduced in 1865 and continued into the seventies and eighties, long and very ornamental handles coming into favour in 1896. This year also saw the introduction of linings of puffed chiffon. Ruched trimmings were popular throughout the century. Carriage riding offered good opportunities for displaying decorative parasols of tussore silk lined with pink or white to cast a becoming glow on pink-and-white complexions. An advertisement in *Cassell's Household Guide* in the 1860s announced that parasols could be cleaned or dyed for one shilling.

By the end of the century jewellery featured every stone imaginable, with moonstones, chrysoprase, turquoise and peridots much sought after. Lockets in the form of 'everlasting hearts' could be plain or gem-studded. Pendant watches set in balls of crystal were pinned to the bodice. Gold chains and necklaces were elaborate and plentiful. Mourning brooches contained hair from the loved one, meticulously plaited into squares like a chess board, and lockets contained faded portraits or miniatures.

High collars, called chokers, were elaborately embroidered with pearls, bugle beads, diamanté, or whatever paste stones were fancied. There were expanding bracelets, dagger brooches, and chunks of jet. Earrings faded in popularity due to trouble resulting from badly pierced ears, but screw-on earrings were a novelty welcomed in 1899. A snobbish fashion was the lorgnette, through which a woman could view friend or neighbour, or scan theatre boxes, with a gesture of disdain. It could be of chased gold or silver, or ornamented with gems for evening.

But the real hall-mark of prosperity was the diamond, worn in abundance on every possible occasion. It was a symbol of the century's wealth and a husband's appreciation of his model wife.

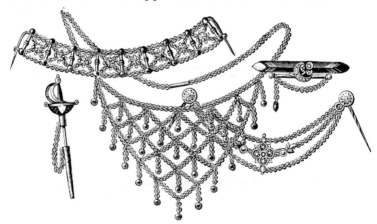

Necklaces, brooch and flower pin 1892

8 ❧ CARE OF CLOTHES

THERE WERE NO automatic washing machines, no electric irons, no dry cleaners except specialists in fur and lace; there were no labour-saving devices whatsoever when it came to caring for clothes in nineteenth-century households. Where neither valet nor lady's maid was employed, responsibility for the master's wardrobe fell on the mistress in addition to looking after her own, plus her children's if she had no nurse, and all household linens and soft furnishings if she had no housekeeper.

In this heavy undertaking she might be assisted by a visiting washerwoman or by a servant-girl, but it was she who added the correct amount of fresh ox-gall to the wash-tub of coloured muslins to ensure the preservation of their colours, or of bullock's gall for the treatment of lace. Only she could apply, drop by drop, the pennyworth of sugar of lead to a pail of cold spring water in which to soak a washable dress for an hour, prior to laundering by hand, or the equally dangerous oil of vitriol used to brighten certain fabrics.

Both sugar of lead and vitriol were violent poisons, as was pearl ash, another popular laundering agent, but all could be bought 'over the counter' for household use. Because of their dangerous properties they were kept well away from accidental handling. Sugar of lead was particularly dangerous if hands were cut or scratched; it could also be absorbed through unblemished skin, though this was not realized for a long time. In both cases, fatal lead poisoning was unavoidable. Vitriol, if used too strongly, would cause dresses to disintegrate, and one drop touching the skin could disfigure for life. (The sale of vitriol was finally banned when women used it for self-protection on the streets, flinging it in their molesters' faces and often blinding them.) Inevitably, the handling of these substances fell to the housewife or, in wealthy homes, to a housekeeper supervising the domestic staff.

Gin was less dangerous and was used extensively as a cleaning agent for clothes unsuitable for washing. It could be bought at Mr Whiteley's famous emporium in Queensway at one shilling and threepence a pint, and at one shilling and sixpence for Harrod's better quality. A large wineglass of it, mixed with a good measure of soft soap to the same amount of honey in two pints of lukewarm water, was excellent for silks, particularly if they were unpicked and laid out in sections. Unpicking dresses prior to washing or cleaning was a common practice, even when hems measured up to five or six yards. Sometimes an elaborate gown contained as many as forty to fifty yards of fabric. All sections of an unpicked garment would be carefully spread on a clean table, smoothing out the creases before scrubbing each side thoroughly with soapy water, then rinsing with clear water. Alternatively, an appropriate cleaning agent was used.

When dry, and pressed carefully with flat-irons heated on the kitchen stove, the garment would then be reassembled, resewn, and retrimmed, for clothes were meant to last and a thrifty housewife made sure that they did. Many fabrics were reversible, and careful laundering made it possible for the gown to be completely turned, presenting a new face to the world. Remaking presented no fears to women accustomed to executing fine needlework. Even when the early sewing machines appeared, many could not afford them or mistrusted them, and still applied every stitch by hand.

Nowadays people tend to smile at the Victorian custom of changing for dinner or supper every evening, but even in modest homes the practice prevailed. It was based not on vanity but on necessity coupled with economy. Day wear became smoke-begrimed in industrial cities and mud-bespattered elsewhere; none escaped the horse-fouled streets, the potholes in country lanes, the dusty town pavements and rough village pathways. Horse-drawn vehicles showered pedestrians with mud, so that men who walked to and from work could arrive home with clothes as soiled as their womenfolk's, and no matter how carefully ladies held their skirts, they could not avoid accumulating inches of dirt. All had to be brushed and cleaned on reaching home, then laid aside for wearing the following day – and even if a garment were not to be worn again so soon, it would not be replaced in the wardrobe until it had been well cleaned.

Not only fashion, but also personal pride, dictated that everything about a lady's toilet had to be immaculate. To be spotlessly turned out, to be as elegant as her purse permitted, to renovate her clothes to keep abreast of fashion, and to know that everything she wore was flawless, was vital whatever her station in life. Not for nothing had

Early sewing machine 1851

she been brought up to regard cleanliness as next to godliness.

Even the humblest housemaid also took a pride in her appearance, striving to emulate her 'betters'; so much so that as prosperity flourished with the advancing century it was frequently remarked that it was difficult to tell who were the maids and who the mistresses. Indeed, as industry and wealth increased, the number of servants correspondingly diminished, lured away from domestic service to factories and shops. Thus many a woman, previously attended by a lady's maid, found herself caring for her own wardrobe.

The large amount of clothing worn by women between 1800 and 1900 had one big advantage – the volume prevented body moisture and its unseen dirt from penetrating beyond the layer next to the skin, so that for the most part all soiling was external, caused by street dirt and air pollution far in excess of the twentieth century. Bathrooms might be scarce, but soap and water were not, and since soap was often home-made there was always plenty of it.

Preventive measures also helped, and training in this respect began when young. Ladies' journals of the day were informative, as were those for daughters of the house. *The Girl's Own Paper*, which ran from 1880 until well into the twentieth century, regularly published articles on deportment and social behaviour, always focusing on the girl's future responsibilities as a wife, one essential virtue being the fastidious treatment of her clothes. She must never forget, when sitting down, that slouching would crease frills and flounces and sashes, and that cane or rush-seated chairs should be avoided unless she was not averse to displaying an embossed design on her *derrière* when rising; that varnished wooden chair frames left an undesirable shine on many materials, especially silks; that white-washed or colour-washed walls could leave a lamentable deposit on skirts if one were so careless as to brush against them. In living rooms there was no such danger since walls were papered (though the popular flocked papers held dust which might rub off), but walls treated with wash were commonplace in public buildings, passages, and kitchens.

Above all, she was urged to move slowly and carefully, for haste could mean damage from doorknobs and latches – besides which, hurrying was unladylike and to run was hoydenish and ungraceful. Even a sudden jerk, when startled, could result in disaster, such as knocking over a cake-stand or spilling tea down her clothes as well as on her hostess's carpet.

But if prevention failed, there were admirable journals to recommend cures. *The Ladies' Treasury*, *The Englishwoman's Domestic Magazine*, *Cassell's Household Guide*, *The Queen*, *The Lady's World*, *The Lady's Realm*, *The Workwoman's Guide* (by A Lady), and that unfailing standby *Enquire Within*, not to mention the estimable Mrs Rundell and Mrs Beeton – all were at hand to ensure that washday was a success and that cleaning by hand need hold no fears.

WASHDAY. Oak wash tubs were preferred to earthenware because they were usually larger, enabling a greater number of compatible garments to be laundered together. Around 1830–40 an attempt was made to produce a washing machine, but this was a cumbersome affair with a rotating wooden drum which had to be operated by a hand-propelled wheel. The weight of it, plus the weight of sodden clothes, made it unpopular. Sturdy servant girls preferred to rub and scrub by hand and probably made a better job of it.

Then came a tub lined with wooden ridges which were intended to reproduce hand-rubbing as the contents were stirred, and another which agitated the clothes between rollers but only succeeded in ripping off buttons and wearing out linens and were again so heavy that they were abandoned. So the 'dolly-peg' or 'washing-dolly' remained the only acceptable tool. This was like a four-legged stool with a pole rising from the middle and a cross-bar handle, which was dumped and twisted in the tubs of wet clothes.

For most of the nineteenth and even into the early part of the twentieth century the washing-dolly and dolly-tub remained the only manual help on washday, apart from a mangle or wringer and a 'copper' in which to boil clothes. The copper was built into a corner of the wash-house or scullery, in either brick or stone, and was lined with a massive copper bowl beneath which a fire could be lit. These splendid copper bowls are now highly-priced antiques.

The physical demands of washday were excessive, due to the weight of sodden clothes, which had to be lifted from tub to tub through the various stages of washing and rinsing. Added to this was the constant emptying and refilling, lifting giant pans of boiling water from fire to tub, then refilling and heaving them back to the fire again – all in an atmosphere of engulfing steam. Feet were protected from soaking floors by country 'pattens' (overshoes raised up by metal rings), but holland overalls provided the only bodily protection. These the model housewife rendered semi-waterproof by applying boiled linseed oil, or by dissolving a pound of glue and a bar of tallow soap in five gallons of water, bringing it slowly to the boil and adding one pound and a half of alum. After soaking in this, the overalls would be hung up to dry, then washed and dried again.

Owing to the many layers of underclothes worn in the nineteenth century, each layer protected the next and only the items worn close to the body required regular laundering, and these were worn only once or twice, in rotation with others, to ensure that they needed no more than a fresh rinse. Only household linens demanded frequent thorough washing and, since linen cupboards were plentifully supplied, these could be saved until a goodly number were ready for the washtub.

The socially snobbish would proudly boast that in their homes a washday was necessary only once every month or six weeks, thereby indicating that their wardrobes were amply stocked, but in middle-class households with servants and the usual large quota of children a fortnightly wash could comprise a formidable number of items, so that laundering, drying, and ironing continued over several days.

No wonder that, when the servant problem became acute, sensible housewives decided on a weekly washday to spread the load. The average woman's wardrobe consisted of both cotton and flannel underwear, dresses in sundry materials, shifts, night gowns, dressing gowns, petticoats, camisoles, corsets both short and long, chemises, shawls, winter vests and combinations, skirts, stockings in wool, silk, and cotton, scarves, gloves, jabots and collars.

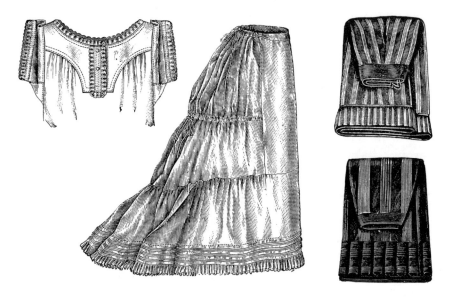

As the century advanced, people of means sent bed linens to laundries, but since these were notorious for ruining delicate fabrics the more precious items had to be treated at home. But it wasn't merely a question of dumping clothes in a tub of soapy water and diligently scrubbing them; unreliable dyes meant that many materials required special attention. Only white cottons and linens could safely be washed in soap and water.

Precarious dyes also meant that when colours had been brightened by various methods, they also needed fixatives to avoid fading. Different colours demanded different recipes for this. For violet, ammonia or a pinch of soda was used in the rinse, though because certain mauves were likely to fade in soda it became a question of trial and error. Green required two tablespoons of vinegar to a quart of rinse; blue, a large handful of common salt per dress. Friar's balsam, both in the wash and in the rinse, was needed for beige alpacas and cream cashmeres. Brown and grey were improved by ox-gall, while black pepper improved the colour of black calico, as did ammonia with other black materials. For white, the rinse would contain the common laundry-blue.

Enquire Within (1878 edition) recommended the country house-wife's practice of washing navy and black linens with peeled potatoes, since soap was apparently unwise for these materials. The potatoes, usually averaging two per dress, were grated into lukewarm water with a teaspoonful of ammonia. After washing in this liquid the linen would be rinsed in cold blue water. No starching was then necessary. Another country practice was to put an infusion of hay in the wash for buff linens, and an infusion of bran for brown ones. A few large handfuls of new ivy leaves added to a quart of bran and a quarter of a pound of yellow household soap, all boiled in water until the soap dissolved and, when cold, strained into the washing water, was an infallible recipe for laundering print dresses. Because of their oxalic acid content, ivy leaves were also an ingredient in the removal of ink and wine stains.

Starch was used warily. Fine muslins and similar materials required only light stiffening with isinglass (a gelatine extracted from fish) which could be bought in halfpenny sheets and broken into small pieces to be dissolved when required. The same edition of *Enquire Within* recommended the use of a tablespoon of 'gum water' added to a pint of starch for stiffening either lawns or thin white muslins. This was made from two ounces of gum arabic onto which was poured a pint or more of boiling water according to the strength required, then bottled for use. Chintzes 'should always be treated in the Oriental manner; that is, to wash them in plain water, and then boil them in congee, or rice water: after which they ought not to be submitted to the operation of the smoothing iron, but rubbed smooth with a polished stone.'

Stiffening for heavy materials could be produced from a knob of glue melted in a gallon of boiling water, then cooled, but this was unsuitable for such things as cotton dresses, which should be wrung in milk, the creamier the better. This was guaranteed to 'produce a desirable stiffening and avoid the heavy creasing caused by starch.'

However, starch was essential for gentlemen's shirts, and the shinier the surface the better, for this discouraged dirt from clinging to the surface. To achieve this gloss was not easy. It required various additives, such as solid paraffin, or borax mixed with gum, spermaceti, glycerine and water. Sometimes a tot of brandy was added to the starch to prolong the stiffness, with a small knob of white wax to prevent the mixture from sticking to the iron. Whatever supplement was used, the faces of the irons had to be protected, and this was most frequently done with an application of kerosene or soap the moment they were lifted from the fire hob.

Most testing of all, and very often daunting to a young bride, were a man's stiff collars, which were attached to the shirt's stiffened neckband with studs; the greater the stiffness and the greater the shine, the greater would be his satisfaction . . . and if the wife cheated a little by using Hebden's Patent Gloss Powder, guaranteed to give a dazzling smoothness at a cost of threepence or sixpence a block, she kept quiet about the extravagance and won her husband's approval.

Another use for starch was in the removal of blood stains, frequently imparted to fine needlework from pricked fingers, or to gentlemen's shirts after shaving. A little paste made from starch and cold water, applied to the spot and allowed to dry, then brushed off, was usually effective and could be repeated if required.

Velvet, being unwashable, needed individual treatment. Rubbing the surface with stale bread was a common practice, and velvet not too heavily soiled could be brushed and then gently rubbed with dry bran, renewed periodically. Benzoin or turpentine could be applied with a piece of flannel, taking care not to flatten the pile, and *Enquire Within* also recommended equal quantities of ammonia and warm water. To raise the pile, the garment was held near the spout of a steaming kettle or hung above a washtub of boiling water.

Alcohol (spirits of wine) was widely used in various forms for removing stains. Eau de Cologne, gin, and many another variant could dispel shiny patches and silk could be revived with a mixture of beer and ammonia in water. Whisky was used for spots of all kinds, after first wetting them.

Spirits of wine was also used for removing wax or tallow stains, a constant hazard before the advent of gas and electricity. Oil spots were dealt with by applying strong alcohol saturated in camphor. Pure alcohol could be bought from any apothecary, as could chloroform to remove grease spots, for which salt dissolved in alcohol was a good alternative.

One particular item very difficult to launder was the all-important corset. Owing to boning, washing was impossible. One method was to brush the surface with soapy water and ammonia but, if this was allowed to penetrate, the stiffening suffered. Fortunately, the corset never came in contact with the body because the chemise was worn beneath it. It was also protected from the penetration of outer dust

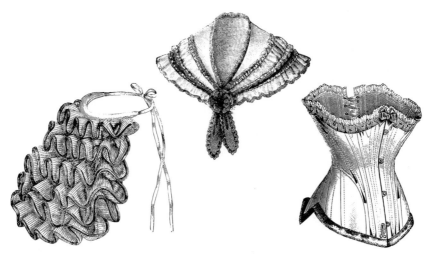

and dirt by a camisole and the usual layers of petticoats. As an additional precaution all fastidious ladies attached an artificial lining to the corset, which could be unstitched and washed frequently.

Similarly, nearly all gowns had detachable collars and cuffs, several pairs being made for each dress. Sometimes collars, such as the wide bertha which spread across the shoulders, were attached to a separate bodice of some thin material worn under the dress, and the collar then folded over the neckline. This, too, made for quick and easy laundering. In such ways a constant supply of clean accessories was at hand, so that an item need be worn only once. Horsehair bustles, covered in cascades of detachable frills, were kept spotless in the same way. The armpits of gowns were protected by dress shields made of rubber or chamois; these were greeted with enthusiasm when they appeared in 1840 and remained in use despite, or perhaps because of, the first unsatisfactory anti-perspirants which came on the market about twenty years later. Many recipes for home-made solutions then appeared in women's periodicals, but none beat a mixture of alum and water though it took a long time to dry and left the skin feeling unpleasantly taut. However, that did not worry fashion-conscious women who were prepared to endure anything in the pursuit of elegance and were thoroughly ashamed of perspiration marks. Even an alarming 1886 recipe, containing chloride of lime as its main ingredient, was widely used until adverse skin reactions and medical condemnation put an end to it.

IRONING DAY. This could be as tiring as washday, but required no protective clothing. The number of flat irons lined up on the kitchen stove was considerable, for the wide variety of materials required a wide variety of temperatures and therefore a wide variety of irons of different weights and sizes. Some would be placed upright before the fire, others on top of the hot ovens, depending on the degree of heat required. Experienced laundresses tested this by holding the iron close to the cheek, or spitting on it. If the spittle sizzled and ran off, the iron was ready; if it sizzled but stayed there, it was not. It was essential to have a good line-up of matching irons for each garment. Being made entirely of metal, their handles became almost as hot as the iron faces and could only be used with a well-padded holder.

A box iron and its metal slug, inserted through a sliding door in the heel; and a flat iron

Smoke and soot from the fire, or a residue of starch, was apt to cling to the iron and meant constant cleaning. A renewed application of kerosene, or soapy water and ammonia, or a wipe over with coarse salt or a sprinkling of bathbrick, all followed by polishing with a soft cloth, usually did the trick, but it required a skilful and speedy touch.

For fragile materials hollow box-irons, heated from within by pieces of red-hot metal, were better than flat irons, and because the face was not exposed to the fire's smoke and soot, they were cleaner and cooler. Their big disadvantage, which led to a final loss of favour, was that the pieces of hot metal had to be placed inside with tongs, and if they were insufficiently hot, the iron was useless, but if too hot the expanded metal could not be inserted.

Narrow rows of frills or pleats needed special goffering irons, and minute frills could be fluted with the aid of a wooden crimping board on which the material would be pressed with a specially shaped rolling pin, but a more popular method was to manipulate a pair of lady's curling tongs, lightly warmed.

LACE. The cleaning of lace trimming was a delicate task, and a lengthy one. The most important tool was a large, straight bottle, thoroughly cleaned to avoid any chance stain from previous contents. This would be tightly covered with strong white linen sewn on with smooth thread. Soiled lace trimming was then wound evenly round the bottle, layering it so that the pattern edge was continuously visible, and securing the ends with a stitch. The bottle was then immersed in cold water early in the evening and left to soak through the night, after changing the water just before going to bed. In the morning, the bottle was placed in an enamel or, preferably, porcelain-lined pan deep enough for it to stand upright, anchored to the sides or handles of the vessel to keep it steady, then boiled in fresh water and white soap. On no account should the pan be any kind of metal, or the lace would be blackened, and a receptacle which was cracked or chipped would leave iron-mould stains.

Boiling lasted until the lace looked really white. The bottle was then taken out and upturned to drain off surplus suds without rinsing. This was important because soapsuds helped to make lace more durable. The bottle was then placed in the sun until the lace dried. Indoor drying was undesirable, so lace-cleaning was always saved for a really sunny day.

Different types of lace required different treatment. Blonde lace, made of silk, was extremely fragile and was often so valuable that only a specialist cleaner would be entrusted with it, but home-cleaning could be undertaken by soaking it for half an hour in a solution of tartar salts, then squeezing it out and leaving it to dry naturally. Cleaning Honiton lace was so expensive that model housewives tackled the job themselves. A flat board was covered with spotless flannel, to which the lace was carefully tacked. Next, well lathered soft soap was rubbed in by hand, then rinsed out two or three times with clean water, and the lace was left to dry on the board. After removal, it was gently stretched to its original size, taking care to keep the pattern symmetrical.

Alternatively, it could be pinned in the same way to a covered board, then dabbed with benzoin. It was even permissible to treat stubborn spots by covering with a piece of clean linen and applying the benzoin liberally, then pressing firmly in the required place and changing to a clean part of the linen as the dirt seeped through.

'The lazy housewife's method' was to soap the lace all over and to pack it in a glass jar containing soft water, but the jar had to stand in full sunlight for twelve hours, which was surely difficult to guarantee in an unpredictable climate. The lace was then taken out and thoroughly rinsed, without squeezing or rubbing.

Cream-coloured lace was favoured in the nineteenth century, rather than white. This was achieved, after washing, by dipping it in cold coffee, or tea for a lighter shade. Sometimes an infusion of snuff was used, or beer and water in a fifty-fifty blending.

Black lace, for which there was always a demand in this age of prolonged mourning periods, had a tendency to look mildewed. Alcohol and borax, or sponging with diluted sal volatile, could prove effective, but bullock's gall in warm water was often more so. An infusion of scalded bran was another alternative, but rinsing in table-beer was best for getting rid of mildew.

Lace was invariably limp after washing, but *Enquire Within* of 1878 sternly forbade the use of starch. It recommended a little gum arabic in the rinsing water, or dipping in a mixture of white wax, white sugar and white soap. Water in which a raw potato had been grated was suggested for lace skirts or similar garments which required stiffening. Honiton lace makers favoured rice water.

Ironing lace was also frowned on, due to the risk of discolouring and destroying the texture. Steaming could freshen some types of lace, but Honiton was rubbed gently with a smooth piece of ivory.

Brussels lace was never washed, but rubbed with a special white powder made from lead carbonate which turned red if exposed for too long. The lace was therefore wrapped in silver paper and hidden away in a tin box. Other lace would be stored in wooden or cardboard boxes and sprinkled with magnesia.

FEATHERS. Feathers could be washed successfully in soft white soap and water, to which a small piece of the dangerous pearl-ash was sometimes added to revive natural colours. (This could fail where dyes had been used.) The feathers could then be dried by rubbing within folded white paper, particularly the absorbent variety used by butchers.

Feathers required curling frequently, particularly in damp weather. Many a woman discovered the folly of using her curling-irons. The safest method was to shake them before a fire and leave them to curl naturally, or to curl them over an ivory knife handle. Another method was to spread the feather face down and run the back of a knife along the spine, but again, success was not guaranteed. Feather-curling was a specialized skill.

Storage was simple – layered with brown paper in an airtight box.

GLOVES. The life of gloves was prolonged by proper care. Because missing buttons and signs of wear were considered shameful, they were attended to at once. Repairs were always done from the inside, either by immaculate stitching or, if holes were small, with 'court plaster' to draw the edges close, disguising any betraying glimpse of plaster on the right side with coloured ink.

White gloves which had lost their freshness were discarded by those who could afford to; those who could not, cleaned them on the hand or on a wooden glove-tree by applying cream of tartar, benzoin, or spirits of hartshorn (or ammonia, the source of which was originally the calcined horns of the hart). For mildew stains, egg albumen was effective after brushing the spots with stiff bristles.

Suede was revived with dry bread; flour could be used, but for obvious reasons was more messy. Chamois gloves would be washed in rain water with plenty of soft soap, then pulled into shape and squeezed through a wringer. After a second rinsing and a second wringing, they were shaken well and hung to dry in the shade. Doeskin needed rubbing with fuller's earth and alum, both dry; it was then shaken in dry bran and alum. A wet method used soapy water or bran tea, then a rubbing with some colouring agent in vinegar or beer – white pipeclay for white, yellow ochre mixed with white pipeclay for yellow, and a mixture of fuller's earth and rotten-stone for darker shades. (Rotten-stone was decomposed limestone containing silicate; it came in a fine powder and could be used as a polisher, or an absorbent.)

Tan leather could be cleaned easily by rubbing with the inside of a banana skin, while black leather responded to rubbing with an orange slice, or with black ink, then with salad oil.

Cleaning gloves at home was, in the main, hardly worthwhile when it could be done professionally for as little as twopence a pair, though in large families even the twopences could add up when each member needed at least a dozen pairs of day gloves alone, all in different leathers for the varying seasons, and twice the number in different materials for other occasions. They were stored in decorative glove boxes, mainly of cedar wood or boxwood, satin-lined and often perfumed, or in drawers between layers of paper to prevent light from damaging the colours.

FOOTWEAR. Sponging the insides regularly with ammonia kept foot odours at bay, but the exteriors required more individual care. Patent leather benefited from a pint of rich cream mixed with a pint of linseed oil, applied lukewarm and left on the shoes for at least twenty-four hours. Cracks in ordinary black leather were repaired with shoe-black then rubbed with beeswax or furniture polish. Alternatively, turpentine mixed with a sweet oil, such as almond, was satisfactory, but a follow-up application of glycerine was wise because it both softened and protected the leather. And all squeaky soles needed a good application of soap.

Cloth-topped boots or shoes could be cleaned with alcohol, which was equally good on white satin evening slippers or on white kid. Storage was usually in holland shoe bags, one to each pair.

STOCKINGS were always hand-washed at home because laundries returned them misshapen by ironing, with both texture and colour ruined by the use of soda and excessive drying heat.

Silk stockings needed rain water with a good soap. They were never rubbed. Rinsing water was improved with a glass of gin, and the stockings were then dried away from heat, finally being polished on the leg with a piece of flannel to enhance the lustre. (Shiny ankles seem to have been admired.) A surprising way of drying them, but one frequently used, was to sew them onto a sheet which was then folded and put through the mangle. Sometimes they were even wrapped in calico and beaten with a rolling pin. All delicate hosiery was given a soak in salt water and dried before wearing, to strengthen the silk; a weak solution of alum served the same purpose.

BAGS. Fabric bags were cleaned in the same way as dress fabrics, though beading and embroidery usually called for professional treatment. Sponging with a weak solution of oxalic acid (the ivy leaf method again) took care of most leathers, but black leather was revived with a mixture of two tablespoons of gin to two of sugar, thickened with ivory black. To this the beaten yolks of four eggs and the whites of two were added, and the well-stirred mixture was then painted on and left to dry.

SHAWLS. Silk, muslin, lace and satin shawls were cleaned in the same way as clothes in the same fabric, but Shetland shawls were washed in soft water to which was added a good quality curd soap to produce a thin lather. Cashmeres and merinos called for a mixture of cold lathered water with alcohol and ox-gall. Colours were set with a rinse containing alum or salt.

PARASOLS AND UMBRELLAS were sponged with the cleaning agents used for silk dresses, but parasols adorned with lace frills and bead embroidery were almost impossible to clean and were therefore used only on 'state occasions' or when the weather was particularly fine.

A disguise for soiled parasols was an 'over skirt' of cascading frills covering the entire frame, in some contrasting but serviceable colour.

METAL LACE TRIMMING AND METAL EMBROIDERY presented problems. The copper in gold lace made it tarnish quickly, so it would then be unpicked, sewn onto a piece of cotton material and boiled in soapy water. After rinsing, it was pinned onto another cloth and left to dry. Tarnish could also be brushed away with the aid of warmed spirits of wine. Another method was to rub it with finely

A parasol with 'over skirt',
and a more informal variety

powdered rock alum, again to be brushed off. The same method was
used on silver lace, using calcined hartshorn.

HATS AND BONNETS. Nineteenth-century ladies took constant care
of their headwear. Hats and bonnets were stored on closet shelves
in individual bandboxes with the crowns well stuffed, or perched on
milliner's blocks beneath covers. These polished wooden blocks
could be purchased in any ladies' emporium for a few shillings, and
lasted a lifetime; to find one now in a hunt for antiques would be
difficult and costly. Storage in this way ensured that hats were
protected not only from dust but from rubbing against one another
and so damaging feathers and trimmings or spoiling the pile.

Meticulous cleaning was undertaken at the end of each season so
that when hats and bonnets emerged the following year they would
be ready for use, although fastidious wearers sometimes gave them
a refresher treatment after their seasonal storage.

In a thorough cleaning, all trimmings were removed and either
treated individually or, if damaged by wind or rain, replaced with

new ones. Straw, particularly the bleached variety known as 'white straw', demanded special attention, for not only did dirt adhere in the weave, but sun discoloured it – and of course rain could ruin the shape. The cure was a small amount of oxalic acid in boiling water, applied with a sponge as hot as could be handled, rubbing vigorously. Then came a cold rinse and the difficult task of restoring the shape throughout a slow drying period. If done conscientiously, the result was a crisp new bonnet.

Leghorn straw hats could be treated in the same way, but with potash in the water. Dust, as opposed to dirt, could be removed with a short-bristled brush dipped in salt water. Discolouration needed bleaching with sulphur applied with a piece of lemon, then the juice washed off. Dingy black straw could either be painted with home-made blacking, or changed to a becoming brown with diluted oxalic acid. An alternative was equal parts of black ink and sweet oil, well rubbed in. Black sealing wax melted in turpentine or spirits of wine could be brushed on to provide a varnish which not only stiffened the straw and made it shine, but rendered it waterproof. Coloured straws could be revived with hot water containing a tablespoonful of liquid ammonia, the brim then being laid out flat and pressed with a warm iron.

Restoring a straw hat made limp by rain meant holding it over steam from a kettle and manipulating it back into shape, then drying quickly. Restiffening entirely needed a stiffening agent, such as beaten white of egg, or starch. Gum arabic was a popular solution; so was a mixture of isinglass, bone dust and ivory shavings. After

Hat box for travelling or storage

applying one of these the article would be held before a fire while pulling it into shape, then hung up to dry very slowly.

Felt was easier than straw to deal with. It could be sponged with water containing strong ammonia or a good portion of soda, or dry-cleaned with benzoin, but with the latter it was important to dry in the open air after sponging with a clean damp sponge. White felt could be revived with powdered pipe-clay; light brown or fawn, with fuller's earth or hot oatmeal; grey felt with warm bran. Both red and grey felts could be cleaned with pearl ash and water, but this pungent poison had to be handled carefully or it could destroy colour.

Silk, crepe, and velvet hats were cleaned in the manner appropriate to the fabric, as were lace and feathers after first being removed from the hat. Honey, soap and gin were again used for silk ribbons, but satin ones could be washed in a thick lather of soap and cold water. Satin ribbons were never rubbed because they were liable to fray. Smoothing was achieved with steam from a kettle, or by placing half-dried ribbons beneath cloths, laying an iron on top, and pulling the ribbons from beneath. Steam was also useful for refreshing artificial flowers, any crumpled edges then being trimmed, but this only worked if soiling was slight. Otherwise they had to be replaced.

In these manifold ways did the model wife or her servants care for her clothes and those of her family. In the days before proprietory cleaning materials, methods were evolved by trial and error and people were often unaware of the dangers of many ingredients, now banned from sale to the public but then obtainable for only a few pence in Harrod's Drug Department and in stores throughout the country. And it should be emphasized that many of these cleaning methods would be not only unsuccessful but destructive if tried on today's synthetic materials.

9 ✒ Out and About
The Carriage Parade

ALTHOUGH THE MODEL nineteenth-century wife appears to have been dedicated to her home, she was by no means house-bound. Whether on shopping trips, visiting relatives, making calls, fulfilling charitable duties or merely appearing decoratively at her husband's side, she needed transport from place to place and this was done in style if she were fortunate enough to have a carriage at her command.

For others, towns provided horse-drawn hackneys catering for several passengers, but these were shunned by a respectable woman if she was alone. The country wife was luckier, for only the really poor could not afford a dog-cart. This was originally intended to transport dogs on a day's shoot, accommodation being provided in a specially designed compartment, but it proved to be a versatile vehicle. The lady of the house used it for shopping or on her round of calls; nannies conveyed their charges in it; and when the railway arrived, by the 1850s, it was sent to meet guests at the station. A smaller version which children could drive, because it was actually drawn by a dog, became popular for a time, but was mercifully banned in London in 1839 and throughout the country by 1855.

At the beginning of the century people of modest means regarded those who were driven, or who drove themselves, as lazy and self-indulgent. This attitude stemmed from the Renaissance, when higher standards of living began to infiltrate the nobility but took a great deal longer to reach those of lesser rank. Wealthy merchants were the first to emulate their betters and they, in turn, became the butt of criticism (or envy). The seeds of carriage-owning snobbishness were well and truly sown in England when the first private coach was built by the Earl of Rutland in 1555. It reached its peak during the Regency period, when bold young bucks terrified pedestrians by racing their curricles in fierce competition with rivals, and with total disregard for people on foot. The carriage driver became lord of the road, travelling in whichever direction he chose, at whatever speed he chose, on whichever side he chose, no matter who or what got in the way.

Stagecoaches and travelling chariots were additional hazards to pedestrians. People riding in them could be as strongly envied as the aristocracy, and as deeply resented. Since the middle of the seventeenth century stagecoaches had plied between the larger cities and, by the turn of the eighteenth, hackney carriages in towns provided additional public transport, but in these no lady would set foot unsquired even during the nineteenth century. She would be molested considerably less on foot, walking briskly, eyes straight ahead, with a no-nonsense look about her. The housewife who kept to her own district was even safer, knowing every inch of the local streets, and the local characters, too.

By the early 1800s, carriage-snobbery was ingrained, pandered to by the landau, the barouche, the post chaise and the gig, all of which remained fashionable for nearly a hundred years. Private conveyances flaunted crests, genuine or otherwise, on their door panels, and although a society woman might pretend to disdain these prestige symbols, she was secretly proud of them because they emphasized her rank, to the humiliation of those of lesser standing.

But perhaps nothing was so envied, nor bore such testimony to wealth, as the privately-owned travelling chariot, used by the rich to journey from their country seats to their town houses, for visits to distant friends or for European tours. A model wife might find such journeys exhausting, but she donned a brave face because she was expected to, or because she secretly enjoyed the awed, admiring, and patently envious glances of lesser mortals – and thought how proud Mamma would be if she could see her dear daughter now.

The types of carriage most favoured for longer journeys were the britschka, Hungarian in origin and becoming fashionable in England around 1818, or the dormeuse, a smaller French version which followed in 1821, for both had extending compartments which converted into beds and were fitted with blinds or curtains for privacy, plus such essentials as food stores, hat boxes, rugs, and 'toilet accessories' which footmen had to empty by the wayside. There were also candle-lit lamps for interior lighting as well as those outside on the coachman's box and the outrider's perch. Spending nights on the road in this fashion held no fears for the model wife because the model husband's sword or pistol was always close at hand. A weapon was considered essential for self-defence when travelling in Europe.

In the more elaborate chariots, equipment sprang to hand at the touch of concealed buttons, as Charles Dickens described with considerable awe when relating his encounter with the 4th Lord Vernon in Switzerland in 1846.

In the first half of the century private long-distance journeys at home were undertaken mainly by personal post chaise, though public ones were available in competition with stagecoaches. Travellers who did not own vehicles on a par with Lord Vernon's were compelled to lodge at posting inns. A patient wife, sore and aching from unremitting jolting over miles of rough roads, which were often no more than rutted tracks, welcomed such overnight accommodation because it gave her the opportunity to repair her toilet and to don a fresh travelling outfit next morning.

This change of clothing her equally exhausted maid had to unpack on arrival, folding away creased and travel-soiled garments in boxes well lined with camphor balls. To avoid a delayed departure the following day these tasks had to be attended to before retiring, no matter how greatly she yearned for the truckle bed allocated to her in attic or cellar alongside other travelling servants – sometimes even a bed shared with two or three unknown to her. Bed-sharing for hard-up travellers or for menials was common practice, but even if the maid had to tolerate the snores of strangers she was at least spared her master's complaints about the high cost of travelling. This grumbling the model wife endured with patience and understanding, knowing that charges were far from low in relation to values of the

Design for a posting chariot by J.W. Peters 1839

time – three shillings and sixpence per mile for each postboy, one shilling and sixpence per mile for each horse.

Posting stops occurred approximately every ten miles or so, depending on the condition of the horses and the state of the roads. Toll fees, plus gratuities for stable hands, ostlers, potmen, wenches who served food, urchins who grabbed the horses' reins, lads who knelt to polish dust-covered boots, inn servants who helped travellers off with their cloaks and made sure they had good seats beside the fire, not to mention the cost of refreshments, added considerably to the final bill.

Stagecoach drivers frowned on private travellers, and equally upon postilions (or postboys) serving the public post chaise, for they despised a vehicle that needed to be driven by an outrider and was therefore more expensive than a coach and team. But the post chaise was faster and the postilion, small and light as a jockey, was highly skilled. He rode on the left-hand horse, his whip guiding the one on his right, and wore a metal shield on his right leg to protect it from being crushed against the shaft dividing the pair. Postilions in royal processions are similarly equipped to this day.

Enmity between postboys and stagecoachmen was proverbial, each scorning the other as being outmoded, and predicting his end. The postboy went first. As toll fees and travelling expenses rose, the post chaise lost favour, though it remained popular with private owners for a long time; but not until the advent of railways did stagecoaches vanish from the roads. In 1831 the railway was in its infancy, but by the 1850s it had replaced the stage and mail coaches for long-distance travel and they were sold off as scrap, or for a few pounds to coachbuilders constructing private carriages for the *nouveaux riches*, leaving the coachmen to seek employment as omnibus drivers, cabbies, stable hands, or road sweepers.

Those who travelled far now went by train. The *hoi polloi* occupied public carriages, while members of the nobility and their ladies, gowns enveloped in protective dust coats and fashionable heads shrouded in clouds of veiling, had their own private carriages with crested doors and a footman perched uncomfortably on a rumble seat outside, smuts marring his immaculate uniform and stinging his eyes. The carriage of a lady travelling alone had to be hitched to the train to ensure that she did not come in contact with undesirable levels of society from whom infections of all kinds might be caught.

Contrary to all predictions, however, the coming of the locomotive did not mean the end of the horse and carriage, but rather its proliferation. Apart from privately-owned vehicles, the number of public ones increased in the cities, and especially in London. Cabs and broughams for hire thronged the streets and packed the areas outside railway stations. Visitors, arriving from the country in growing numbers, needed conveying to their destinations. Non-carriage-owning residents of the capital also needed transport around town. Not all would use the horse-drawn omnibuses or hackneys which, in rush hours, were swooped on by commuters who were now able to work in the city and travel in daily from the suburbs.

Dr Tivoli's patent omnibus on the Paddington to London Bridge route *c*. 1860

No well-brought-up young lady, or wife careful of her reputation, would set foot on an omnibus. If she had no carriage of her own, she would order a brougham, taking care to pronounce it 'broom' as evidence of her refinement. If economy forced a respectable woman to use an omnibus, she would be careful not to ascend the stairs. Only 'fast' women in quest of gentleman passengers did that.

The world of carriage and horse became a vanity fair worthy of Thackeray, typifying the false values and snobbishness of the day. A household was judged not only by the style and quality of its carriages, but by their number – not to mention the quality of the horses, for which high sums could be paid and which sometimes required more servants in the stables than there were in the house. Such things were carefully assessed by a marriage-making mamma, who knew that seven or eight carriages would be at her daughter's disposal should she land the much-coveted rich husband. Only with such a retinue would social status be underlined.

Less affluent households had to make do with one carriage for the head of the family, one for his wife, a governess cart or dog-cart for transporting children and nurse, and usually a gig for the elder son of the house, for young men liked to cut a dash. In large households, domestic staff took it for granted that when the family they served was absent they had the right to convey kitchen friends back home in one of the carriages, even if a wagonette for the use of servants stood in the stables.

For the model society wife a stylish carriage was as important as the fashionable clothes she wore. Coachwork had to be highly polished, harness gleaming, brasswork sparkling, coachman and footman impeccably groomed, and her page a miniature replica of the senior stable servants from the crown of his shining silk hat to the toes of his shining knee-length boots.

In London, main thoroughfares would be jammed with carriages, particularly fashionable Regent Street where the centre of the road would be monopolized by stationary vehicles. Stable servants, yawning on their perches, would wait for hours while their mistresses dawdled round the shops or visited friends in fashionable squares, attended musical recitals in society drawing rooms, or (among less model wives) amused themselves with secret assignations of which their servants pretended to know nothing. It was the privilege of the upper classes to indulge in whatever recreation they fancied for as long as they fancied, and the privilege of their stable hands to jam the middle of the roads, or wherever they could pull in, to the inconvenience of other traffic. The important thing was that Milady had to be waited upon, and the affluent wife accepted it as her due.

In wealthy households, a large retinue of coachmen, grooms and stable boys were employed so that their mistress could drive out in style, even if only to parade for an hour or so in competition with others. Every afternoon a thousand carriages or more drove repeatedly along the Ladies' Mile in Hyde Park, round the Serpentine, and back to Hyde Park Corner. Others would join the parade as a finale on their way home from shopping or from calling on friends and acquaintances on At Home days.

Scene in Belgrave Square by Eugene Lami

Regent Street at the height of the Season 1866

This self-conscious display reached its height during the Season (Easter to July). High fashion marked it and pedestrians would flock to see it, poor people walking all the way from the East End to gape at the rich. It was the greatest show on earth, and free. They could even see gorgeously dressed ladies driving themselves, for to be a good whip attracted not only admiring male eyes, but admiring male comments, such as 'a cut above, b'Gad!' or 'well bred little fillies', which didn't mean the horses. Either coquettishly or haughtily the ladies would then flick a light whip adorned with a tiny parasol on the crop, a wholly useless decoration but as pretty as a toy poodle or an outsize frilly rosette.

A liveried groom sat on the rumble seat, or rode respectfully behind. He was not only a fashionable accessory, enhancing her elegant turn-out, but a necessary adjunct, at hand to deal with any emergency involving horse or vehicle – which was not uncommon since there were no rules of the road. It was a free-for-all in which the most skilled or the most belligerent won.

These self-driving ladies were, for the most part, among the younger set. Older ladies – mainly dowagers and duchesses, or famous actresses and notorious society mistresses, of whom the model wife would naturally disapprove – preened beneath beautiful parasols while being driven by coachman or groom, with a pair of footmen, or one footman and a tiger, behind. But all had one thing in common – they were there to be seen and admired, confident that they outshone every feminine rival in sight.

The curricle 1803

The tiger, fashionable with the curricle in Regency days, was revived with its successor, the cabriolet, later in the century, but many people remained loyal to the curricle, a two-wheeler believed to have hailed originally from Italy. It had been popularized by the Prince Regent and, apart from being smart and speedy, it was easy to control. It was drawn by a pair and considered safer than a single-horse vehicle. The ladies' curricle had great appeal because, being low slung, it was easy to climb into even with voluminous skirts, which could then be spread to advantage. Unlike the 'broom', its construction displayed a lady's whole ensemble.

Her tiny tiger sat proudly on his diminutive rear seat or, in the case of the cabriolet, on a minute platform, adding to the model wife's elegance. The footman who drove her was always over six feet in height, a stipulation for all footmen. Both servants had to be perfectly proportioned and hold themselves straight as pokers.

It was the tiger's duty to hold the horse's reins while the footman opened the carriage door and helped his mistress to alight, having already leapt up the steps of the house she was visiting and wielded the knocker, for no lady could be expected to perform such a task, soiling her gloves and demeaning herself in the process. The carriage door would then be opened with a flourish, a pair of small, carpeted steps placed to receive the lady's foot, and a rigidly bent arm held out to support her hand; carriages, especially those with very high steps, could lurch perilously during the occupant's descent.

If his mistress were going shopping, the footman would go ahead to open the doors and, if bidden, follow her through the store to carry her purchases, always walking deferentially behind. If the weather were bad, or if she enjoyed emphasizing her social status for the benefit of passers-by, she would wait in her carriage while her footman summoned the proprietor or, at such stores as Fortnum & Mason in Piccadilly or Mr Whiteley's famous emporium in Queensway, a senior department manager who would promptly emerge, bow low, take Madame's order and rap commands to a servile assistant hovering at his heels. Goods would then be brought out for her inspection, which would be conducted unhurriedly even when blocking the traffic or keeping the deferential assistants standing in the rain.

On returning home, an immediate duty of the footman was to wash all the coins left in his mistress's purse in case they should have picked up germs from tradesmen or saleswomen. And several times during the outing he would have had the far less pleasant task of scraping dung and mud from the hems of her trailing skirts, which could pick up as much as two inches of filth as she walked from shop to shop or crossed the roads. This was due not only to dust rising from the granite setts in the roads and the weight of horse-drawn traffic passing over them, but to the resulting deep ruts which overflowed with mud after rain. Some streets became quagmires, made worse by the ever increasing amount of horse dung which made London and other cities stink like gigantic stables.

A delicately nurtured female might screw up her nose at the odour, holding a perfumed handkerchief to her nostrils, but the coachman's wife, living in the mews behind the house, was accustomed to it. The wife of a married groom would even welcome it, for one much-coveted 'perk' – the sale of horse manure to out-of-town market gardeners – was exclusively her husband's and well worth having. A good load of horse manure was as valuable as money in the bank, so it was garnered in heaps in mews or coachyard until large enough for despatch. Two or three weeks' storage meant a very good sale, and the flies and stench were therefore accepted with equanimity.

Not even the coachman or his wife would complain, though both ruled the roost in this tight, enclosed world behind 'the big house', he professionally and she domestically, for it was her job to look after and feed the stable staff as well as her husband and family. For this reason she was often glad when senior stable servants married and had wives to look after their limited accommodation.

It was as important that a woman wedded to a coachman should be the model wife, as it was for the mistress of the house, for in their different ways the responsibilities were equal. The coachman's wife knew her place, and kept to it. She knew her duties, and carried them out. She saw that her husband was wakened in time to supervise the preparation of carriages and horses for daily use, that sleepy stable lads and unmarried grooms were roused. Work began in stables and mews as early as five a.m. in the summer and only slightly later in winter. Stalls had to be cleaned, horses groomed and given their fodder, carriages and harnesses thoroughly inspected, cleaned, and repolished, before breakfast could even be thought of.

The daily chores of a coachman's wife included keeping an eye on all sleeping accommodation in the stables, as well as the cramped coach house quarters occupied by herself, her husband, and their children. It was therefore not surprising if she became as great a matchmaker as any socially ambitious mother, encouraging senior stable servants to marry and thus lessen her load.

The stable servants' breakfast, served in the crowded loft used as a communal mess room, was always eaten hurriedly because a carriage might be required by ten o'clock and the lengthy business of wheeling it out and harnessing the horses would take at least fifteen minutes. The vehicle then had to be driven round to the front door of the house. Surging horse-drawn traffic, and the possibility that it might block the exit from the mews, had to be allowed for.

When a carriage was ordered for a second or third time, the process of re-harnessing had to be repeated because the vehicle could not be allowed to stand out in the mews area, gathering dust and blocking the passage of others, nor could horses be returned to confined stalls wearing harnesses which could chafe.

A coachman's wife rarely got out and about, so rarely saw life beyond the mews, for she was not officially part of the household staff and was therefore restricted to her own quarters. Because working hours were erratic, the model coachman's wife had to be prepared to serve something on a platter when time permitted a servant to sit down to it. She also washed their clothes, in addition to looking after her husband's uniform. Grooms were responsible for preserving their own liveries and were allowed to clean and press them in the basement kitchen of the big house, and even to wash at the scullery sink.

Social life in this city world of horse and stable was inevitably confined to the dark, cobble-stoned, ill-ventilated area behind the tall terraced houses of elegant squares and fashionable streets. To such mews drifted out-of-work coachmen and grooms, hoping to pick up an odd job or at least a bite to eat. They rarely failed if the coachman had the right kind of wife.

In the country, conditions were different. Stable blocks attached to country mansions could be immense. Usually built round a large quadrangle, they could contain as many as forty or more stalls, all roomy, all immaculately kept, and very often superior to the accommodation of stable staff, whose lowest members slept on straw in lofts above. Such things as steam baths, or bathing facilities of any kind, were unheard of for them, but were considered essential for valuable horses. Sunny positions facing south were favoured for the siting of stables, and equally important was good ventilation.

Country-house stables were divided between carriage horses, riding horses, and hunters, and included stalls for visitors' horses. There would also be a harness room. (In cramped town mews, harnesses and other equipment had to be hung on any available wall.) The bigger country estates also had grooming sheds, and a smithy in which a farrier shod the horses. In every way, the animals were given preferential treatment, whereas the men who looked after them were often poorly fed and poorly housed. Although country stable hands fared better than their town counterparts, insofar as they breathed cleaner air when out of doors, many drifted to the warm camaraderie of crowded city mews, where a model coachman's wife tolerated bad tempers and bad language, and cared for the small boys taken on as stable lads.

Lads being trained from childhood to step into the shoes of the immaculately uniformed grooms regarded them with awe, for they themselves were often street arabs, pushed out into the world by parents glad to be rid of them; urchins who had wandered into the mews to find a corner in which to sleep, or the offspring of former jockeys now destitute. The model wife of a coachman mothered them all, though she might shout and swear and bandy stable jokes as bawdily as any of the men.

Wages for stable staff bore no comparison with the value of the horses and equipment they cared for. Head coachmen, even in the stables of the nobility, could be paid as little as £52 per annum. The wages of an under-coachman averaged around £35 annually, and footmen between £25 and £35 according to first, second, or third ranking, but 'perks' swelled these receipts. By tradition, a coachman was entitled to wheels that were no longer sound enough for use, which he could sell to tradesmen for their carts. So neither the coachman nor his wife begrudged the groom's private dealings in horse manure.

Both coachman and groom expected a cut from the buyer when a horse was sold. They also extracted commission from corn chandlers, coach builders engaged on repairs, harness makers and saddlers, and it was easy to overcharge for items such as lamp oil, axle grease, polishes, cleaning materials, and other essential purchases for the stables.

This was the backdrop to the glittering show in Hyde Park, Mayfair, Belgravia, and what was then fashionable Bayswater, but there was another side to it. Deceit was prevalent in the carriage world; everything was geared to preserving the façade of wealth and grandeur. The horse that held up its apparently proud head was forced to do so by a savage bit attached to a bearing rein. Foaming mouths caused by pain were ignored by gracious ladies, but model wives from the suburbs who came to town to gaze on the model wives of high society would wince at the sight, as did more and more compassionate people.

Most cruel of all was the docking of horses' tails, a mode prevalent in Regency times and revived in the 1870s. This involved the amputation of vertebrae in the tail. A hot iron then seared the stump. Sometimes it was also cut on the underside to sever the tendon that pulls the tail down, then tied to a weight suspended from a pulley to hold it upright. No thought was given to the creature's agony, or to the fact that it had lost its much-needed protection against flies. So-called justification for this horrific practice was that it prevented the horse's tail from tangling with the reins or flinging dirt on the driver, but such excuses only served to make protests more vociferous.

In the country, the most popular hours for driving abroad, apart from morning outings, were from four to seven o'clock in the summer, and from three to five in winter. London had its own particular times for public parade, which, it seemed to provincial folk, was indulged in all day long.

To take part in this fashionable display, a bride-to-be would be well drilled in carriage etiquette. She was already aware that a man escorting ladies offered his right arm to the most senior and

'Taking up your party' from *The Lady's World* 1887

conducted her to the carriage first, opening the door with his left hand and then handing her inside. The ritual was performed with each lady in turn, in strict order of seniority. Unmarried elder sisters squirmed beneath it, for it painfully emphasized their damning spinsterhood and advancing years.

Rules for ladies when entering and descending from carriages were clearly defined. A hostess had to alight after her guests, unless convenience dictated otherwise, in which case she would explain the reason for such discourtesy and crave their pardon. When ascending, the hostess would stand aside for her guests to enter first, but if she were only calling to take a friend for a drive, she would wait in the carriage while her coachman or footman announced her arrival and then conducted the guest to the waiting carriage. She was also aware that any gentleman who *was* a gentleman must throw away his cigar and sit with his back to the horses (a position accorded to the youngest member of the party when no gentleman was present). If he should err in either respect, an arched eyebrow could be used to good effect.

Rules concerning social acknowledgements when out driving were to be strictly adhered to. Smiles, nods, and bows were permitted

'A combination of agreeables. Saturday afternoon – west wind and sunshine – room for one, say to Hurlingham and back, or anywhere you like.' George du Maurier in *Punch*, 1888

A light park phaeton, from the 1851 Exhibition catalogue

from landau, brougham, cabriolet, vis-à-vis, curricle, phaeton, barouche, berline, calèche, the clarence (named after the Duke of Clarence) and the ever popular victoria (named after the Dear Queen), but such greetings could only be delivered according to rank or familiarity. Social ostracism would result if a lady of lower degree greeted a lady of a higher one with whom she was barely acquainted, as some jumped-up females dared to do. Even if they were acquainted the first greeting had to come from the lady of higher rank, or next time they met the 'cut' would be delivered.

Rivalling the popular ladies' curricle was the park phaeton, similar to the victoria but lacking a coachman's box. It was appreciated by stout ladies because it had originally been designed for the corpulent George IV to facilitate access and descent.

The barouche, another park-driving carriage, accommodated up to four passengers and was therefore favoured by ambitious mammas displaying a trio of eligible daughters (with a fourth squeezed in if necessary); but it was a fair-weather vehicle because it had only one hood, leaving the other end of the carriage exposed to rain. Not surprisingly, it was supplanted by the landau, which had hoods at both ends; the snag was its cost – around £200 – but persuasive wives might prevail upon their husbands to buy such an expensive vehicle because it could be used in both town and country.

One of the biggest status symbols in the park parade, and around the fashionable squares, was a well-trained Dalmatian dog, decorated with a handsome brass collar bearing insignia which looked very much like a family crest (some were indeed genuine). This animal trotted in perfect unison with the horses, but behind the carriage, and if a lady did not own one it could be hired from kennels for an hour or two. Dalmatians were also supplied by dog trainers working in conjunction with job-masters.

Equally important were the colourful, costly liveries of servants. Senior stable servants, such as coachmen, footmen, and grooms, were usually provided with free liveries twice a year, one new set being essential for the Season if they were not to be eclipsed by those from rival households. These uniforms included state liveries complete with snowy wigs, white buckskin knee breeches (satin for evening), white stockings and shining tricorne hats; and, for daily wear, frock coats, striped waistcoats, top hats, great coats for winter use, and top boots which had to be kept highly polished. Coachmen's frock coats had side flaps; the grooms' had none.

The liveries of tigers and pages were miniature replicas of their seniors', usually handed down from others who had outgrown them; but never let it be whispered that they were bought second-hand. They would be discreetly purchased from livery suppliers who reconditioned rejected uniforms, making them look as good as new.

The satin waistcoats of stable servants were worn with immense pride. They were vividly coloured and vertically striped (horizontal stripes for footmen when indoors). Coats were ornamented with gilt or silver livery buttons embossed with a coat of arms if the family possessed one. Footmen's white silk stockings were padded with shaped 'falsies' for skinny calves.

Another symbol of an employer's status (and thus his wife's) was the black leather cockade on a footman's or coachman's highly polished top hat. Originally this had indicated an appointment to the Crown or the rank of officer, but the popularization of carriage life and the competitive hiring trades of job-master, livery supplier, and hatter reduced this emblem to a mock trimming.

Vanity was further pandered to by the addition of false tails if the horses' natural ones were sparse. Loud mirth from pedestrians, and humiliation for the proud passenger, would result if a false tail accidentally became dislodged.

Such incidents could never embarrass the owners of finely bred horses, for which people of means paid handsomely. The more expensive the equipage, the more diligently was it cared for and the less was it used. Both horses and carriages had to be cherished and preserved to maintain the necessary air of opulence, and no first-class horse was allowed to travel more than fourteen miles a day at a maximum of ten miles per hour, which was well below its capacity.

Inevitably, such horses became as lethargic as their mistresses, stepping out only to feature in the park pageant.

It was an artificial world into which sordid commerce inevitably intruded in the shape of the ubiquitous job-master, from whom horses and carriages could be hired. He proved to be a godsend to less privileged, but socially ambitious, women, for he brought the fashionable carriage parade within their grasp. Housekeepers and ladies' maids, cooks and thrifty female servants who managed to save enough from their meagre wages, could rent a fashionable hat and cape for a shilling or two from the pawnshop at which they temporarily hocked their own drab daywear, and hire a brougham for an hour's drive in Hyde Park during the Season. It might be only once a year, but it was worth saving for.

The 'broom', of French origin, was the favourite vehicle for this occasion, being small and enclosed, a two-seater with plate glass

Lord Lonsdale's brougham 1880

windows which revealed only an elegant head and shoulders, concealing shabby boots and skirts behind its well-painted and sometimes falsely-crested panels. Instances abounded of ladies' maids being spotted along the famous route, wearing their mistresses' clothes when they were out of town, and of menservants jauntily smoking their masters' cigars while lolling negligently in a hired carriage. Lords and ladies for an hour, they blessed the job-master who thus elevated them. But clients who hired a carriage for the Season, or for a month, a week, or even a day, did not always agree. Job-masters varied, and it was not always certain that the coachman who went with the elegant turn-out would remain sober, or the pseudo-footman not decamp with one's purse, or even worse.

Many were the stories of carriages, hired complete with glistening harnesses, artificial flowers in silver-plated vases, and every apparent refinement, that sooner or later betrayed serious faults such as springs protruding through seemingly well-upholstered seats and broken axles or C-springs, resulting in demands from the coachman for the cost of emergency repairs and even, in some cases, total abandonment of the vehicle. Battles with the job-master were frequently doomed to failure.

Even so, with ever-rising costs, many former carriage owners resorted to hiring vehicles from reputable job-masters, whose numbers constantly increased, driving the less honest ones out of business.

Life was very different for the woman who did not own a carriage, who came from a lower stratum and was forced to use the socially stigmatized omnibus or, from the 1860s, the horse-drawn tram, regarded as even more undesirable. As for the 'open' hansom cab, its unsavoury reputation was earned from ladies of the town who beckoned from it to prospective clients and, on being joined by them, directed the cabby to an address with which he was possibly already familiar and for which he would then double the fare. A respectable woman who hailed one took a grave chance, earning ribald remarks from cabbies and from male pedestrians alike, and even running the risk of being joined by a stranger when held up in traffic.

Working women, and those of straightened means, had no choice but to travel by omnibus or tram, for there was no alternative form of public transport until the underground railway opened – the Metropolitan line in 1863 and the City and South London in 1890. Even when the bicycle became available it was an expensive thing to buy. So public transport flourished, and on both buses and trams women were short-changed unscrupulously. Any dispute over the fare would be suppressed by threatening thugs, who were there for the purpose and were skilled pick-pockets into the bargain. It was also not unknown for well-dressed ladies to be seated on outside

The Bayswater Omnibus (detail) by G.W. Joy 1895

seats to lend an air of respectability to the vehicle, thus convincing unsuspecting women that it was safe to step aboard.

An additional hazard was the discomfort and slowness of omnibus travel. Average speed was five miles an hour and space was uncomfortably restricted. The fact that vehicles were supposed to carry only ten to twelve passengers inside, plus ten to fourteen outside on the upper deck, was consistently ignored, and conductors (commonly known as Cads) took fares but provided no tickets as proof of payment. They could therefore accuse a complaining passenger of non-payment, forcing her to pay again or leave the bus. In addition, they pocketed much of the proceeds, which they shared with the driver.

Interiors were dark, hot, and smoke-laden, the windows blocked by advertisements. They were also odorous and rarely cleaned. In winter, floors were covered with straw which rapidly became mangled underfoot and heavy with filth deposited from road and pavement. No wonder many women envied the men who, by tradition, occupied the open-air seats upstairs, and that they even thought it worth risking their reputations to join them!

Inevitably the four-wheeled enclosed cab was preferred to the open-fronted two-wheeled hansom by unescorted women who could afford them, but there was also the hackney carriage, not to be confused with the public hackney catering for several passengers. The hackney carriage was usually the discarded coach of some nobleman and for this reason appealed to socially ambitious people until decaying grandeur and shabby or broken harnesses spoiled the picture. So cab design came into its own, producing a two-wheeled cabriolet in which the driver sat beside the passengers. The shape of the hood earned it the soubriquet of 'coffin cab'. Then came the bulnois, with a door at the rear – unpopular because it provided easy access for bilkers, the equivalent of present-day hitch-hikers except that they did not pause to thumb a lift and could be unpleasantly aggressive if asked to dismount.

Even a three-wheeler made its appearance, but the only cabs to remain consistently popular were the four-wheeled clarence and the two-wheeled, open hansom. The clarence, commonly called a 'growler' because of the noise it made on stone or concrete roads, was a four-seater, larger than a brougham, and since it had a luggage rack on the roof it could be safely used by servant girls removing their boxes to new situations, by old ladies on their way to visit relatives, and by any unattached woman with luggage to testify that she was a traveller who was likely to be met at her destination.

The hansom was favourite with courting couples. They could enclose themselves with a screen, draw curtains across the windows, and the driver, who sat behind and above the cab, could spy on them only through the limited vision of a trap door in the roof. Stepping into it demanded agility because the first step was high and very small, and the skilful twist of the foot required to climb further could result in damaged clothes unless negotiated with caution, and in physical discomfort for the stout and the elderly.

As the century progressed, the lack of control over traffic and the growing number of horses and vehicles involved in street jams (plus the pall of smoke hanging over cities, which sometimes left vehicles fog-bound) fanned the growing resentment of those who considered it their right to behave as they wished on the roads. Even when it was decreed in 1835 that drivers should keep to the left (so chosen, legend has it, because coachmen carried the whip in the right hand and signalled with it), affluent people still considered they could do as they pleased and clung to their legal rights when it came to leaving their carriages wherever they wished, for as long as they wished.

By law, cabs had to give way to carriages on the road unless obstruction could be proved to the satisfaction of magistrates, whose notorious bias, as drivers or aspiring drivers of carriages, quashed the majority of court cases. So traffic chaos continued to be as impossible to control as the insanitary conditions of the streets due to accumulated horse droppings, and the increasing number of fatal accidents. Frustrated passengers, having paid off drivers with the intention of proceeding on foot, could find themselves trapped between rocking coaches and stamping horses; one slip in the mud and they were crushed beneath wheels or hammered underfoot by iron-shod hooves.

But those who despaired over the state of the roads and the sufferings of horses and human beings, might have taken heart, as would the model wife bemoaning the filthy condition of her skirts, had they known how soon the horseless carriage was to transform their world.

10 ❧ STEPPING HIGH
Grace and Elegance in the Saddle

To QUALIFY FOR REAL ADMIRATION in the park parade it was necessary to be more than an expert whip, or a decorative passenger lolling in an elegant carriage. A good seat on a horse was as essential as wearing a superbly tailored riding habit, and no one was more qualified to perfect this 'seat' than J. Rimmell Dunbar, 'Professor of Horsemanship', whose treatise on Park Riding appeared in 1859.

Though his attitude towards London's riding schools was patronizing, his expertise on the most stylish form of horsemanship was unquestionable. So, too, was his reverence for the nobility and his adulatory attitude toward royalty:

> Who that has seen can ever forget the magnificence of that scene which Rotten Row presented to the admiration of the world, at the commencement of the present reign, when a young and beloved Sovereign sought relaxation from the cares of State in equestrian exercise in Hyde Park, or who could have witnessed the spectacle of that Royal Lady mounted on her favourite horse, passing through lines of her loyal subjects, without feeling that in the mighty but youthful Sovereign of the greatest empire in the world, they saw – as was said of her illustrious predecessor Queen Elizabeth –
>
> > 'Our Gracious Queen
> > With grace and dignity rode through the host,
> > And proudly paced that gallant steed as though
> > He knew his saddle was a royal throne.'

It was the ambition of all fashionable lady riders in Rotten Row to compare favourably with the highest in the land, but the ordinary riding school, with its circumscribed indoor arena, failed to accustom them to wider outdoor areas, nor did it teach more than the rudiments of what this presumably self-styled 'Professor of Horsemanship' called the Menage type of riding – the basic, adequate, but wholly undistinguished method which he likened to that of times long past. 'This, for school riding, is quite correct,' he admitted with some condescension, but added that his own instruction went beyond the point at which the schools left off. And indeed it did, for he specialized in the Grecian Seat, the distinctive feature of which was the total relaxation of the rider's body – 'riding disunited' while her horse remained 'united', meaning that the rider sat at ease while keeping her horse under perfect control.

> For Park Riding, we consider this elegant attitude on horseback to be the most graceful ... and when learned from the instructions of a professed and experienced master [it] exhibits the perfection of equestrian art.

Dunbar extolled this style of riding as being particularly suitable for displaying the grace and beauty of womanhood – which was enough to send to the doorstep of Riding House, Motcombe Street, Belgrave

From *The Lady's World* 1887

Square, any woman who wanted to be seen and admired in the park parade and could afford his tutorage.

Even experienced horsewomen, particularly those who had learned the old-fashioned Menage method, believed the most important thing to master was a firm seat in the saddle, whereas a knowledge of the operation of the hand on the horse's mouth was the greater essential. In the hand all excellence lay, for it was by this that a horse would be governed and guided. 'A good seat' would come next.

Another important thing to remember was that the rider should always be obeyed by the horse, not mastered by him, and that a horse well broken-in readily performs every action when properly commanded. A good park horse should be obedient to the hand and therefore always ready to perform correctly. In addition, he had to be of middling size, with good feet and legs, supple shoulders, a long, thin mane and tail and a well-raised neck; he had to have breeding and courage, be full of spirit and action, but at the same time quiet, safe, and steady; and ideally, never under five years old. The head had to be carried on a level with the shoulders, and he should have been taught to move forward, backward, or sideways. His mouth should be both 'sensible and tender, light and loyal – a fine fresh mouth'. And he should be ridden with the greatest ease and exactness, 'making him display the most elegant attitudes'. In the eyes of J. Rimmell Dunbar, elegance in the horse was the perfect foil for elegance in its rider.

Some horses, however well trained, would be slow to obey the hand and therefore the heel was needed to supplement it, but if the rider applied the spur too violently the horse could interpret it as punishment and react either in distress or defiance, thus leading to accidents with other riders. The undesirability of making such a spectacle of herself in Rotten Row was enough to horrify any socially ambitious lady. She went riding, first, to be admired, second for exercise, but never to be ridiculed. Her aim was to stand out against the background of what was considered the most magnificent school for open air practice in the world,

> where may be seen the realisation of the poetical picture of a perfect horsewoman: A lady riding her palfrey, even as some beautiful water-fowl pressing onward with the tide, seeming in the eye of fancy, by the concord of its motion with the undulation of water, to be a portion of the stream on the surface of which it floats, there is such a beautiful harmony between the rider and the horse.

The Professor was apparently as flattering in his approach to the ladies as he was unctuous in his attitude to royalty, but any woman taught by him could always be sure of acquitting herself well in the saddle.

One of the first requisites was to mount gracefully. She should approach her horse with good temper, resolution, firmness, and confidence; she should display no fear; she should speak to her mount and pat him affectionately on head and neck, taking care to make him understand who was mistress. This last gesture could be aided by spotless gloves and delicate perfume, which apparently earned any horse's respect.

The lady could then proceed to mount. Always she should imagine an unseen audience, silently applauding. With them in mind she would approach her horse with her habit held gracefully in the left hand, taking the reins from the groom with her right. She would then place her right hand, holding the reins and whip, on the crutch of the saddle, raise her left foot into the groom's hands, place her left hand on his right shoulder, and rise in one fluid movement. If properly executed the effect was eye-catching. As soon as she was comfortably seated she would arrange her habit while the groom guided her foot to the stirrup. A slight pressure of the left leg and a gentle yielding of the bridle hand would then intimate to the horse that she wished to proceed.

The Professor's advice covered not only the control of the horse at different paces, and the rider's posture, but also how to transfer the reins from one hand to the other or rearrange her habit or her hat while cantering.

A lady also had to learn how to shake hands with a friend while riding, for part of the enjoyment along the Ladies' Mile was meeting others and demonstrating one's ability to perform this action without faltering or breaking the horse's rhythm. It called for balance and again for the transfer of the whip and reins to the left hand in order to leave the right hand free for greeting one's acquaintances.

An even greater test was caressing the horse when in the canter, something every lady liked to do before admiring watchers. Again she had to change her whip from right to left hand without losing her balance, then lean forward to reach her horse's ears and head, patting his head and neck and speaking to him in a kindly voice.

Alternatively, she could lean backwards, again without losing her balance, in order to pat him at the rear, or sufficiently far sideways to see his hooves and then to pat him on the side. All these actions would have to be conducted gracefully if they were to win appreciative comments as she rode by.

Professor Dunbar liked nothing better than teaching his pupils in the open spaces of Hyde Park, taking them through their paces when backing, or dropping and recovering the reins, altering the stirrups while cantering, and finally stopping – an essential perfection in riding.

To do this the pupil had to throw herself backwards at the moment the horse's forelegs were coming to the ground at the end of a cadence, then press the horse's side with her leg and, with the reins drawn to the body, propel the animals' haunches forward so as to bear on the bit. Skilled pupils performed this twice – a double *arret* which always earned praise and marked them as worthy to ride in Rotten Row.

And finally there was dismounting, the supreme test of grace and skill. To do this the lady disengaged her habit from the saddle and her left foot from the stirrup and, by moving her right leg out of the crutch, sat sideways. Putting the whip into the left hand, this time point downwards, she then extended both hands to the accompanying gentleman as if she were taking a letter offered on a silver salver by a servant and, leaning slightly forward, she descended, taking care to alight delicately on the toe or the ball of the foot to break the shock. This time the groom stood at the horse's head.

An alternative method was to extend her right hand into the gentleman's corresponding one, her left hand holding the habit and his left hand supporting her right elbow as she alighted. The habit was thus kept clear of the feet and her descent was both light and graceful, finishing with a delicate dancing step.

Dunbar's manual contained a long list of Golden Rules culled from the celebrated Treatise on Horsemanship by the Greek historian Xenophon, *c.*438–*c.*354 BC. Among them were the following:

> Never approach your horse in a passion, for anger never thinks of consequences, and forces us to do what we afterwards repent...

(This was, of course, superfluous advice to ladies who would never dream of displaying bad temper in public, since it was not only a sign of bad breeding but marred the beauty of the face.)

> Never contend with a horse upon that point which he is prepared to resist.

A lady ought never, if it can be avoided, chastise her horse; let some one else undertake the breaking him of any vice.

The business of riding is to display beauty, it strengthens the body and improves the carriage.

Should you get confused between carriages, trust your horse to get you out, but see that he takes you not too close to injure your leg.

Horses are fond of music and it much refreshes them.

Insisting that Park riding ranked as a first-class exercise for health and cheerfulness, the Professor also claimed that because it was enjoyed in the open air it could not lead to fatigue, and that riders were never in fear of taking cold, coupled with which was the enjoyment of an agreeable landscape in conversation with a friend, or in solitary contemplation. But solitary contemplation was not the motive which brought fashionable ladies to ride in Hyde Park. It was the 'done thing', of which they were inordinately conscious.

Invalids, however, were no doubt encouraged by his belief that the heat of the horse's body was beneficial to them, and that nothing could be of greater benefit to the ailing than to ride in the morning air. People in good health were also encouraged by his insistence that riding kept them so, and his avowal that riding was a lesson in deportment, 'adding grace to the fairer sex', brought him eager pupils.

The major part of Dunbar's teaching seemed to cater for women, but he did not entirely overlook the gentlemen, to whom he was forever stressing the importance of riding etiquette. 'Gentlemen may ride at a hand-gallop, as it is a gentleman's pace, and corresponds with the canter of the ladies.' Reminding them that the hand-gallop was the only gallop permitted in Rotten Row, he also emphasized that the gentleman rider should always approach a lady rider on the off or right side, and that when riding in company with her he should remain on her right, holding his reins and whip in the right hand, leaving his left one free to render any assistance she might require.

On no account was a gentleman to ride between two ladies riding together, or pass a lady too quickly or too near, for fear of alarming her horse. It was 'the height of bad taste and imprudence, if not something worse, for a gentleman to ride at a gallop past a lady on horseback, or to pass on her left side. Always keep to the left side when meeting objects of any description. When overtaking and passing them, keep to the right. When in a difficulty in passing an object, the gentleman always leads.'

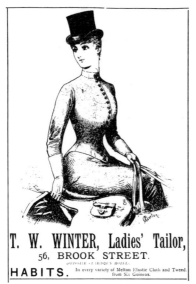

LEFT An advertisment from *The Lady* September 1887
RIGHT Ladies' riding habits from *Harper's Bazar* 1873

However well a lady might acquit herself in the saddle, perfection could never be reached were she badly dressed. Ladies' riding habits were therefore of supreme importance and could be made more eye-catching by the quality of the material and tailoring. Mohair was popular for riding on chilly days, with grosgrain and heavy silk materials for warmer weather.

The lady's riding habit appeared in France in the seventeenth century. In the early days it was worn with long full petticoats, but by the nineteenth century these were replaced by under-trousers long enough to strap beneath the instep (spelt 'trowsers' in America). Short knee-breeches with top-boots, discreetly concealed by the riding habit's flowing skirts, were an alternative. Hair was drawn back and brushed close to the head into a small bun at the back, which well displayed elegant little riding hats adorned with small, upstanding plumes or larger ones swirling about the crown, or with swathed silk or chiffon falling into folds at the back.

Nineteenth-century women's riding habits had increasingly full skirts; the coat was based on a man's, though a favourite French style retained a small upstanding collar, close buttoned and revealing a smart bow at the throat, and had plain inset sleeves adorned with braid. By 1894 leg-o'mutton sleeves were back in fashion, even with riding habits, but the popularity of braid trimming on riding clothes never really went out of date.

By mid century, America was designing well-tailored women's riding clothes. English styles were closely copied, made of grosgrain, velvet, wool, mohair, or whatever material was considered suitable for active exercise.

Tall beaver hats swathed with gauze or veiling, or highly polished felt ones of similar style, became fashionable in the 1870s. They were extremely becoming, but the small hat with a pill-box crown, designed earlier in the century, remained popular for park riding. This was also swathed with gauze or tulle, but less and less with plumes. The tall beaver with close veiling over hair and face, and always in shining black, was exclusively for the hunt.

The riding corset, a rigidly-shaped, whale-boned and tightly laced affair guaranteed to display the hourglass line, was indispensable though to wear it must have bordered on torture. In the 1880s came the basque, the tightly-fitting jacket buttoning up the front and styled to fit snugly over the back of the bustled skirt. With an open style basque a waistcoat was a smart accessory.

No well-dressed lady would take to the saddle without the proper accessories. These consisted of long riding gloves, usually gauntleted; pins designed as stirrups, horseshoes, riding crops or hunting horns, to be worn on the collar or, if the jacket had open revers, on the cravat, which was always snowy white and immaculately tied. The riding crop had to be well made and adorned with a well-designed and sporting handle, usually in the shape of a horse's head, a fox, or a hound, carved in bone or ivory, or chased in silver and gold. This could be displayed when meeting friends and acquaintances whom one desired to impress; a costly handle would put to shame one fashioned merely of wood. After all, one of the reasons for stepping high in Rotten Row was to eclipse others, down to the smallest detail.

Collar pins for riding habits

. . . For better for worse,
for richer for poorer . . .

AMONG THE WOMEN RIDERS whom respectable wives would ignore along Rotten Row were the successful prostitutes who, by the middle of the century, began to flaunt their beauty and their prosperity there. With blazing self-confidence they either drove in costly carriages adorned with motifs subtly suggesting crests, or flaunting their initials (often daringly entwined with others to indicate their link with some noble name), or rode on splendid mounts with saddle-cloths similarly adorned. No hired hacks from riding stables for them! They rode well, tutored by the best masters and demonstrating their skill with all the tricks of horsemanship extolled by 'Professor' Dunbar. Their ability to stoop gracefully from the saddle to greet an admiring pedestrian or, even more skilfully, to drop the reins and lean backward on their hands, thus displaying the provocative outline of waist and bosom, gave rise to much jealous criticism and accusations of brazen exhibitionism.

Their presence along the Ladies' Mile outraged Society, as it outraged the upper echelons of provincial cities where facilities for park riding were also available, but public protestations and condemnation in the press achieved precisely nothing. Such women were, according to some observers of the period, a necessary evil that had to be tolerated; according to others, a scourge of which the nation should rid itself.

Self-righteous voices in the correspondence columns of *The Times* and other esteemed journals protested that wives and daughters could not be taken to the opera or to the theatre without being brought face to face with whores thronging the foyers, lolling from boxes to smile and wave to men in the audience, promenading during intervals to attract attention, and turning the most respectable bars into places where no respectable female could be taken.

Even one side of Regent Street was traditionally accepted as the territory of the Ladies of the Town, so that refined women hurrying into the shops had to tolerate insulting overtures from male pedestrians. The long route from St Paul's Churchyard through Fleet Street, the Strand, the Haymarket, Regent Street and Portland Place to Regents Park was notorious and many husbands and fathers forbade their wives and daughters to set foot in the area. Into disreputable Windmill Street and the network of alleys and streets around the Haymarket, known by night as Babylon, no women other than prostitutes would set foot after dusk.

Large provincial cities were equally well supplied with commercial sex, and all dockland areas swarmed with it. No wonder, cried the prudes, that foreigners were shocked, when visiting Britain, to find themselves unable to walk along many famous thoroughfares without being accosted at every step and that, on returning home, they expressed their disgust at the Englishman's double moral standards.

That these double standards existed, in an age that attached so much importance to propriety, even the most sheltered of wives could not fail to realize, but the model wife, reared to a distaste for immorality, would do what she had been taught to do when confronted with anything unpleasant – look the other way. This may have been difficult when faced with evidence that many husbands (though by no means all) had one code of behaviour for their wives and another for themselves. In the opinion of many a nineteenth-century husband the place for a wife was on a pedestal as a model of decorum, respectability, and motherhood, and there he was content to leave her while he satisfied his lusts elsewhere – or perhaps a wife reared to frigidity drove him to it?

Among respectable Victorian families, delicacy in sexual matters meant that this aspect of marriage was something for which ambitious mammas never prepared their daughters, just as they never prepared them for the secrets of the marriage bed. A bride had to be unsullied and untouched, which meant pure in body and innocent in mind. Even her literature was circumscribed. Many novels, such as those by Charlotte or Emily Brontë or George Eliot, were strictly forbidden in case they polluted a young lady's thoughts and morals, and were labelled by some critics as coarse, low, indelicate and vulgar, even when they were acclaimed by the general reading public.

In narrower circles, gentle females were allowed to read only the most chaste literature – which meant the dullest and most pious, for Evangelical strictures were still very widely heeded. They were obligingly supported by Charles Edward Mudie, a lay preacher and writer of hymns, who founded a circulating library in 1842 which, by 1850, had become the biggest in the land and therefore the most influential, establishing him in the powerful position of self-appointed censor. No volume that he personally considered to be of doubtful taste or dubious influence was ever admitted to his shelves. Also in the 1850s, a stern Methodist named W. H. Smith, founder of a rapidly expanding business as a book vendor on railway stations, banned all books, journals, or newspapers that he deemed offensive.

Delicately nurtured females could be sure of finding on such shelves only works sentimentalizing the role of dutiful wife and devoted mother, forever emphasizing that a woman should be a Madonna, not a Magdalen, for was there any figure more maternal or more pure than the Virgin Mary? Thus idealized, but often lonely and unhappy along with many other women in the same situation, this saintly figure on her saintly perch was regarded with possessive pride by many a Victorian husband because she symbolized the sanctity of his home but, all too often, he was content to let her remain on her pedestal while he sought less virtuous companionship.

Defenders of the erring Victorian male have argued that his hypocritical attitude was prompted by a sense of guilt, a secret awareness that man was a sinner but woman – the real woman as opposed to the fallen woman – was not, but it seems more likely that his

LEFT The young bride was expected to be a model of purity and innocence
RIGHT The model wife had to turn a blind eye when her husband chose to seek less virtuous company

insistence on revering motherhood was a nod in God's direction, a bid for approval when the time came, a sign that he had cherished his wife and done his duty as a father and provider.

There was, however, another side to the coin. Although moral standards were strict and largely adhered to in the middle and upper-middle class, the sanctity of family life was regarded as a bourgeois ideal among some higher levels of society. Irregular liaisons entered into by either husband or wife were often condoned by members of the 'smart set', providing they were handled discreetly and avoided scandal. At all costs, the eleventh commandment – 'thou shalt not be found out' – had to be observed. Divorce was the ultimate disgrace, barring them for ever from the Royal Enclosure at Ascot, and to the idle rich no other form of social ostracism could be so damning as that.

But even in elevated circles, as well as in more average ones, there were countless devoted and faithful husbands, many loving parents and happy marriages; though the fact remains that infidelity held greater perils for a wife than for a husband. Fall from her pedestal, and where would she land? Any property she owned on marriage had become her husband's. In return, he had contracted to support her. One lapse from grace on her part, no matter how extenuating the circumstances, and that support would be withdrawn. She would be dismissed from his home and denied access to his children, for they were *his* children, not hers. Her property would also remain his. Therefore however unfaithful *he* might be, she was forced to accept it if only for economic reasons. Nor would the law favour her should she voluntarily leave her husband, no matter how great the provocation.

Before the Divorce Act of 1857, even if a husband's guilt had been proved, and the marriage terminated as a result, the innocent wife would still be denied access to her children and the husband could do with them what he willed – send them to live with his parents or even his mistress and ensure that the mother never saw them again. Although the Custody of Infants Act of 1839 had done a little, but very little, to rectify this cruelty, clever lawyers could often find loopholes through which the father could wriggle, and unless the wife remained a model of conventional respectability sympathy would be for her husband.

In 1879 the estranged husband of Annie Besant, the theosophist and free-thinker, sought a court order to reclaim the custody of the daughter assigned to her under the Deed of Separation drawn up in

1873 (the son being assigned to the father), declaring his wife to be an unfit parent on the grounds of her anti-religious writings, including the notorious Knowlton Pamphlet on birth control, in 1877, of which she was co-author.

Even the 1857 Act had helped women very little, for it enabled a man to divorce his wife merely on the grounds of her adultery, but demanded that a wife should provide undeniable proof of her husband's guilt in rape, sodomy or bestiality, or of adultery linked with incest, bigamy, cruelty or desertion.

In short, she was trapped. To break her marriage vows would mean a broken life, rejected by family and friends, without money or any means of support, ill-educated – for academic knowledge was widely deemed unnecessary and even undesirable in a woman, with the result that money was predominantly spent on the education of sons rather than daughters – and unable to obtain a position even as a nursery governess or housekeeper because no respectable home would employ her.

The only source of money, if she could use her needle well, was piecework in the clothing sweat shops, sewing trousers at eightpence a pair – less, if her stitching was imperfect – and completing perhaps no more than ten or so a week; or the collars and wristbands of shirts, plus buttonholes and four rows of hand stitching down the front, for twopence-halfpenny per shirt. Even fancy needlework, offered to 'ladies in reduced circumstances', would yield only four shillings and sixpence for some weeks of stitching – as Annie Besant experienced after legal separation from her husband.

Something even less elegant was the only alternative for the majority of women. If lucky, they could become washerwomen to large households where a laundress could work at her dolly-tub in an out-house and never set foot across the threshold or meet any of the occupants; or, in the north of England, they could become orange-women peddling fruit in the streets and markets of Liverpool or Birkenhead among notoriously rough women who would close ranks against anyone who was plainly not one of themselves. For less than a pittance that would not keep body and soul together, they could clean the floors of the textile mills. Very late in the century 'lady typewriters' were employed in offices, but this required training and vacancies were few; in any case, lady typewriters were often the daughters of proprietors, working for the family business.

The only profitable alternative for a destitute woman, to which she might eventually be driven to avoid starvation, was prostitution,

A refuge for the destitute: the women's ward of a hostel for the homeless, London 1870, from *The Lady's Newspaper*

and she would be lucky indeed to become one of the comparatively few 'kept women' in congenial surroundings such as St John's Wood or Chelsea – and then only for as long as her charms lasted.

The Married Women's Property Act of 1882 was the first merciful concession towards a Victorian woman's independence, for at last she had the right to retain her money and possessions. Even so, the chains could still tighten were she to chafe against them, for although, after 1852, a man no longer had the right to force a deserting wife to co-habit with him by issuing a writ of habeas corpus against anyone who sheltered her, until 1891 he retained the right to kidnap and imprison her and no writ of habeas corpus could be issued against him.

Little chance of success, therefore, had any woman who refused to submit to the dominating male. It was surely a masculine voice which declared, in 1869, that a woman of good breeding always felt complacent in submitting to the superiority of a member of the opposite sex? Many a woman could have contradicted that, for to be loved and cherished was one thing, to be trapped and tyrannized was another; but with so much at stake, so much to lose, the average woman dare not risk a breakdown in her marriage, nor contribute to it in any way.

The writings of William Acton, a medical man apparently much heeded in the 1850s, confirmed the current view of female sexuality.

'As a general rule,' he wrote in 1857, '... a modest woman seldom desires any sexual gratification for herself. She submits to her husband's embraces, but principally to gratify him; and, were it not for the desire of maternity, would far rather be relieved from his attentions.'

He also claimed that many young men formed their ideas of women's sensuous feelings from what they had experienced with low women, 'in casinos and other immoral haunts', who were expert at faking strong passions even if they did not feel them. To these experiences Dr Acton attributed the late marriages of many Victorian men, arguing that they were reluctant to commit themselves to a lifetime of demanding passion, and anxiously reassuring them that many females never felt any sexual excitement whatever and that 'no nervous or feeble young man need be deterred from marriage by any exaggerated notion of the arduous duties required from him'. The best mothers, wives, and managers of households, he insisted, knew little or nothing of sexual indulgences, and 'love of home, children, and domestic duties are the only passions they feel'. If this was meant to reassure a timid husband, it also encouraged the strongly sexed one to indulge himself elsewhere and to look upon his wife merely as a domestic chattel.

With such attitudes prevailing, small wonder that sex was taboo as a subject for home discussion and that many a bride went to the altar totally ignorant of what lay ahead. Ambitious mothers, inhibited by convention, were content that their marriageable daughters should retain their innocence to the bitter end. For many brides that end was bitter indeed, for shock could lead to disgust and disgust to instinctive retreat. Girls from the country or the slums, where parents sometimes begat children as blatantly as animals mating in a field, entered into marriage with their eyes wide open, but the ignorance of girls from sheltered and respectable homes was the result of what is seen today as a totally false idea of delicacy and refinement.

No century saw genteel affectation swell into competitive gentility so greatly as the nineteenth. Avid contenders in the social race were the middle and upper working classes, whose increased prosperity encouraged successful tradesmen and artisans to send their daughters to exclusive boarding academies for young ladies. Here they studied elocution, deportment, dancing, feminine arts such as pen-painting on silk, sketching in pastels, painting in water colours, and singing to their own piano accompaniment. As testimony to the school's high educational value, they also learned bad French. Sheltered, pseudo-refined, they finally emerged with all the delicate airs and graces of a lady and with absolutely no knowledge of sex.

Even menstruation was something for which many girls of all classes were totally unprepared, and consequently found terrifying when it happened. The body and its functions were not subjects for discussion in respectable home. If instinctive curiosity made a young lady wonder whether more lay behind the attraction of man to woman, she would be fobbed off with marriage manuals such as Mrs Caddick's *Bride's Book*, or Clara Balfour's *Whisper to a Newly Married Pair*, neither of which mentioned anything so crude as sexual intercourse, presenting only a picture of domestic bliss in a household run efficiently by the model wife.

Later manuals, even though claiming to be more enlightened, merely hinted at what was to come and unfailingly suggested that it was an ordeal that had to be endured, a virtuous woman's sacrifice on the altar of duty. However, since dear Mamma (so delicately mannered and refined) had experienced it, it obviously couldn't be very shocking, probably no more than sleeping beside one's husband and exchanging chaste kisses ... so divinely romantic! But often a girls' romantic dreams were shatted by reality, and the shock could be violent, leaving a stunned bride wondering bitterly why she had not been told that the bridal paraphernalia and all the elaborate preparations for marriage were to lead to such an invasion of the modesty she had been taught to cherish, and often to pain and humiliation as well.

Since modesty in the bedroom was as important to the Victorians as modesty outside it, the sight of nakedness was avoided. Even if sisters shared a bedroom, they would undress beneath voluminous nightgowns with their backs to each other, hiding their bodies. In many marriages, the husband undressed and donned his nightshirt in an adjoining room and did not enter the bedroom until his wife was ready to receive him in billowing nightgown and frilly cap.

Embarrassment over nudity seems at variance with the custom of nude bathing. Eric Trudgill, in *Madonnas and Magdalens*, says:

> Bathing, especially at the seaside, presented problems for the Victorian prude, since until the adoption of swimming costumes in the 1870s, bathing machines were the only protection for outraged modesty; and the correspondence columns of the press each summer were full of bitter complaints about the shameless seaside cavortings of loose women and unblushing men....

He also cites the evidence of Francis Kilvert, the chaste young West country clergyman:

> In his diary for the seventies [Kilvert] is both lyrical about the delights of nude sea bathing and indignant about 'the detestable custom of bathing drawers' that was becoming *de rigueur*. At Seaton in 1873, he notes with scant embarrassment, he scandalized the beach by being unaware of the new convention. But in fact he did not scandalize everyone: '. . . the young ladies who were strolling near seemed to have no objection'. And this was, or rather had been before the adoption of bathing drawers, one of the mysteries of the age, that ladies at the seaside seemed to throw off all prudish apprehensions as they did their shawls and wrappers. In the major resorts, crowds of perfectly respectable women thronged the gentlemen's part of the beach, within a few yards of the bathing machines, quite unconcerned by the sights before them. 'There they sit,' commented the *Saturday Reveiw*, 'happy, innocent, undisturbed – placidly and immovably gazing at hundreds of males in the costume of Adam. . . .'

Annie Besant, in her autobiography of 1893, admits that when she married at the age of twenty she was as ignorant of sex as a child of four, and as unsuspecting. From physical shock, plus the subsequent disillusion caused by a husband who believed that a man had exclusive rights in all matters and a woman none, she fortunately emerged clear-eyed and courageous, intelligent enough to look back on her upbringing and recognize the potentials in her character which had been smothered by hypocrisy and cant.

'All girls have in them the germ of passion,' she wrote, adding that its development depended on 'the surrounding influences of education', meaning home influences in the main since most female education was negligible and gave the mind no encouragement to think for itself. 'I had but two ideals in my childhood and youth, round whom twined these budding tendrils of passion; they were my mother and the Christ. I know this may seem strange, but I am trying to state things as they were . . .'

Annie Besant's mother was Anglican, her father agnostic. He died when she was five. Between mother and daughter was a deep bond of affection, which remained unbroken despite future events. Perhaps the mother was over-protective, even possessive, for she dismissed more than one offer of marriage for her daughter without even telling her, on the grounds of her 'youth and childishness'. Annie was also forbidden to read love stories and, being reared to obedience, accepted his mother's strictures in everything. Not surprisingly, her daydreams were untouched by the average hopes and fears of girlhood, and inevitably '... as my girlhood began to bud towards womanhood, all its deeper currents set in the direction of religious devotion.'

In an almost fanatically religious age, and with the figure of Christ as the ideal man to be loved and worshipped, this too was not surprising. Many highly impressionable young women were attracted by the emotionalism of religion. '... my inner life ... was absorbed in that passionate love of "the Saviour" which really is the human passion of love transferred to an ideal – for women to Jesus, for men to the Virgin Mary.' And to prove that she was not exaggerating Annie Besant listed passages from the Bible in which she and other emotional girls could find escape and daily delight:

> Let Him Kiss me with the kisses of His mouth; for Thy love is better than wine ... The King has brought me to his chambers ... May the sweet and burning power of Thy love, I beseech Thee, absorb my soul.
>
> ... may my soul ever languish and melt with entire love and longing for Thee. Let it desire Thee and faint for Thy courts ...
>
> Oh, that I could embrace Thee with that most burning love of Angels!

When Annie's mother finally accepted an Anglican minister as a suitable husband for her daughter, the marriage proved disastrous.

That such an upbringing and experiences were not unusual was confirmed by many letters which later came before Annie Besant in the course of her work as an advocator of birth control. Her comment that many marriages were doomed from the outset by the traumatic effect of the wedding night on an ignorant bride and, all too frequently, by the man's callousness and clumsy ineptitude violating 'a young girl's sensitive modesty and pride, her helpless bewilderment and fear', was also well substantiated by 'the passionate gratitude evidenced by letters from thousands of poor married women ... thanking and blessing me for showing them how to escape from the veritable hell in which they lived.'

However, despite the fact that some social historians seem to concentrate on the disappointments and frustrations and hypocrisy of nineteenth-century marriages, there is plenty of reason to believe that many wives loved their husbands dearly and not only learned to accept the physical side of marriage but to find pleasure in it, and

A portrayal of happy married life. The Harden family at Brathay Hall, 1827

plenty of evidence that many marriages turned out happily and that the family circle was united and affectionate. This was confirmed by an old lady approaching ninety who told me many years ago, with some amusement, of her Victorian mother who considered herself so enlightened that she resolved not to shirk her duty on the eve of her daughter's marriage. After some hesitation, the mother finally blurted, '*My dear – always oblige your husband in the bedroom!*' On being asked in what way, she could go no further, but embraced her daughter tearfully and fled, scarlet with embarrassment.

The daughter's marriage was supremely happy. She became the mother of seven, and none, she confessed with fond indulgence, needed so much mothering as her husband – and judging by many stories of nineteenth-century gentlemen, such was often the case.

It was not unusual for a man who had lost his mother to take a wife mainly to replace her. Thomas Carlyle was not the only Victorian who made his wife unhappy for this reason. Jane Carlyle's childlessness does not appear to have dismayed him; he was the one she was expected to mother, so their sterile marriage is hardly surprising. It is known that in old age he would peer hopefully at visitors and murmur, 'Is that you, dear Mother?'; never, 'Is that you, dear Jane?'

Many men of note seem to have regarded their mothers as the embodiment of ideal womanhood, resulting either in difficult marriages or in unions with women much older than themselves. Tennyson was one who did eventually see and acknowledge the reverse side of his own maternal 'angel woman', but it is difficult to reconcile Robert Browning's adoration of his mother – so strong that on his own admission he could never be in a room with her without wanting to sit with his arm about her, and that, as in childhood, his bedroom adjoined hers and the door was always left ajar – with the swashbuckling lover carrying off Elizabeth Barrett from Wimpole Street.

Elizabeth was not the first older woman to play a part in Browning's life: her six year's seniority was less than Eliza Flower's nine and Fanny Haworth's eleven. But perhaps his love for Elizabeth was based on a chivalrous protective instinct toward frail and aging womanhood. (The maternal influence again?) Whatever its basis, their love for each other was evinced by their happiness together.

Elizabeth Browning gave birth to a daughter, but there were many childless unions between younger men and older women. Some Victorian wives may have envied them for that, for although childbirth gradually became less hazardous as the nineteenth century progressed, for many it was an agonizing and often prolonged nightmare in which there was no relief from pain. Physical inactivity, unbalanced diets, restrictive clothing and tight lacing were contributing factors. Nevertheless, in the main, women delighted in their children and large Victorian families were usually happy.

Fashion dictated that at eighteen a girl's waist should measure no more than eighteen inches; at nineteen, an inch more; at twenty, with yet another inch to match her years, her waistline had reached the permissible limit. Thereafter, if she took any pride in her appearance and wished to maintain the unnatural figure so admired by men, she dare not exceed it. By twenty-five her chances on the matrimonial market were considered to be over, so it was vitally important to retain youthful measurements by stringent control, however uncomfortable and however painful. The ideal was to appear fragile and dependent, to emphasize a man's strength and to arouse his protective instincts. The pretence was equally important after marriage, for any husband would be proud to display on his arm a wife whose femininity stressed his masculinity, whose waist was as small as a girl's. Fashion gave no thought to the possible physical harm caused by unnaturally produced curves, or to restrictions that could cause later trouble in childbirth.

Medical knowledge was mercifully expanding, but loss of babies at birth or shortly afterward was still commonplace. To have 'borne twelve and buried six' was almost routine, though not always due to childbirth problems; childhood diseases could also take their toll. But for the mother childbirth itself was considered a danger from which only God could really deliver her. Women were unanimous in their dread of it, including Queen Victoria, who had no great fondness for children anyway; not until they were growing up does she seem to have found their company in any degree interesting.

Queen Victoria's opinion of childbirth was: '. . . it is such a complete violence to all one's feelings of propriety (which, God knows, receive a shock enough in marriage alone!)'. And in a letter to her daughter the Princess Royal in 1858 she wrote: 'What you say of the pride of giving life to an immortal soul is very fine, dear, but I own I cannot enter into that; I think much more of our being like a cow or a dog at such moments; when our poor nature becomes so very animal & unecstatic . . .' Perhaps the most significant of these statements is the one in parenthesis concerning the shock of marriage, but if the Queen's marital night was as traumatic as it frequently proved to be for virgin brides in those days, the experience appears to have left her with no permanent distaste for sex. Those subjects who looked upon their queen as a model of decorum and moral rectitude would either have been profoundly shocked or greatly relieved to know that she is reputed to have referred to the marriage bed as 'a foretaste of heaven'.

Not until 1847 were anaesthetics considered suitable for use during labour, and even then they were regarded with doubt and suspicion. Many wives declined them because they feared the unknown, many a husband forbade them for fear that the child might be harmed or stillborn, that the mother's brain might be affected by the fumes of chloroform, or that it might even kill her; and religious voices were raised against them, declaring that Divine Will would condemn women who tried to flee from the curse placed upon Eve in the Book of Genesis. That she would 'henceforth bear children in sorrow' was interpreted as God's ordinance that she should do so in pain for evermore. Not until the Queen herself chose

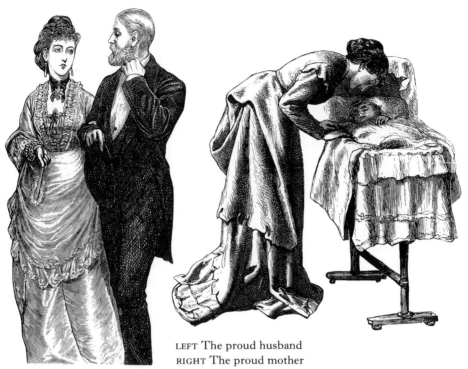

LEFT The proud husband
RIGHT The proud mother

to have an anaesthetic when giving birth to Prince Leopold in 1853, and praised 'that blessed chloroform' afterwards, did other mothers follow her example, encouraged by her statement that she found it 'soothing, quieting, and delightful beyond measure'. At least one aspect of frequent childbirth was much improved – for those who could afford it. The poor could not.

Survival of both mother and child was also increased by Lister's introduction of antiseptics in 1860. Previously derided by the medical profession and others, he was proved right by results and many mothers who would have died in childbirth lived to bless him.

Ironically, there was another aspect for which a woman, worn out by pregnancies, had cause for gratitude – a husband's recourse to commercial sex. As a method of birth control it was second to none, though many wives regarded it as obnoxious. For the man's part it had the advantage that an illegitimate offspring was no concern of his; he could disclaim all responsibility, for it might well have been begotten by some other man. But a wife's pregnancy was different. The outcome was a responsibility he was forced to shoulder and indeed often wanted to, as he built up a fine family to feature in a silver frame in the parlour – the model husband, the model wife, and their model children.

Another factor that contributed to many a wife's aversion to the sex act and to her continuous fear of renewed pregnancy was the widespread lack of knowledge about contraceptive methods. Only in 1880 did this particular fog begin to clear. Until then self-induced miscarriages were usually, and dangerously, resorted to and crude abortions were by no means unknown even among the well-to-do.

The idea of contraceptives should have represented hope; instead, it largely met with mistrust and even greater religious opposition. Not only were peoples' consciences troubled, but immense fears were fired by doctors' warning about health hazards. Terrifying diseases, many with names incomprehensible to the lay person and therefore all the more frightening, were listed in a medical document of 1879 entitled *The Moral And Physical Evils Likely To Follow If Practices Intended To Act As Checks To Population Be Not Strongly Discouraged and Condemned*. Among these were galloping cancer, leucorrhoea, hysteralgia and hyperaesthesia of the genital organs, ovarian dropsy, mania leading to suicide, nymphomania, and sterility. Such a list was enough to put any woman off contraception, though the final one – sterility – might well have been welcomed by those to whom childbirth was almost an annual event.

The growth of feminism was inevitable; the slowness of it not surprising. Financial dependency, fear of being a social outcast, religious enslavement, and the difficulty – for some, the impossibility – of shedding ingrained ideas of feminine delicacy, kept many women firmly entrenched in the old order. Insulated from the world, safe within the walls of their over-furnished and cluttered homes, they glimpsed no sordid realities, nor wanted to. With their children about them and the daily demands of domesticity to occupy their minds, with their consciences clear because they did their duty on the altar of matrimony whenever their husbands demanded it, they were attuned to a pattern of existence which most of them accepted passively, and many with contentment.

Trained throughout their lives to be modest and self-denying, always taking second place to men, such women allowed the rhythm of their lives, whether happy or not, to engulf them. Some developed neuroses known as 'nervous disorders' (which they probably were) and, taking to bed or couch, became permanent invalids, as Elizabeth Barrett did until rescued by Robert Browning. This was called 'going into a decline', though in her case it was due to an accident in girlhood that would have been considered minor today, from which a dominating father and misguided doctors prevented her from recovering normally; but for many women invalidism, real or otherwise, was often an escape route from domestic misery, or a ploy to become the centre of attention in the household.

To such women, whether invalids or not, female emancipation meant little. Let others fight for it; let nothing disturb their safe, secure world. They preferred not to know about the restaurants, playhouses and music halls with near-naked dancers or insalubrious entertainers where some, but not all, husbands spent their evenings. The majority of women lived for their homes and children because they wanted to; they loved them. This was what they had been reared for, so what would they do with emancipation even if they had it, and what was 'feminism', anyway? Weren't they feminine enough?

The average Society wife was even more content with her world of entertaining and being entertained, of carriage driving and park riding, of calls and At Home days, drums and kettledrums, servants and nannies, and visits to the opera and theatre followed by suppers in fashionable night spots. Why change the order of things when life was safe, comfortable, and well organized?

And why, they wondered, should other women grumble about social restrictions when there were a number of places to which even a husband on a limited income could take his wife and family? The theatre may have deteriorated from the position it held in the previous century and become, as many people declared, nothing but a place of iniquity, but respectable people could still go to see Sir Henry Irving in a fine melodrama such as *The Bells*; and similar entertainments like *Maria Marten; or the Murder in the Red Barn* and *East Lynne*, could be seen in London and the provinces. There was also the bioscope and the newly invented and very exciting dioramas and panoramas and cycloramas, all splendid for family treats. There were pleasure grounds such as Cremorne Gardens in Chelsea, and the Highbury Barn where a husband could take his wife to dine and dance until it lost its dancing licence in 1870 and closed down the following year. The Argyll Rooms in St James's were equally respectable until the inevitable invasion of prostitution forced them to close in October 1857; they were re-opened in October 1858, only to become notorious again.

For all classes, throughout the century, there were family gatherings at home, or at the houses of relatives and friends, with games, charades, choruses round the piano and individual renderings of songs, parlour tricks, amateur dramatics, and laden plates of home-cooked food. Fathers would read aloud to their families while wives and daughters did their needlework or practised their drawing.

A popular form of family entertainment

Recitations from Shakespeare or other dramatists necessitated much censorship, and many bowdlerized editions were published.

There were also family picnics, with well-stocked hampers and exciting drives into the country; and the museums in South Kensington, built from the profits made by Prince Albert's inspired Great Exhibition of 1851 in Hyde Park, became very popular. When the magnificent Crystal Palace, in which the exhibition had been housed, was moved to Sydenham in South London and erected on an even larger scale, families could attend daily performances in the Concert Hall which seated four thousand, or in the Opera House which seated two thousand. There was also the Great Orchestra Hall which accommodated four thousand people as well as a gigantic pipe organ, worked hydraulically. On Thursday and Saturday evenings in the summer magnificent firework displays drew families in their thousands, and in the surrounding park, on an island in the lake, were life-size models of prehistoric monsters among the trees.

A family picnic c. 1840

There was plenty of entertainment available for the ordinary, middle-class woman who wanted to escape from domesticity, and those who had both leisure and money found it hard to understand the demand for more freedom and independence. But the poorer housewife, the really poor, silently supported the cry for female emancipation, despite being powerless to do anything about it. To rail about inequality or to demand better wages could mean the loss of her meagrely-paid factory job or her underpaid piece-work at home. Besides, with all those children to feed and a husband who ruled the roost, she had enough on her hands day in, day out, so there was nothing to do but accept her lot and pin her hopes on those who spouted revolutionary ideas about liberation and women's rights and electoral reform, which few believed would ever come. Politics were for men, not for women, a belief underlined by the general (male) view that only an intelligent (male) understanding could possibly be capable of judging such issues.

The really poor wife could do little but accept her lot . . .

Thus women with feminist aspirations were continually thwarted by traditional beliefs, traditional codes: '. . . trained from childhood to believe that for man, and man alone, she must live, that marriage must be not only her highest, but her only aim on earth, as in it is comprised the whole of her destiny,' wrote Anne Richelieu Lamb as early as 1844. Her book *Can Women Regenerate Society?* brought down wrath and scorn on her head, but it planted seeds that were to contribute to the slow growth of sympathy for the new, radical woman who wanted equality with men in all spheres – social, political, educational, professional, and even sexual.

However, such total emancipation was not supported even by the most sympathetic. Limited equality was one thing; complete equality was another, so woman was destined to wait a long time and to fight a long time to be recognized as an intelligent human being who could also be a mature and enlightened mother – and a lover too, free of the stigma of lewdness and licentiousness, hypocrisy and cant.

Meanwhile, she had her children . . .

12 ❧ THE NURSERY SCENE

O may our house be still a garrison
Of smiling children, and for evermore
The tune of little feet be heard along the floor ...

(R. L. Stevenson – *Before This Little Gift Was Come*)

I N 1820 A TOY SHOP WAS OPENED in London's Burlington
Arcade by a family named Morel, whose descendants owned
it until it closed in 1951. Its fame spread worldwide. It was a
magic grotto to generations of children and is remembered with
affection even today for its enchanting window displays of miniature
toys that attracted grown-ups as well as youngsters.

Morel models are now collectors' pieces. Children treasured them,
as children tend to treasure anything small and easily handled, in
whatever generation they are born. A miniature could be cradled
in the hand or carried in the pocket – though nineteenth-century
discipline forbade bulging pockets, stressing that they were not
designed to hold pebbles, bits of string, dead beetles or glossy
chestnuts picked up on daily walks with nurse, nor even for hands
to be thrust into. Gloves, not pockets, were designed for hands, and
no well-behaved or well-dressed children would walk along the
streets dragging their garments down at the sides. Pockets were to
accommodate handkerchiefs, nothing else.

As a special treat parents would take their offspring to Morel's,
letting them glue their noses to the window before entering the
magic grotto to pick perhaps one, at the most two, eye-catching toys,
for material indulgence was something virtually unknown to most
nineteenth-century children. In many upper-class homes they were
reared against a nursery background where fond nurses would allow
them to make as much noise as they liked. Here they were well away
from their parents until the hour set aside for them to descend to
the drawing room to be petted and fussed over, or to be reprimanded
about bad behaviour which had been reported by an over-zealous
nurse. Devoted parents would come upstairs to say goodnight to
their children when they were tucked up in bed; to read a story to
them, or sing a nursery rhyme. But in some respects children in
poor, overcrowded homes often fared better as part of the family

scene, under their mother's feet all day and seated round the family table to share the family meal at the end of it.

In an upper-class household and, later in the century as prosperity boomed, in upper-middle-class ones as well, a children's nurse was considered an absolute necessity and she, in her turn, considered it her right to have at least one nurserymaid and often two. Sometimes the size of the family necessitated both a head nurse and an under-nurse.

In many families the mother tutored her daughters, also her sons when small, though most upper-class families employed a governess. Older sons were taught by tutors or by their fathers before going to school. Consequently many households had a schoolroom as well as nurseries, and together these sometimes occupied a whole floor.

Nursery furnishings depended very much on what might be available in the household, the barest necessities being deemed adequate. Often furniture from the main part of the house, which had become unfashionable or worn and not worth selling, was relegated to the nursery. The floor was usually bare or covered with linoleum. Sometimes there were rush mats which could be rolled up by the nurserymaid and taken outside to be brushed, and there might be a hearthrug or a strip of carpet before the fire. Day-nursery windows were often uncurtained, but those of the night nursery might be shrouded in dark drapes of some hard-wearing material. In spartan households window curtains in the night nursery were considered

The nursemaid

The governess

an unnecessary extravagance. Not until the century was on the wane did grown-ups begin to think that children might enjoy and even thrive better in light and cheerful rooms, touched with colour and with some concessions to childhood tastes and childhood interests, and with warm floors.

The day nursery inevitably contained a large clothes closet, sundry ill-matched chairs, a big deal table in the centre of the room which the nurserymaid had to scrub nightly, and a cupboard for toys. In some there might be an eighteenth-century hanging cradle suspended from the ceiling, a relic from earlier generations, in which the newest addition to the family would be placed, safely out of harm's way. A later, more sophisticated cradle was a wooden affair fitted with a clockwork spring which could produce automatic rocking. Later still, in 1888, came the 'hammock berceaunette', which was actually a small bed suspended between four short, sturdy pillars, with curtains which could be drawn round it to shut out light from sleepy eyes. And of course there would be Nurse's rocking chair, favoured by motherly women who liked to take their charges on their knees to comfort them, or to rock them to sleep when fretful.

The most prominent item in the nursery was the huge fireguard on which clothes were aired – and even set to dry in wet weather. The resulting steam would ruin a little girl's ringlets, painstakingly produced with curl papers the night before, so that she would have to endure hot curling tongs to create the corkscrew curls which Mamma would expect to see when her children came downstairs.

In the night nursery, next door to the day nursery or close by, Nurse slept with the youngest of her charges, the older ones sharing the nursemaid's attic room. If the family was large, other children would often sleep with the upper servants. That children of a family should sleep with the domestic staff was a centuries-old custom. Sometimes sisters and brothers also shared bedrooms. Only in very grand houses might older children have their own rooms.

In contrast, an indulged child of doting parents might share their room, sometimes in an alcove which also accommodated the nurse. In some middle-class households this continued up to an age when the child should certainly have slept elsewhere, resulting in rebellion and night fears when banishment finally came.

In most homes only the fire in the day nursery was lit; a nurserymaid had to haul the coals upstairs from the coal cellar. If a child were sick, the nursery fire would be maintained throughout the night and its cot placed there, a nurserymaid curling up in an armchair beside it, or the child would be taken into the head nurse's bed, but either was an indulgence observed only in times of crisis.

At the start of the century, the belief that it was desirable for a mother to breast-feed her child was finally being accepted, but the earlier practice of hiring a wet-nurse was still by no means disapproved of. 'Happy indeed is the child who, during the first period of its existence, is fed upon no other aliment than the milk of its mother, or that of a healthy nurse,' advised that all-knowledgeable manual *Enquire Within* as late as 1878. It then went on to recommend, as a supplement to this natural diet, biscuits or stale bread boiled in an equal mixture of milk and water, but emphasized that this was not advisable during the first *week* of life. It also stipulated that even the purest of water was never to be given until the latter part of a child's first year, and then only occasionally, '. . . and if this cannot be procured, a light and well-fermented table beer might be substituted.'

Well-to-do eighteenth-century mothers had rarely, if ever, nursed their own children. Wet-nurses had been the accepted rule, and babies had even been fed broth or ass's milk almost from the day they were born, but at the start of the nineteenth century some middle-class mothers did begin to nurse their own children. Impoverished mothers had always done so, and for this reason the upper classes considered it socially degrading and clung stubbornly to wet-nursing. If 'nursing out' proved necessary because the hired woman could not leave her own family to 'live in', the situation was accepted because someone had to suckle the child whenever it cried, be it night or day; many people interpreted crying only as a sign of hunger, despite a newfangled theory that it was the only way in which a child could communicate. So the newborn child would be handed over to a wet-nurse to take to her own home, sometimes for up to a year (cases had been known for even longer periods) but generally for two or three months until the child was weaned.

The hazards of 'nursing out' were the risk of infection from a home less well cared for than the child's, or that the wet-nurse might prove to be neglectful. Even so, some society mothers apparently considered such chances worth taking because a wife should naturally put her husband's interests before her own *and* her children's; to absent herself from his side because yet another baby needed to be breast-fed was quite out of the question.

A wet-nurse released the mother from responsibility and enabled her to take up her social life again, happily dismissing the views of a certain Dr Buchan, aired in 1793, which declared that a mother's milk was the best food for an infant and that children who might appear to thrive without it succumbed to childish diseases more easily and more dangerously. These views had been heeded up to a point, but although still quoted they were still largely mocked. Who would heed the opinions of a man who had also declared that women's heads were so filled with the *expectation* of pain during childbirth that they brought much of it on themselves, and that if they discarded their stays and learned to relax during pregnancy the birth of a child would take place far more easily? This was considered as ridiculous as his views on the use of swaddling clothes, on which he blamed the convulsions of many an unfortunate baby.

Swaddling bandages, in which newborn infants were tightly swathed from the moment of birth, could be as long as eight feet and sometimes more. The habit persisted long into the nineteenth century, even though disciples of Dr Buchan decried it, echoing his belief that it was practised by nurses simply to demonstrate their knowledge and efficiency.

Enquire Within even gave advice about the fact that little boys, when released from swaddling, could be seen to have erections as they screamed and struggled to exercise their bodies: 'In the first years of infancy, many expressions of the tender organs are to be considered only as efforts or manifestations of power.' This was meant to reassure ignorant adults who feared, as some did, that it indicated lasciviousness later in life.

Many age-old superstitions persisted amongst ignorant nurses. A baby that frequently smacked its lips was believed to have been born with some unsatisfied craving which the mother had experienced during pregnancy. The remedy was a little sacramental wine. And for thrush, a live frog sewn in a muslin bag and given to the child to suck was considered a certain cure, the frog drawing off the thrush and dying in the process. That sucking a live frog might make the child choke was not even contemplated, nor was it considered possible that some of these country-bred notions might contribute to the high rate of deaths in early childhood.

At the beginning of the century, when customs and beliefs from the past still abounded, the mistress's 'personal woman' was frequently expected to care for the children as well. She often attended the actual birth and to her the newborn child would be handed – and from her, if she were a countrywoman, more superstitions would be handed down: that a child would rise in the world if it were immediately carried up to the top of the house or, as a substitute, held aloft while the nurse stood with it on a chair; or that a child who later developed rickets could be cured if the mother or nurse passed it through the cleft trunk of a tree, preferably hazel or ash, to another person waiting to receive it. These were only two of the superstitions which died hard.

From an advertisment for pears Soap in *The Lady* 1887

Baptism also had its share of age-old beliefs. The ceremony usually took place a month after the birth, at the most six weeks, and if the baby did not cry during the service the nurse would pinch it, firmly believing that a child who failed to cry at its christening met with an early death, or, alternatively, would not be rid of the Devil.

Dr Buchan had thought little of nurses, condemning them for letting their charges cry too much and thus causing ruptures, and for relying on remedies like Daffy's Elixir, which also persisted well into Victorian days. It consisted of aniseed, juniper berries, carraway seeds, senna, and jalop, soaked in alcohol and water and finally mixed with treacle and water before giving the required dose. It was considered second-to-none as a remedy for colic because it had been used as long ago as the reign of Charles II, and administered to the king himself by the royal physician.

Among other remedies never absent from the nursery cupboard were Godfrey's Cordial and Dalby's Carminative. Such preparations were frowned on by Buchan and his nineteenth-century advocates, who propounded theories about good food, fresh air, exercise and cleanliness; but every traditionally-minded nurse worth her salt ignored them, and every mother too unless she was prepared to run the risk of losing her much-valued nurse. Until mid century it was firmly believed that bathing a child too frequently was bad for its health; daily cleansing of visible areas of the body was considered sufficient. Nor would all underwear be discarded at night, even in the summer unless Nurse judged the weather sufficiently warm and windows were kept tightly shut; fresh air was considered dangerous – as was adding fruit and vegetables to a child's diet, which was also being suggested by progressive advisers.

Not until well after mid century did nursemaids have to carry cans of hot and cold water from basement sculleries to upstairs nurseries every day, for the babies' baths. The bath would be placed before the nursery fire, and towels would be warming on the fire-guard. Baby powder, usually containing fuller's earth, would also be close at hand, with items from the medicine cupboard which Nurse considered indispensable, such as Dr Gregory's powder for bowel disorder. This was an unpleasant pink mixture that smelled as horrible as it tasted, which even the sternest Nanny would com-passionately administer in jam or syrup, or floating in a saucer of milk like a slimy pink island, to be swallowed at one gulp. If nausea and retching followed, this was considered a good sign because when it passed the child would feel better. This much-hated medicine was still given to children well into the twentieth century, as was sulphur and treacle (the good old-fashioned 'brimstone and treacle') on cold winter mornings. The green sulphur powder produced an unattractive colour when stirred into the rich, dark syrup, but the sweet treacly flavour made it palatable.

Other nursery standbys were blackberry syrup for coughs, cinnamon and tar water for internal upsets of all kinds and, as another and certainly more acceptable cure for thrush, borax blended with honey for rubbing on baby gums. Every nurse had her own individual remedy for teething troubles. Many favoured massaging the gums with something hard, such as a bead of amber or coral (both believed to have healing properties) dipped in carrot juice.

Nursery diet was plain and, because of its repetitiveness, dull. A child had to be ailing to escape the daily monotony of boiled mutton with boiled potatoes, followed by either milk or batter puddings. In large households, greatly to the vexation of Cook, this dull nursery fare had to be prepared in the kitchen, although it was the job of a nurserymaid to carry the laden trays upstairs.

In mid century it became customary, in smaller households, for older children to join their parents for the midday luncheon, accompanied by their governess who kept a strict eye on their table manners. Here they fared better, sharing the more interesting menu served to their parents. In such homes younger children and nursery staff also fared better because the kitchen staff was not sufficient to cope with separately prepared meals, which meant that nursery portions were carved from the dining room joint, always far more tasty than boiled mutton. The nursery allocation was then sent upstairs with more appetizing accompaniments.

Only when ill were children indulged with such food as roast chicken or veal, along with jellies and claret. Alcoholic beverages were not frowned on for children, who could be given ale with their midday meal and mulled wine and water at bedtime.

Exercise and fresh air was provided by an afternoon walk with nurse or nursemaid pushing the youngest children in one of the new perambulators. Perambulators were not in general use until well after 1850 and rivalry between nurses in the matter of these status symbols was keen, the latest and most costly models being the envy of all – particularly the mid-century three-wheeler with two large wheels at the handlebar end and a smaller one in front, in which the child faced forward beneath a fringed canopy, usually round in shape like an eastern potentate's sunshade. Looking much like a Bath chair, this perambulator could carry another child seated on the forefront. Coachwork was always of wood. The costly vis-à-vis either had an overlay of plaited wicker or was wholly made of it, and had four wheels. In this vehicle the baby faced its nurse but the two front wheels, beneath its head, were smaller than the rear wheels, giving an unbalanced appearance although it was advertised as 'The Newest and Most Thoughtfully Designed Child's Perambulator, Ensuring both Safety and Comfort and a Pleasure to Propel.' It could be covered with a hinged hood, the height of which increased its top-heavy appearance.

A selection of Victorian baby carriages

Within the area of the park where nursemaids congregated a strict hierarchy existed; the social position of employers was bestowed upon their respective nursemaids, one from an earl's household taking precedence over one from, say, a mere baron's. And at no time would a lesser nursemaid from a lesser household have the audacity to sit on a park bench which traditionally belonged to one from a higher household. This snobbishness prompted the custom of calling each other by the names of their employers. If Lizzie Smith were employed by the Duke of Cholmondeley, she would be addressed as Nurse Cholmondeley, never as Nurse Smith. Only by her charges might she be called by the affectionate name of 'Nanny'.

Alongside the proud nurse pushing her baby carriage walked brothers and sisters, often both looking remarkably alike because very young boys as well as girls wore dresses with sashes, white stockings and laced-up boots and wide-brimmed straw hats. The children would walk decorously until reaching the park, when they would be allowed to play games of tig or battledore-and-shuttlecock

A small boy (*left*) was often dressed in skirts like his sister

on the grass, or spin a diabolo until it flew into the air to be caught again on a length of twine stretched between two handles; or they would spin tops or play with skipping ropes on a pathway well within the nurse's line of vision. If they were lucky, there might be a swing or see-saw in the garden at home. Thus, it was considered, children gained ample exercise; too much would make them boisterous and unmanageable.

Slightly older children were dressed in formal, adult styles for much of the century, often with many layers of complicated underwear. The advice of reformers that stays for girls should be discarded and looser clothing adopted was viewed by nurses and mothers as ridiculous: boned stays supported a child's back and waist and abdomen, and plenty of body-hugging clothes 'helped to keep the cold out'. It was not until after 1880 that an easier style of dress, reminiscent of Regency days, began to appear.

Girls and boys were generally expected to be little ladies and gentlemen, not hoydenish romps. Disobedience would bring punishment, from their nurse if they had erred only slightly, from parents if their behaviour had to be reported. And punishment could be unpleasant, such as being shut in a dark cupboard for a prolonged period, or in a cold, empty attic with nothing but dry bread and cold water brought to them until they repented of their sins. (The many sentimental stories about cruelly punished children held more than a grain of truth, though such tales always pointed some moral, usually religious.)

Every model wife and mother knew how important it was for her children to learn how to conduct themselves when out of doors, how to walk properly and how to modulate their voices in the street, for people would think that children who hopped and skipped and prattled shrilly had been badly brought up. In improving the deportment of older children, particularly girls, the manual *Enquire Within* called for particular study in 1878:

> WALKING – To walk gracefully, the body must be erect, but not stiff, and the head held up in such a posture that the eyes are directed forward. The tendency of untaught walkers is to look towards the ground near the feet; and some persons appear always as if admiring their shoe-ties. The eyes should not thus be cast downward, neither should the chest bend forward to throw out the back, making what are termed round shoulders; on the contrary, the whole person must hold itself up, as if not afraid to look the world in the face, and the chest by all means be allowed to expand. At the same time, everything like strutting or pomposity must be carefully avoided. An easy, firm, and erect posture is alone desirable. In walking, it is necessary to bear in mind that the locomotion is not performed entirely by the legs. Awkward persons rock from side to side, helping forward each leg alternately by advancing the haunches. This is not only ungraceful but fatiguing. Let the legs alone advance, bearing up the body.

Straight backs were encouraged by the use of backboards, on which girls had to recline for an hour or so daily. These folded flat for storage; when opened, the board locked on a slope and a foot rest prevented the body from sliding downwards. At this angle the full length of the spine was supported. A backboard for younger children could be a flat piece of wood tied to the body from shoulder to hip; adjustable straps encircling shoulders and armpits enabled the arms to be moved. Uncomfortable as it must have been, this type of backboard could be worn without unduly hampering movement. Records show that a more sadistic version had protruding poles which passed in front of the wearer's elbows to pull the shoulders back. Thus drilled, carriage, posture, grace and poise would come naturally to a young lady when launched upon the marriage-market.

Punishments meted out to children were very much in keeping with the Victorian theories of 'spare the rod and spoil the child' and 'children should be seen and not heard'. Nor did such punishments cease when they reached schoolroom age, or even later. For six months in 1869 *The Englishwoman's Domestic Magazine* published an interchange of correspondence between mothers, comparing various methods of thrashing their daughters. The correspondence continued unabated until the widely read *Saturday Review* focused attention on the sadistic relish revealed in the letters, condemning both the writers and the magazine that published them.

Even in families where affection was strong, physical punishment was resorted to, often until the late teens, yet records left by governesses, such as the famous diaries of Miss Weeton, contain plenty of evidence that spoilt children were by no means unknown. Some seem to have been the products of indulgent parents who regarded their children as playthings to be shown off before visitors, allowing them to grab sweetmeats and sip their parents' wine at will, while guests looked on with polite, taut smiles. But why worry? The nurse or governess could always be held responsible for any disaster and be ordered to deal with the little darlings accordingly.

Physical punishment was frequently resorted to in many households

Others, like the Armitage children Miss Weeton had to cope with, 'though well ordered by their parents, when out of their sight are as unruly, noisy, insolent, quarrelsome, and ill-tempered a set as I ever met with.' The governess considered the eldest girl, aged seven, to be the black sheep: '... punishment or reward make no lasting impression; I fear she is naturally depraved. Though seven years of age, she has no ideas of common modesty; it is wrong to inure children to stript [sic] entirely in the nursery, whilst washing.' So indulged were the Armitage children that they seemed 'not to know what obedience was', but by the time she left them, Miss Weeton had won their very real affection.

In God-fearing households belief in Heaven was fostered by daily household prayers, which had to be attended by every member of the family, plus the staff, assembled in hall or dining room. Chairs were placed in rows for servants to kneel to, while members of the family knelt together in a group. The master of the house conducted the prayers, read aloud the Bible lesson and the day's Collect followed by more prayers, delivered a homily on dutiful and righteous living, then murmured a final blessing. The older children were then expected to learn the Collect by heart and repeat it to their father later.

Sunday was a depressing day, consisting of morning and evening church-going with endless prayers and even longer sermons, Bible classes (the forerunner of Sunday schools) in the afternoon, all shops closed, tolling church bells and an overall atmosphere of gloom. Games of any kind were strictly forbidden, and of course 'Sunday-best' clothes were worn; stiff and uncomfortable as the day itself. As relaxation before nursery teatime, chairs would be drawn up to the big deal table, and verses from a children's religious book, such as *The Peep of Day*, would be laboriously copied out.

> Satan is glad
> When I am bad,
> And hopes that I
> With him shall lie,
> In fire and chains
> And dreadful pains.

Isaac Watts's *Divine and Moral Songs for Children* produced some formidable lines for them to remember, among which was a verse guaranteed to terrify any child:

Then let me always watch my lips,
Lest I be struck to death and Hell,
Since God a book of reck'ning keeps,
For ev'ry lie that children tell.

John Ruskin recalled the Sabbath as the gloomiest day of his child-hood, spent mainly in a church pew which he found 'an extremely dull place to keep quiet in'. Children's toys were locked away in nursery cupboards (in 'liberal' households Noah's Arks were excepted because they were associated with the Bible) and the only books allowed, between church services, were those with a moral theme, such as *Pilgrim's Progress*, or Mrs Sherwood's stories from *The Fairchild Family*. These tales, written between 1818 and 1847, of a family of three children, much loved by their parents and enjoying a very happy home life, were expressly planned to point morals, as some of their titles indicated: 'The All-Seeing God', 'Sad Story of a Disobedient Child', 'Story of an Unhappy Day', 'Story of Ambition; or, The Wish to be Great'. Some of them were extremely frightening, and even the adoring father and mother of the happy Fairchild children inflicted harsh punishments which seemed at complete variance with their parental devotion, stressing that parents not only had the right to chastise their children physically, but that children should accept it, not with protest, but with penitence. Scarcely a nursery shelf lacked Mrs Sherwood's book.

Nor did it lack Maria Edgeworth's stories, with their ill-concealed educational intent mercifully lightened with humour, or the books of Dorothy and Mary Jane Kilner, all of which appeared in the late eighteenth century and were therefore free of the early Victorian sermonizing and moralizing. *Little Stories for Little Folks*, *Memoirs of a Peg Top*, and *The Life and Perambulations of a Mouse* were three much loved Kilner books. But on the whole children's literature during the early years of the century could scarcely be called carefree. Mrs Sherwood made a return with *The Infant's Progress*, a story steeped in missionary fervour, then animal stories began to make a tentative appearance, but it was not until mid century that children's books began to be really entertaining.

Happily, this started with the return of fairy stories. They had been banned by educationalists at the beginning of the century, but made a welcome reappearance in 1843 in *The Home Treasury of Books*, a series containing all the old favourites like 'Red Riding Hood' and 'Cinderella' and on sale in small editions at sixpence and

Family prayers *c.* 1850

a shilling. This was followed in 1846 by the first English translation of Hans Andersen's fairy stories under the title of *Wonderful Stories for Children*. The same year saw Edward Lear's *Book of Nonsense*. After that came a flood of memorable children's stories, including Hoffman's *Shockheaded Peter* (*Struwelpeter*) in 1848, and an anthology, *Fairy Tales of all Nations*, in 1849. Thackeray's *The Rose and the Ring* followed in 1855 and Charles Kingsley's *Water Babies* in 1863 (many children wept over this unhappy story). Most successful of all was Lewis Carroll's *Alice's Adventures in Wonderland*, published in 1865 and followed six years later by *Through the Looking Glass*. And so came a merciful flood of outstanding books for children, including such worldwide classics as *Uncle Tom's Cabin*, *Black Beauty* and *Treasure Island*, accompanied by periodicals and magazines such as *The Infant's Magazine* and *Little Folks* aimed solely for entertainment and, not surprisingly, highly popular.

Although John Ruskin was so impoverished for toys that the only playthings he could ever remember possessing were a cart, a box of building bricks, a ball and a bunch of keys, the average nursery was plentifully supplied. Dolls' houses and rocking horses, battalions of toy soldiers, drums, bugles, bows and arrows, marbles (said to have been introduced to England by the Romans), ninepins, model shops of every description complete with their miniature wares, and much-loved soft toys, peepshows, toy theatres, Jack-in-the-boxes, hobby-horses, windmills, musical boxes and mechanical toys were all to be found. In large families the collection of toys could be vast, owing to the innumerable aunts, uncles, and family friends who sent presents for Christmas and birthdays.

And, of course, for little girls there were dolls of every description: wax dolls and china dolls; rag dolls and celluloid dolls; dolls with real hair, dolls which opened and shut their eyes, dolls with their own small trunks filled with clothes, and dolls which could cry 'Mammaaa!' and 'Papaaa!'; and even the small china penny dolls of which Morel's was never out of stock.

Whatever the nineteenth-century nursery lacked, it was certainly never starved of toys. Nor, in the average home, were children starved of parental love, particularly maternal. Daily involvement with the life of her children was both essential and rewarding to the model wife, content in her devotion to husband and family.

Sources Consulted

ADBURGHAM, ALISON *Liberty's: A biography of a shop*, Allen & Unwin 1975

Annie Besant: An Autobiography originally published 1893; republished by Theosophical Publishing House 1939

BEST, GEOFFREY *Mid-Victorian Britain 1851–1875*, Weidenfeld & Nicolson 1971

BLUM, STELLA (ed.) *Victorian Fashions and Costumes from Harper's Bazar: 1867–1898*, Dover 1974

BRANCA, PATRICIA (ed.) *The Silent Sisterhood: Middle class women in the Victorian home*, Croom Helm 1980

BRIGGS, ASA *A Social History of England*, Weidenfeld & Nicolson 1983

BROWN, IVOR *Jane Austen and her World*, Lutterworth 1966

CHESNEY, KELLOW *The Victorian Underworld*, Temple Smith 1970

CUNNINGTON, C. WILLET and PHYLLIS *A Handbook of English Costume in the Nineteenth Century*, Faber 1970

DAVIDOFF, LEONORE *The Best Circles: Society, the Season and Etiquette*, Croom Helm 1973

DELAMONT, SARA and DUFFIN, LORNA (ed.) *The Nineteenth Century Woman*, Croom Helm 1978

Diaries of Hannah Cullwick, 1866–1873, Virago 1984

DUNBAR, J. RIMMELL *Park Riding*, London 1859

Enquire Within, 1878, 1892 and 1894 editions

EVANS, HILARY and MARY *The Party that Lasted a Hundred Days*, Macdonald & Jane's 1976

EVELEIGH, DAVID J. *Firegrates and Kitchen Ranges*, Shire Publications 1983

— *Old Cooking Utensils*, Shire Publications 1985

FLICK, PAULINE *Old Toys*, Shire Publications 1985

GERNSHEIM, HELMUT and ALISON *Edward VII and Queen Alexandra*, Muller 1962

GLYN, ANTHONY *Elinor Glyn*, Hutchinson 1955

GOLBY, J. M. (ed.) *Culture and Society in Britain 1850–1890*, Open University 1986

HELLERSTEIN, E. O. *et al* (ed.) *Victorian Women: A documentary account of women's lives in nineteenth-century England, France and the United States*, Harvester Press/Stanford University Press 1982

HORN, PAMELA *The Rise and Fall of the Victorian Servant*, Allan Sutton 1986

HUGGETT, FRANK C. *Carriages at Eight: Horse-drawn society in Victorian and Edwardian times*, Lutterworth 1979

KING-HALL, MAGDALEN *The Story of the Nursery*, Routledge 1958

LANSDELL, AVRIL *Fashion à la Carte*, Shire Publications 1985

LOFTS, NORA *Domestic Life in England*, Weidenfeld & Nicolson 1976

LONGFORD, ELIZABETH *Victoria R. I.*, Weidenfeld & Nicolson 1971

New System of Domestic Cookery, A by A Lady (Mrs M. Rundell), 1819

NORTON, GRAHAM *Victorian London* (for London Weekend Television) Macdonald 1969

NUNN, JOAN *Fashion in Costume 1200–1980*, Herbert Press 1984

PERRY, GEORGE and MASON, NICHOLAS (ed.) *Rule Britannia: The Victorian World*, Times Newspapers 1974

RUSKIN, JOHN *Praeterita: Autobiography*, Oxford University Press 1978

SAMBROOK, PAMELA *Laundry Bygones*, Shire Publications 1983

SHERWOOD, MARTHA *The History of the Fairchild Family*, 1818–47

SMITH, D. J. *Discovering Horse-drawn Carriages*, Shire Publications 1974

STRACHEY, LYTTON *Queen Victoria*, Chatto & Windus 1921

THIRKELL, ANGELA *The Fortunes of Harriette: from the 1825 memoirs of Harriette Wilson*, Hamish Hamilton 1936

TRUDGILL, ERIC *Madonnas and Magdalens: The origins and development of Victorian social attitudes*, Heinemann 1975

Tyrwhitt-Drake Museum of Carriages, The, Maidstone Corporation, Kent

VICINUS, MARTHA (ed.) *Suffer and Be Still: Women in the Victorian age*, Methuen 1975

WALKLEY, CHRISTINA and FOSTER, VANDA *Crinolines and Crimping Irons: Victorian clothes – how they were cleaned and cared for*, Peter Owen 1978

WEETON, MISS E. *Journal of a Governess, 1807–25*, 2 vols, ed. Edward Hall, Kelley Publishers, USA

Index to Text